Metro

'Fascinating' Simon Evans, *Choice*

'It's more than a musical memoir. Black paints a vivid portrait
of simmering rainbow.................. the Second World

War . . . This is also an intelligent and affecting account of life as a black child in a white family, feeling "like a cuckoo in somebody else's nest" . . . Britain's original "rude girl", she approached her job with a fearlessness and determination that carried her through a subsequent acting career . . . She takes few prisoners, which is what you would expect from a woman who has spent a lifetime taking a sledgehammer to race and gender barriers. With *Black by Design*, one hopes she will get the recognition she deserves' Fiona Sturges, *Independent*

'There's plenty of "on the road" tales to please 2-Tone fans, but this is ultimately the story of a brave, intelligent woman's struggle to make sense of the nasty world around her' Lois Wilson, *Mojo*

'A complex self-examination of the dichotomies of Black's life . . . a valuable social commentary' Ian Abrahams, *Record Collector*

PAULINE BLACK

BLACK BY DESIGN

A 2-TONE MEMOIR

A complete catalogue record for this book can
be obtained from the British Library on request

First published in this paperback edition in 2012 by Serpent's Tail
First published in 2011 by Serpent's Tail,
an imprint of Profile Books Ltd
3A Exmouth House
Pine Street
London EC1R 0JH
website: www.serpentstail.com

ISBN 978 1 84668 791 4
eISBN 78 1 84765 762 6

Designed and typeset by Crow Books

Printed and bound by
CPI Group (UK) Ltd, Croydon, CR0 4YY

10 9 8 7 6 5 4 3 2

Grateful acknowledgement: Quote on pp 387–8 is from *The Velveteen Rabbit*
by Margery Williams. First published in Great Britain in 1922. Published by
Egmont UK Ltd London and used with permission.

For Jane (1950–2008)

CONTENTS

PART THREE
BACK TO BLACK

ACKNOWLEDGEMENTS

Everything I have to say about my particular life's journey is written in these pages. It is too late to qualify or worry unduly about what I have said. Suffice to say that I believe it to be the truth.

Much of this book is based on personal diaries, memories or oral family histories. I have tried to give a truthful approximation of what was said to me or relayed by a third party. For the sake of privacy, some of the characters that appear are composites of people I have known and in a few instances names have been changed.

My thanks to author Tony McMahon for initially introducing me to his literary agent, Oli Munson, who generously signed me to Blake Friedmann and suggested that I should consider writing my memoir. Oli singularly nursed this project through, from tentative beginnings to finished draft manuscript with careful readings, kind consideration and thoughtful observation during those periods when occasionally my inkwell ran dry. I also thank him for introducing me to Serpent's Tail publisher Pete Ayrton and my dedicated editor, John Williams, who both showed enthusiastic support while shepherding *Black By Design* to a final manuscript. Thanks also to everybody else at Serpent's Tail, particularly Rebecca Gray and Ruth Petrie for firm attention to detail and Anna-Marie Fitzgerald for her unstinting organization.

Thanks to Nella Marin and Linda and Pick Withers, who provided safe London havens during my theatrical years and those friends who supported, encouraged and listened to me during the writing process, especially Esme Duijzer and Paven Kirk, who generously read my scribblings at an early stage and provided useful feedback. Thanks also to members of The Selecter, both past and present, who have provided me with a surrogate, if sometimes unruly, family for over thirty years.

My fond gratitude goes out to the Vickers family, Murphy family, Adenle family and Hamilton family, without whom my tale would never have been told. Four families spread across three continents to tell one story. I love and respect them all.

Lastly, my heartfelt thanks to my wonderful husband, Terry, who supported, listened and encouraged me when I wailed, railed and cursed while bringing my story to the page, and who helpfully provided the solution to many a lapse of memory on my part. I love you dearly.

PART ONE

WHITE TO BLACK

ONE

A WHITE LIE

1958, aged 4

My earliest memory is of vomiting the breakfast contents of my stomach onto a pile of starched white sheets that my mother had just finished ironing. I succeeded in Jackson Pollocking all of them. She was not amused, but then again it was her own fault: she shouldn't have told me that I had been adopted.

It was the late summer of 1958 in Romford, a newly expanding market town in the county of Essex, famous for the stink of its Star brewery, 'a night down the dogs' at the local greyhound racing stadium and as the one-time residence of the infamous Colonel Blood, the only man to have stolen the Crown Jewels, even if only temporarily. This backwater suburb was only fifteen miles north-east of London's buzzing post-war metropolis, but a light year behind in terms of progressive thinking.

My mother was astute enough to know that, since I was about to start infant school, I should be told the truth about my origins, just in case my new pale-faced schoolmates asked me why I was brown when my parents were white. I had noticed that I was different, but I hadn't realized that it was any kind of a problem. Well, nothing much is a problem at four years old, other than not getting what you really want for birthdays and Christmases.

'Why didn't you tell me you felt sick,' screamed my mother, as she landed a huge smack on my right leg, grabbed me by the arm and sent me upstairs to my bedroom as punishment. 'As if I haven't got enough work to do,' she shouted as I howled my way upstairs.

I sat on my bed, running my hand over the large red handprint on my calf. The mark on my skin felt hot and tender, but the indelible print her words had left on my being was cold and hard.

In her defence, I have to tell you that she was taking Purple Hearts at the time, aka Drinamyl, a potent combination of amphetamine and barbiturate, a form of prescription 'speed' that was doled out by GPs from 1957 onward for menopausal women. It was also the drug *de jour* of the soon to come swinging '60s, loved by the Mods and Rockers that my mother's generation would so vehemently hate.

Since her marriage to Arthur Vickers at eighteen, she had

4

spent nearly two and a half decades bringing up four sons, Trevor, Tony, Ken and Roger. She was now a 'woman of a certain age' who tired easily, but was still expected to fulfil a monotonous list of housewifely duties without the abundance of today's labour-saving devices. So drug companies made it their business to invent various potent little pills to help such women get the jobs done quicker. How else could women achieve the 'perfect fifties family home' that Hollywood films popularized and spouses expected? Unfortunately these little 'pick-me-ups' made her hopping mad about the least little thing.

I jumped off my bed and stared at my tear-stained face in the dressing table's triptych mirror. I looked different. Then I understood why. I was now a little 'coloured' girl who didn't have a real mummy and daddy. This new piece of information didn't fit me. It was like trying to insert the last piece into a jigsaw, only to find that it belonged to another picture.

My brain buzzed with all the new words that my mother had used. She had said that my 'real' father was from a place called Nigeria. Apparently he had dark-coloured skin. My 'real' mother had been a schoolgirl from the nearby town of Dagenham. No mention was made of the colour of her skin, so I assumed that she wasn't 'dark coloured'. This 'darkness of colour' was said in such a way that I instinctively knew that it wasn't seen as a good thing.

Until then, the only thing that had marred my blissfully ignorant existence was my hair, which was alternately described as 'woolly', 'wiry' or 'fizzy' by three curious old aunts, all named after various fragrant flowers. Their cold, arthritically knobbed fingers, like the gnarly old winter branches on bare trees, loved to grab handfuls of it when they visited.

My least favourite aunt, named after the thorniest flower, usually dripped disappointment like a leaky tap whenever she talked about me. 'Ooh-er,' she invariably said as she rubbed a section of my hair between her forefinger and thumb, testing its texture, 'I thought it was going to feel like a Brillo pad, but it's soft, just like wool.'

Just to put her into context – she had sent me a golliwog for my first birthday present, which, ironically, I cherished for much of my childhood.

Another aunt, whose name evoked a tiny purple flower with a golden centre, was kinder and helpfully suggested to my mother: 'I heard that you can tame all that fizz with a wet brush.' She always used the word 'fizz' instead of 'frizz', as if I was an unruly bottle of pop that had been shaken too much.

My third aunt, who was named after a fragrant flower that grew in valleys, was the only one of this sisterly triumvirate who thought my hair was pretty, but she was half blind. Her cloudy eyes had the same distant, yet myopic look that all cataract sufferers share. 'Just like candy floss,' she would say, as she patted my hairy confection.

Now it seemed that not only my hair was a problem, but the colour of my skin too. My mother had told me that I was a 'half-caste', a polite term back then; politically correct phrases like mixed race, dual heritage, people of colour, Afro-Caribbean, Anglo-African were as yet unknown in those halcyon days of fifties post-war Britain. The ownership of colonial overseas dominions allowed British citizens to exercise their God-given right in calling a spade a spade. You could even get away with saying 'wog', 'nigger' or 'coon', especially if you wanted to practise a 'colour bar' in your local pub or club. Those 'darkeys' had to be kept out at all costs.

As I grew, I began to understand that these derogatory

terms were standard in our family when describing a black person. Slowly and surely, I realized how un-level the green and pleasant playing fields of England really were, but I was a resourceful child and quickly learned to ignore the colourful jibes hurled by complete strangers on the street when I was unaccompanied. I always considered 'jungle-bunny' the funniest insult I ever heard. I used to wonder how the users of this phrase could be so misinformed. Didn't they watch Desmond Morris's *Zoo Time* programme on children's television? Rabbits didn't live in the jungle; they preferred more temperate climes. I soon understood that 'getting it all muddled up or just plain wrong' is the main stock in trade for any good racist worth their salt.

Black people were still a rarity on the streets of Romford. Nobody ran up and touched you for luck any more – as my mother explained that she and her school friends did the first time that they saw a black man – but being the only black kid in school did make me an automatic target for some of the more uncharitable children who made monkey noises in the playground or school corridors. When I mentioned it to my mother, she would say things like: 'Just tell them that sticks and stones may break my bones, but names will never hurt me.'

It was her attempt at elastoplasting the hurt but, believe me, that jingle is hardly an incisive retort when going head to head with the local primary school bully. A playground thug rarely wants an in-depth discussion about the pros and cons of trans-racial adoption in modern society. The laser-like precision with which such kids seek out the soft underbelly of their object of derision, before putting the metaphorical boot in, must stand them in good stead for future careers as managers or stand-up comics. Almost instinctively I empathized with the ugly or fat school kids who suffered the same kinds of verbal abuse. Being marginalized at such a young age makes children defensive and prone to moodiness. I was good at both.

'Don't sulk,' my mother would bark at me. 'What have you got to be miserable about? You should think yourself lucky that you've got a good home. Lots of little girls like you haven't, you know.'

What she really meant was that I should consider myself lucky that I had been adopted. It never occurred to her that having your history erased and replaced with somebody else's version of it was a dubious kind of luck. Adoption is like having a total blood transfusion; it may save your life in the short term, but if it's not a perfect match, rejection issues may appear much later.

In the tiny microcosm that I inhabited as a child, the word racism hadn't yet been invented. The concept was alive and kicking, but in the absence of a name it thrived like an inoperable cancer. Ignorance breeds ignorance, particularly when newspapers run inflammatory headlines about being 'overrun' or 'swamped' with people of a different race. It wasn't just black people, the Irish got it in the neck too, and the Poles and the Italians, but blacks were highly visible on British streets, therefore they took the brunt of the opprobrium. I frequently heard stupid comments from family members or friends about their brushes with members of the black community.

My mother's nephew, Alan, was a gas meter reader in Stoke Newington. His job allowed him into people's homes, so he got to see things that were hidden from the general population. He was always welcomed with open arms whenever he turned up at family gatherings such as funerals, weddings and christenings, because his lurid tales livened up even the most sombre occasions. He brought news from far-off frontiers, the kinds of places that white people ordinarily feared to tread. He confirmed their worst fears.

After liberal quantities of beer he would grow red in the face and begin to wax lyrically: 'You should see the way some of them darkeys live. Twenty to a room. Take the doors off the hinges and sleep on them, some of them. Have to pick my way across the floor to the cupboard just so's I can read the meter. 'S wonder I don't fall over sometimes.' Such insights aroused audible intakes of breath from the adults.

'And the smell of their cooking. What do you think of this then?' he would say conspiratorially, comically looking over each shoulder for effect. 'I saw loads of open tins of cat food on the kitchen table. Not a cat in sight.'

When his audience looked at each other uncertainly, as if they didn't quite understand what he was driving at, he would land the punch line. 'That's what they eat.'

'Oh,' the audience would collectively murmur, finally satisfied.

The stories were always the same. Nobody seemed to notice the repetition or the little black girl listening in alongside.

All Our Yesterdays, a bleak documentary television series about the Second World War, was also on permanent repeat throughout my childhood, just like Alan's stories. Once I'd seen Alan in his gas meter man's uniform, his blond hair sticking out of the back of his peaked cap, his moustache small, oblong and freshly trimmed. He reminded me very much of the peaked-cap, rain-coated men who stood by watching as filthy, skinny people in stripy pyjamas were herded into squalid rooms full of bunk beds. The dour commentary explained that these uniformed men were Nazis rounding up the Jews. When pictures of lifeless bodies being bulldozed into freshly dug pits appeared on the screen, my mother would leap up from her armchair and switch the television off. 'Enough of all that. We don't need to see all that again.'

But I did want to see it all again. I was fascinated. I'd never seen real dead people before, particularly not being so unceremoniously buried. Their arms and legs flopped around like rag dolls. From what I could understand at the time, being Jewish was similar to being 'coloured'. Nobody much liked you if you were either. Even then I realized that being 'different' could lead to bad things happening.

After one of Alan's sessions at a distant relative's wedding, I asked my mother why these 'dark people' – my mother's terminology (she didn't seem to be able to say 'darkeys') – had to sleep so many in a room. Without missing a beat she replied: 'That's the way they live. They're not like us.'

I wasn't sure whether she included me in that 'us'. Indeed, sometimes I couldn't quite figure out where I fitted into this inequitable equation. I implicitly understood that most of the white people I knew thought that most black people were not as clever as them. I think it was this erroneous assertion that first ignited my somewhat competitive nature when I was a child. I considered it my duty to prove them wrong by making myself as clever as possible. This did not make me popular with my youngest brother Roger, a prototypical 'Dennis The Menace', who became, probably understandably, jealous of my early achievements.

I was dispatched to piano lessons when I was five, because my Aunt Violet thought I might be musical. 'They're always singing and dancing when you see them on the telly,' she said knowledgeably.

Roger and me in Clacton, 1957

'Why don't I get sent to piano lessons?' Roger asked whenever he heard me practising on the newly purchased upright piano. Nobody had the heart to tell him that he could barely read and write coherently at the same age as I was taking my Grade 2 piano exam. It wasn't that he had any yearning to play the piano. He hadn't even thought about piano lessons until then. He just couldn't bear the fact that I played well after only a few sessions. Surely he was cleverer than this little black girl who had usurped his coveted position of 'youngest' in the family? As soon as he left secondary school at fifteen, he became a Teddy Boy. In his late teens, a local beehived girl hurried this drape-suited, pencil-moustachioed rebel without a clue up the aisle. She later produced a niece and nephew for me. When the children were old enough to talk, they frequently referred to me as 'chocolate aunty' – out of the mouths of babes.

My oldest brother Trevor, a hard-working, upright, Duke and Duchess of Windsor-admiring fellow, had married a winsome, auburn-haired secretary the month before I was born and immediately moved into the new home they had saved up for, so I never really knew him.

Tony, the next in line, eighteen years my senior, was doing his National Service when I arrived in the family. He often joked that when he took me out for a walk in my Silver Cross pram, many older women would peer at me and then disapprovingly glance at him in his army uniform and say: 'Look what you've brought back with you from overseas.'

Then there was Ken, my always smiling, happy-go-lucky brother, thirteen years my senior. He was always a bit of an outsider. He had been adopted too, although he was white. It drew us together as I got older, but he was married and had left home by the time I was eight, so we never got the chance to swap notes on what adoption meant to either of us.

■ ■ ■

Despite the undercurrent of racism that pervaded British society in the late fifties, I made friends easily with many of my white schoolmates. Just as well because there were no black pupils at the primary or secondary schools that I attended. I was good at reading, writing, spelling, music and running and therefore I was much in demand for netball, school sports days, reading the Bible lesson at School Assembly and tinkling the ivories at my mother's behest whenever she thought that visiting relatives had stayed too long. I could clear a room with the opening bars of Beethoven's *Pathetique Sonata*.

Many of my girl friends at school were in the Brownies. I wanted to be too, but apparently it wasn't possible to join unless I first attended Sunday School at the local church where the Brownie meetings were held. I badgered my mother for weeks until she relented and promised to enquire about enrolment. I remember standing by her side while she had a heated conversation with a woman just outside the door of the church's adjoining hall. The door was ajar and I peeped inside. I recognised a few of my friends among the horde of little girls running around the small room in their smart brown and yellow uniforms. I could hardly wait to do the same. It was winter and there was snow on the ground. I was aware that a lot of breath was condensing in the freezing air between the two women. Suddenly my mother grabbed me by the arm and hauled me off down the road towards home. She looked very angry, so I didn't dare ask when we could buy my uniform. I later heard her talking to my Dad: 'That bloody woman wouldn't take her for the Brownies or even the Sunday School. She had the bloody cheek to ask me why we adopted a coloured girl and not one of our own. Call themselves Christians? Don't know the bloody meaning of the word.' I'd never heard her swear so much.

Calmly, my Dad said: 'If she's not good enough for their church, then their bloody church isn't good enough for us.'

It was my half-blind Aunt Lily who eventually offered to take care of my religious education. She took me along to the local Salvation Army Hall on Sunday mornings. The only thing I liked about the Sally Army were the women officers' bonnets, the old-style ones with the heavy grosgrain ribbons that tied in a huge black bow under the right side of the chin. The severity of their stiff black form edged with red, as if the cloth had been dipped in the still warm blood of Christ, was intoxicating. Even the raddled old face of the Brigadier's wife became beatific in a Sally Army bonnet. One day I plucked up enough courage to ask if I could have one, but to my bitter disappointment, I was told that it took years of dedication before anybody got a uniform and bonnet to wear.

Annually, the Sally Army had what they called an 'International Pageant' and all the kids had to dress up as somebody from each of the different countries in the world. They had no black children, so they were overjoyed that they had finally found somebody who could wear a grass skirt, hold a cardboard spear and paint the ends of a white bone on either side of their nose. This costume was supposed to signify a native from deepest, darkest Africa; apparently national boundaries were unimportant for black people. Even then, I was precocious enough to refuse point-blank when offered the raggedy old skirt. I screamed and created such a fuss that I was never asked again.

I acquired a very special friend at school when I was nine. Her name was Dorothea – Thea for short – and she was the middle one of three sisters from the Hawthorne family. Both parents were teachers. Her mother was a lecturer at a London art school and her father taught English at a local secondary school. Her mum wore shift dresses and Capri pants in vibrant pinks, yellows and purples, sometimes with crazy geometric patterns. Long red curly hair tumbled over her shoulders. Kitten heels adorned her shapely feet. She oozed an indefinable cool. My mother wore pastel-coloured Crimplene dresses with matching dinky hats and gloves, topped off with an assortment of badly hand-knitted cardigans. Unfortunately she oozed uncool like a thawed-out burst pipe.

Inside their house was light and airy, our interior was dark and old-fashioned. They had real art in sleek wooden frames on the wall; not just any old art, but modern art, modern inexplicable art. In our house there were a few faded prints in gaudy filigree frames of *Bubbles* and *Little Lord Fauntleroy*, picked up at jumble sales. A mahogany-framed sepia print of *The Return from Inkerman*, visibly stained in one corner, a depressing heirloom left to my mother by her dead father, was displayed above the hearth. It complemented the drab, overstuffed room with its flowery wallpaper and multi-coloured swirly carpet.

Thea and her sisters romped around their home as if it belonged to them as much as to their parents. Nobody told them to be quiet if they offered up an opinion on something they'd seen in the newspaper or on the television. One afternoon when I was invited round for tea, Mrs Hawthorne gave me a bowl of pasta. I watched in horror as they spooned the white wriggly food into their mouths.

'What's wrong?' Mrs Hawthorne asked, as I sat staring at my plate.

'I don't like it,' I said.

'Try it first. It's Italian, darling,' she said helpfully. She called everybody 'darling'.

'I'm not allowed to eat foreign muck,' I chirped up, because that's how my mother referred to foods from other cultures. In fact, 'foreign muck' was her pet phrase when confronted with any food she didn't like, even Mulligatawny soup.

Thea and her sisters laughed. Her mother told them to be quiet. I knew I'd said the wrong thing. Mrs Hawthorne took my plate away and made me tinned spaghetti on toast instead. Just like my mother made at home. The Hawthornes put a whole new spin on my concept of 'them' and 'us'.

We lived in a three-bedroom, semi-detached house which had been bought by the local council after the war. We were the only family in the street who paid rent for their house and our next-door neighbours, the Greens, never let my parents forget this. Not by saying anything, that would be too rude, but just by gesture or nod; this was enough to keep the Vickerses in their place. My mother compounded the rent-paying felony by telling our neighbours that we lived in a 'privately owned council house'. A definite oxymoron!

Mr Green, a tall, upright and distinctly uptight man, went to work in the City every morning wearing a bowler hat, crisp white shirt, striped trousers and carrying an umbrella. His wife, Mrs Green, a homely woman, would spend the day laundering his shirts so that a fresh one was available every morning. You could set your watch by Mr Green's departure to catch the bus, from which he would alight at exactly 8 a.m. directly opposite Romford station, where he caught the 8.10 a.m. to Liverpool Street, which enabled him to be at his desk for precisely 9 a.m. Mrs Green liked to relate these kinds of details to my mother across the garden fence as she pegged her washing out.

Dad, a short, balding, slightly tubby man with stained brown teeth from incessant smoking, left a full hour and a half before Mr Green, clad in brown overalls, a donkey jacket and flat cap, to drive six miles to Dagenham, where he clocked in with a punch card. As a mechanic, he was cleanly efficient, but the work was difficult and dirty. Dad constantly smelt of oil, which congealed in a black mass under his nicotine-stained fingernails, and no amount of Swarfega could shift, whereas the no-nonsense carbolic aroma of Lifebuoy soap noticeably enveloped Mr Green when you passed him on the street. Despite Dad's sartorial shortcomings, I loved him implicitly. I loathed Mr Green explicitly.

Dad grew vegetables to supplement the meagre household budget, whereas Mr Green could tell you the Latin names of the flowers he grew. The only time Mr Green had a lengthy conversation with Dad was when he complained about the squawking of our chickens, which lived in a makeshift wire run at the end of our long back garden. The chickens disappeared the next day. When I asked about their whereabouts, my dad explained that he had given them away, because they needed too much upkeep. The next time I spoke to Stephen, the Greens' oldest child, across the garden fence, he imperiously informed me that his dad considered it 'common' to keep chickens. I wondered if there was a list somewhere that let the unwary among us know when we were doing something that was considered 'common'. I asked my mother if she knew where I might find it.

'Common, common,' she repeated, sounding very much like a squawking chicken, 'I'll give them common. Just who do they think they are? Don't take no notice of that stuck-up lot,' she muttered, her face as purple as a boiled beetroot. 'Wait till I tell your Dad what he said.'

But she never did. We ate a lot of chicken stew in the following weeks.

To avenge this slight against my family, I plotted my revenge on the Greens. One afternoon, when they were out, I got the idea to dig up Mr Green's prized gladioli. I had recently planted some seeds in the small patch of garden previously occupied by the chicken coop. Dad said it was my very own little patch to grow anything I wanted. When nothing grew after a week, I became impatient, so I thought I would 'borrow' a few ready-made plants from next door. They had so many flowers that I didn't think they would miss a few. How wrong can a young girl be?

The terrible deed was done while my parents took their habitual Sunday afternoon nap. The only problem was that gladiolus plants are very tall and although they stood proud in Mr Green's flower bed, they took on the appearance of the leaning tower of Pisa once replanted, particularly since I had dug them up without their root balls. I managed to prop them against each other in a delicate balancing act, but as I stood back to admire the fiery redness of the flowers, a loud screech went up next door and I heard their back door slam shut. I had been so engrossed in finding a solution to my tilting flower problem that I hadn't noticed the unexpected return of the Greens. The next minute, an angry Mr Green appeared, striding down the garden path, gobs of spit and invective flying from his mouth, his arm outstretched, finger pointing just like Donald Sutherland's in the last frame of *Invasion of the Bodysnatchers*: 'Wait till your father hears about this, you little thief. I might have known you'd turn out like this.'

I wasn't sure what he meant by that last remark, but suffice to say, my mother's punishment was swift and accurate. I didn't venture into the garden for the remainder of the summer.

Instead I begged my mother to let me spend more time at Thea's house. She always allowed me to go because she was secretly pleased that I'd made friends with somebody who lived in a posher area than we did. My mother was a closet snob. If only she had known the reality of what the Hawthornes' three free-spirited daughters were allowed to get up to, then she might have thought twice before letting me go round there. Fortunately she was never privy to the mayhem of their birthday parties, dressing-up boxes, impromptu dancing and poetry recitals in the garden, picnics up in their tree-house, home-made puppet shows, zooming up and down their sedate cul-de-sac on rollerskates or picture painting on the huge pine-wood table in their vast kitchen. Their life seemed such fun and my home life seemed so dull by comparison.

The Hawthornes would pile into an old blue VW camper van bound for the Pembrokeshire coast in the summer holidays. Sometimes they even went to France. Bliss. I was so jealous. How I wished that I could have gone with them. I got a week in a bed and breakfast in Clacton-on-Sea with my mum, not something you bothered bragging about!

But the star attractions at the Hawthornes were the bookshelves in the living room, which were crammed with books and LP records. The ceiling-high shelving unit housed large books, with glossy covers bearing names like Picasso, Dali and unpronounceable French words in huge print on their spines. The only books in our house were the ones I got from the library each week. Even more interesting were the rows of LPs that occupied the shelf nearest to their sleek new radiogram, which housed a cocktail cabinet in the underneath cupboard. Sometimes Thea's mother would play these records while she painted. Her easel was a permanent fixture in the living room. The smell of turpentine was the only air freshener. When she was painting, us children were banished from the house to play in the garden. Thea and I would peer through the window at her as she boogied round the living room to weird-sounding music, which Thea informed me was called jazz. Her paintings didn't look like anything I'd ever seen before, but the music seemed to complement the brightly coloured zigzags that she seemed fond of spreading all over her canvases.

Once I sneaked into the living room when she was out. I eagerly ran my finger along the book spines, randomly alighting on one and then trying to read the title. *To Kill A Mockingbird* was my favourite one. Next I peered at the photos on the fronts of the LPs. Some of the cover photos were of black people, mostly men, some playing piano or trumpet or saxophone. One LP cover in particular caught my eye. I pulled it out of the stack for a closer look. It depicted a close-up photo in profile of an attractive-looking black man. His hair was heavily greased and combed back from his large smooth forehead. Half the photo was stained in sepia and half was in black and white. 'The voice of Langston Hughes' was written on the sepia half, the words 'voice' and 'Langston' in yellow type, the other words in white. I was suddenly startled by a familiar voice: 'Why aren't you outside with the others?' Mrs Hawthorne asked.

'I'm sorry,' I stammered, my cheeks hot with embarrassment at being caught in the living room unsupervised.

'Don't be,' she said lightly. She was unlike any other adult I had ever met. She treated kids like equals, never talking down to them.

'I like looking at all the coloured people in the photos,' I offered by way of explanation.

'He's very handsome, isn't he,' she said, gesturing towards the photo on the LP cover. 'But he's not coloured, darling. He's a mulatto like you, see his wavy black hair?'

She elegantly slipped the record out of the cover and put it on the turntable. She poured herself a drink from a brown bottle in the cocktail cabinet and bade me perch on the sofa with her. As she sipped from her glass, a man with an American accent intoned a poem while music played in the background, very much like the stuff she listened to all the time. He kept talking about rivers. I couldn't understand all that he meant, but it was one of those moments in life when you know to pay attention because somebody is at last taking the trouble to tell you something.

'This is Langston Hughes,' Mrs Hawthorne said, handing me the cover of the LP. 'Isn't he wonderful?' I'd never heard anybody refer to a black man as wonderful before. Mrs Hawthorne was a strange lady, I thought. But the solemnly spoken words stilled the air in the room. I felt as though I was making a connection with something that had been lost to me. But the feeling was fleeting and passed as soon as the poem ended.

Many years later I bought the same album in a tiny record shop in Laguna Beach on the west coast of America. The discovery of the poem's name, 'The Negro Speaks of Rivers', written on the back of the sleeve, was a vivid reminder. When I finally managed to listen to it again, I was catapulted back to that day in Mrs Hawthorne's living room. Even though I had been a child, there was something in the choice and cadence of the words which conjured up an eternal river that demanded my total immersion in its depths, a symbolic baptism into an underworld where I instinctively knew that I belonged. This river and its many tributaries was a metaphor for black life, depicting the journey of Africans from their homelands into slavery in the New World and beyond. But I didn't know that then.

Mrs Hawthorne lifted the stylus from the record after Langston Hughes had said the final words of the poem, 'My soul has grown deep like the rivers.' Her eyes glittered as she turned to me and simply said: 'Beautiful.'

She returned to her easel. Soon she was lost in her work. I ran back outside to play. The word 'mulatto' rang in my ears. She had pronounced it 'moolatto', in that weird, higher-pitched way that people have when they say a foreign word. Only a few months before I had seen that word written down, but I had pronounced it mullet-o, like the fish, but with an extra 'o' at the end.

■ ■ ■

Most weekends my parents and I were obliged to visit one of the many elderly relatives. That's what happens when your mum and dad are already middle-aged when they decide to adopt. This particular afternoon we were at the home of my Aunt Rose, a spotlessly tidy house near Elm Park. My mother and she spent much of the afternoon roasting themselves to the colour of cooked lobsters on plastic recliners in the remarkably well-kept back garden, while their husbands worked on an old second-hand Humber that my uncle had just bought. I feigned a headache to avoid having to listen to the gossipy nonsense that was normally shared between the two women. My mother suggested that I go indoors and lie on the sofa in the sitting room. My aunt didn't seem to like this idea.

'I thought you would have liked this hot weather,' she snorted. Lots of people said exactly the same words to me every time the sun came out, as if I never got uncomfortably hot like everybody else.

In the end, she relented, but not before barking at my retreating back: 'Don't touch anything.'

How well she knew me! I liked to snoop. I had reached the conclusion that grown-ups were always hiding something; they always had some little secret about themselves that with just a bit of delving into their private nooks and crannies would usually elicit an illicit treasure trove. My home piracy was generally a strategically coordinated affair, requiring stealth, a steady nerve, colourful imagination, abundant opportunity and, above all else, a healthy disregard for the victims.

Once alone in the sitting room and having satisfied myself that the ladies were deep in conversation, I decided that the bookcase looked an interesting place to begin. Usually adults liked to hide their more fascinating reading material behind the boring stuff like cookery books and the Bible. I had often found copies of *Reveille* and *Tit-Bits* in some of our other relatives' bookcases. These cheap paper magazines always had photos of pneumatic, scantily clad young women, usually artfully posed, on their front covers. My two youngest brothers also hid such stuff under their beds, so I was familiar with the genre. I always wondered why the women in these cover photos didn't have wobbly bits and hairy underarms and legs like the bathing-suit-clad ladies who sunbathed on the beach at Clacton.

As I noiselessly slid the glass frontage aside, I noticed that the Bible was sticking too far forward for its relative size. Carefully removing it, I delved into the shadowy interior. I immediately hit paydirt. I withdrew a large, slightly shabby and obviously well-thumbed book. A damp, mushroom smell clung to it.

The cover image scorched my eyes. A huge, well-muscled, half-naked black man proudly stood with his sinewy ebony arms on his hips. The lower half of his body was clad in loose, white cotton trousers, but his eyes were downcast, despite the arrogance of his stance. Beside him stood a young, white, fiery red-headed woman in a yellow and white silk Victorian crinoline dress, her soft, white hand possessively hooked into the crook of his arm. Her blue eyes upturned towards him, stared with an absolute purpose. There was no doubt that she was in control.

Above the picture was a banner headline in red: MANDINGO, and some blurb about the contents being 'terrifying and horrifying', 'a wonderful novel of life on a slave-breeding farm'. Underneath it said that millions and millions of copies had been sold.

So why hadn't I heard about it? From the look of the cover, I suspected that I wouldn't find it in the local library. I traced the word 'unabridged' with my right index finger, wondering what it meant, before my hand strayed towards the picture of the bare-chested man. Suddenly my palm felt clammy and stuck to the shiny front cover. As I flicked through the book, I noticed that there were faint lipstick smudges on the tops of some of the pages, where my aunt's finger had probably brushed against her lips before licking its tip to facilitate turning over each leaf.

My mother was fond of calling my Aunt Rose a 'lady of leisure'. Mostly out of jealousy I think, because my aunt's husband, Leonard, had a good, white-collar, number-crunching job at the Electricity Board. He and his wife enjoyed ballroom dancing, holidaying abroad and bridge nights. My aunt changed the flowers on the altar at the local church twice a week and went to WI meetings. Now I knew how she spent her leisure time.

On an initial, cursory inspection it seemed that the book was full of 'rude' bits – the only way, at that age, I had to describe people kissing each other. As I read on, a frightening story emerged about how white people in America bought black people at auctions and forced them to work on their cotton plantations in a place called Alabama. If they didn't work they were whipped. Was this true? Could the home of my much-loved zany (I loved that word, so American) TV shows like *I Love Lucy* and *Mr Ed* really have been a place where black people were owned, bought and sold like animals, just a hundred years before? I avidly read for an hour and a half on that hot afternoon, completely undisturbed. While my mother and Aunt Rose broiled in the back yard, I learned that the black man on the front cover was a slave who loved his white master's wife. This upset everybody and the black man was horribly punished. It happened in 1830. Unable to separate fact from fiction in those days, I decided that perhaps history was interesting after all.

My imagination whispered that this story was similar to what might have happened between my 'real' father and mother. They had made a baby, just like the white lady in this story. According to the book, this baby was called a mulatto. I put the book back where I found it. I felt inexplicably afraid.

When we got home I looked up the word 'mulatto' in a dictionary. It said it was the offspring of a female horse and a male donkey. I imagined my 'real' mother munching a carrot in a field somewhere in Dagenham and my 'real' father hee-hawing somewhere in Nigeria. I was so upset that I had to take the next day off school.

Later, when I heard the way that Mrs Hawthorne had said the word 'mulatto', I reappraised it. She made it sound like it was a good thing to be. It was devoid of animal connotations on her lips. I tested the word on my mother.

'Where did you hear that?' she asked suspiciously.

'Mrs Hawthorne told me that's what I was.'

'Oh, did she. Trust her to put those kind of ideas in your head.'

What ideas, I wondered?

■ ■ ■

The Hawthornes moved nearer to London that autumn. I never saw any of them again. Mrs Hawthorne's paintings may have been lost to the art world, but I know I owe her a profound debt for helping me find the first glimpse of my black heritage on that sunny afternoon in 1962.

When I was in my twenties, after my Aunt Rose suddenly

died, I discovered that she was not really an aunt after all, but just a friend of the family. After her funeral, I eavesdropped on some juicy gossip about the adventurous sexually charged past she had led in a tiny village in Suffolk during the post-war years. Apparently she was rather partial to many of the American GIs, who were stationed at the nearby airbase. A former neighbour, who'd come all the way to Romford from Suffolk for the burial, saucily said to his male friend: 'She'd blow any of them Yanks for a pair of silk stockings and a packet of fags after the war, even them darkeys.'

I couldn't help smiling amid the sad faces.

At birth my mother was unfairly named after a clinging, parasitic plant, instead of a flower. Ivy James was born in 1911 in Cotleigh Road, Romford. She had been a sickly child and spent part of her childhood in a convalescent home near Clacton-on-Sea. Her formal schooling had stopped when she was twelve and she had then got a job as a ladies' maid to a doctor's family in the posh area of Romford, known as Gidea Park.

Her duties entailed taking care of two young girls. Often she would stand in Rise Park dreamily staring through the wire mesh perimeter fence into the huge back garden of an imposing house. She talked fondly about her days in service. Her favourite story was about how she used to take the children to and from school in a pony and trap. If the pony defecated en route then she was expected to step down from the trap and collect the steaming pile in a bucket for her employer's rose garden. A small shovel was stored on the side of the vehicle for this express purpose. One day the pony almost ran off down the road with the children in tow while she was engaged in her odious task. I think she nearly lost her job over that particular escapade.

She loved children, particularly babies. One day when I was about eight, a young blonde woman knocked on our front door holding what at first looked like a bundle of old clothes, but on closer inspection turned out to be a baby. Her name was Joy. My mother invited her in and immediately took hold of the baby and cooed and clucked over him. Joy told her that the baby's name was Sylvan and he was nearly a year old. I got the impression that my parents had been expecting her. My dad perked up no end when he first set eyes on her, particularly after she told him that she had once been part of the Tiller Girls dance troupe. Like most red-blooded males of the time, my dad was no stranger to their high kicking, scantily clad routine at the start of *Sunday Night at the London Palladium*, a schlocky '60s variety TV programme. Joy's statuesque body jiggled harmoniously with her Monroesque good looks, as she walked around our living room on her impossibly long legs. It was obvious that she had been aptly named. The upshot of her visit was that the household gained baby Sylvan in exchange for Joy paying my mother thirty shillings a week.

Every fortnight she visited her son for two hours on a Saturday afternoon. Sylvan's father accompanied her only once, when his son was nearly eighteen months old. He was not formally introduced by Joy and remained nameless throughout the short visit. I was entranced by the colour of Sylvan's father's skin. It was blue-black and shone like a mirror. His tombstone-white teeth seemed almost perfect compared with my mother's yellowing National Health dentures. I was told not to stare and to get on with my piano practice, but my concentration was shot. Mandingo was in the house and sitting on our sofa!

Joy had just bought a new record which she popped onto the turntable of our radiogram. I watched enthralled as she and her partner did 'the twist', a new dance craze, to Chubby Checker's eponymously titled song in the middle of our living room. It proved all too much for my mother. Just before the young couple left to catch their train back up to London, she took Joy into the kitchen. I tagged along holding Sylvan, who was bawling his head off because he didn't like being separated from his mum. I distinctly heard my mother say: 'Please don't bring your friend with you again. Goodness knows what the neighbours will think.'

Joy eventually got tired of my mother's rudeness and took Sylvan away after a year. My mother bawled her eyes out for days after he left. She had grown to love the gorgeous little boy. I wasn't sorry to see him go. His skin was a lighter brown than mine, almost white, and visitors constantly remarked about the good fortune of this. I didn't like how I was unfavourably compared to him and in the end grew to dislike him. In retrospect I was obviously jealous of the poor little fellow. He had a 'real' mum and dad, who hadn't given him away. I wondered whether I would have been given up for adoption if I'd been lighter like Sylvan? These dark thoughts had been troubling me ever since I had found out a secret about myself while riffling through my mother's personal things.

My mother objected to how much the local hairdressing salon charged for a perm, so she preferred to have the noxious chemicals, supplied by the Twink home perm company, administered to her thinning tresses by a non-professional, namely her friend from across the road, Lil Batty, who expertly turned her iron-grey hair into poodle curls in exchange for a good gossip over numerous cups of tea and cream cakes. It was a biannual event and usually took about two hours. That meant I was free to have a good snoop in the large chest of drawers in my parents' bedroom. My absence was rarely missed.

During one such adventure, I discovered an interesting box full of dark brown, rubbery, bullet-shaped things. There was a white paper label on the front of the box, which instructed my mother 'to insert one twice a day'. To a young child this was like discovering hidden treasure. What were they, I wondered? Where did she put them? While my tiny mind raced with possibilities – mostly of the 'can you eat them' variety – I noticed a sheaf of papers tucked at the very back of the drawer, the contents of which haunted me for the next thirty-three years. Inside was a khaki brown registered envelope from 'Eileen Magnus' addressed to my mother; it bore a return Dagenham address on the reverse side. On closer inspection, the other documents turned out to be my adoption certificate and court papers.

The adoption certificate had the name 'Belinda Magnus' written in perfect script. I noticed that this person had my exact birth date. Instinctively, I knew that I was this person. I also thought that Eileen was my real mother.

Eileen was the same name that had been inscribed on the flyleaf of the book *Treasure Island* which had been given to one of my brothers as a present. Feverishly, I ran and fetched the book from my toy cupboard and read the inscription, 'To Kenny, happy birthday 1954, Eileen'. My tiny heart raced as I traced the handwritten words with my finger.

■ ■ ■

I have a photo of my dad lying on his back on the grass in the grounds of a large Dr Barnardo's home in Dagenham. He is wearing a dark '40's-style suit, with a white shirt, and a grey trilby hat pulled down over his eyes. He looks just like Humphrey Bogart in a gangster movie. I'm about eighteen months old, wearing a frilly white organza dress, lace-topped, white knitted socks and white kid leather boots. I'm sitting astride his legs, facing him. He is smiling up at me and I am smiling down at him, with that slightly quizzical look that I seem to have in all childhood photos, as if I am wondering whether the love that is on offer is real. One thing is for sure: I really loved my dad in an uncomplicated way. We had an understanding; he thought I was fabulous and I thought he was too.

My dad and me, 1955, in the grounds of Dagenham's Dr Barnardo's Home

At work, he fixed articulated lorries. He called them 'arctics'. He often got words wrong, but I loved him all the more for it. He worked for Silcock and Collings, who transported new Ford Motor Company cars on these huge lorries to distribution sites all over England. Sometimes one of these lorries would drive past me on the way to school. I felt so proud that he made these gargantuan beasts well when they got sick. At least that was my understanding of what he did for a job. I used to tell people, when I was very young, that he was an 'arctic doctor'. They probably thought I was daft.

Before becoming a mechanic, he had been a long-distance lorry driver for Rediffusion television manufacturers. He'd travelled far and wide with that job. Sometimes he was away all week, returning on a Saturday morning, just to disappear down the local pub, the Parkside, for opening time. He would stagger home for the football results in the afternoon after closing time. At 5 p.m. my mother would serve up a large bloater fish done in vinegar for his tea. It came with bread and butter on a tray, so that he could carry on watching television while he ate. Our family didn't do lunch and dinner; we, like most working-class people at that time, did dinner and tea. That was a major difference between the working and middle classes.

My dad was working class and proud of it. He was the thirteenth son of an itinerant pig man. His mother had died giving birth to him in June 1912. I'm surprised that she didn't give up the ghost sooner, considering how many children she had. His father quickly married a formidable countrywoman from Clacton-on-Sea. As the youngest, my dad grew up a softhearted country boy. During their courtship he used to ride a motorbike all the way to Romford from Clacton, just to see my mother for the afternoon, and then go all the way back. That was quite a journey in those days, no bypasses and new roads to get you there quickly. After they married, my mother moved with him to Weeley, near Clacton, but she hated it. She was a town girl and Dad's stepmother was at great pains to let her know this at all times.

Later Dad's father would take up employment as a pig man near Enfield and Barnet in the 1930s. Dad seemed to be very fond of that area and would drive through it at every available opportunity, eschewing motorways and dual carriageways in and around London, just so that he could point out what used to be countryside or allotments and orchards, instead of row upon row of houses. He would have a tear in his voice as he moaned about how built up the area had become.

He adored cars or indeed any motorised transport, buses, coaches, lorries; they were all grist to his mechanical mind. He knew what was wrong with a car within a few seconds of starting the engine. He liked beer and Vera Lynn, and always voted Labour. I considered his political affiliation very principled of him. Indeed, I never saw him display any prejudice towards people just because of the colour of their skin either. Once I heard him say that he had stood up for a West Indian man he worked with, whose workmates had complained about him to the foreman. My dad refused to get drawn into the dispute. 'He does his job well and knows what he's doing, unlike some of 'em that wants to see him gone for some reason or another,' was all he would say, when he related this story to my mother.

She, on the other hand, displayed her prejudice as fear. Her most constant fear was that I would 'go the way of poor Janet Sparks'.

Posing on my dad's Wolseley in 1955 outside our house

The 'Janet' in question was the adopted daughter of my mother's best friend, Mrs Sparks. Janet had been five years old when she had been removed from Barnardo's orphanage to become the only child of the Sparks family. My mother had first met Mrs Sparks while shopping in Romford market. They had hit it off immediately because they were both convinced that they were doing their bit for the good of the Commonwealth by adopting two young strays, both of whom had been left behind after their respective fathers had flown the coop.

While our mothers conversed, Janet and I stood to one side silently staring at each other. She was of West Indian origin, tall and lissom, lightly tanned with glossy, curly brown hair, casually pushed back with a red plastic Alice band, and hanging in tendrils all the way to the small of her back. Janet was the kind of girl who, even if she'd been wearing a sack, would still have looked a million dollars. I envied her on sight. Although she was only fifteen, she already stood about 5' 9" in her stockinged feet. I was only nine at the time. How I longed to be as grown-up as she was.

Mrs Sparks invited my mother and me to her house the following week and a firm friendship sprang up between them. We visited often for lunch during school holidays. Then one day we found Mrs Sparks in floods of tears when we visited unexpectedly. Her usually immaculate appearance was dishevelled, as though she'd been crying for days and hadn't bathed or fixed her hair. Ordinarily, her black-dyed hair would be backcombed and upswept into a gravity-defying bouffant, reminiscent of Elsie Tanner, a much loved character in Britain's favourite soap of the '60s *Coronation Street*. On that particular day, her hair lay like damp horsehair on her heaving shoulders, grey strands creeping through at her temples. 'I can't talk today,' she said curtly. 'You'll have to come back another time.'

She quickly shut the door, leaving us standing on her doorstep. That was the last we ever saw of her.

My mother tried to communicate by phone and letter, but all to no avail. Not to be deterred, she travelled all the way to the eel and pie shop in Bow where she knew that Mrs Sparks did some part-time work. On arrival there was no sign of her. My mother discreetly asked the skinny young woman serving behind the counter whether she knew what had happened to her. The shop was empty after the lunchtime rush, so the woman was well inclined to chat.

It transpired that Mrs Sparks had left her job some weeks ago, but the woman had heard on the grapevine that her daughter Janet was six months pregnant by an unemployed West Indian drug dealer and now lived in a squat in Ladbroke Grove. Warming to her theme, the woman said that the Sparkses had warned their errant daughter that if she came home with a black man, they wouldn't open the door to her. Since Janet had refused to visit them without her boyfriend, they cut her off completely. How cruel, I thought. How could they ever have really loved her?

During my teenage years, Janet was held up as an example of a 'girl gone bad' because she had been ungrateful and gone the way of the 'dirty girls'. This mantra was dinned into me for so long and so hard that I was completely paralyzed in the presence of black men for some number of years after I left home, as bizarre as that sounds. It was as if both our adoptive mothers fervently wished to breed the black out of us. By then there was a generation of these kinds of well-meaning women doing just that to a new generation of 'coloured' children. I don't know what happened to Janet Sparks and her baby. I wish I did.

So, why did my mother choose a black child if she had so much antipathy towards black people? Didn't it occur to her that my 'colour' was going to be a future issue, which couldn't be swept under the carpet and ignored? The initial decision to adopt a child into the family had been made after my mother developed a facial paralysis known as Bell's Palsy, which had rendered the left side of her face like the molten wax drips on a candle that has been left in a draught. The viral infection of her facial nerve destroyed not only her looks but her confidence too. She was reluctant to go out in public in case people stared or poked fun at her. Her health began to deteriorate as she became more reclusive.

Our family GP, a rotund and florid whisky-drinking Scotsman, Dr Donald, decided, in his wisdom, that what she needed was something to take her mind off her appearance. How about a new baby? Babies were considered a common panacea for all womanly ills in the '50s. Unfortunately, my mother had had a hysterectomy after the birth of Roger, so technically another child was impossible. So Dr Donald helpfully suggested an adoption.

In those days, prospective adoptive parents were invited to view a row of available babies and then asked to choose one. That is so scary. As a child, I often wondered what would have happened if I hadn't been chosen, or indeed, if I had been picked by somebody else. Presumably people just walked up to a crib and said: 'Ooh, that one looks nice, we'll have that one, please.'

Fortunately for me, the other children available for adoption on the day that I was chosen were boys. After rearing four boys already, my parents desperately wanted a girl. So much so that they didn't care what colour it came in. This child supermarket, where I was on 'special offer', was called Sunnedon House in Coggeshall near Braintree in Essex. Coggeshall is a picturesque, sleepy little village, full of quaint clapboard houses, whose garden gates whisper to each other of gentler times; a perfect place to hide the disgraced pregnant young women who came there to give birth.

I've since discovered that back then the countryside was awash with 'Mother and Baby Homes', most of them run by the church. Such Christian do-gooders thought that depriving a bastard child of its identity would be beneficial in the long term, even more so if it was a 'coloured bastard'. The mother's shame was hidden and the child relocated to other benevolent families or orphanages – problem solved – a win-win situation for all those involved. The sweet smell of charity perfumed the rank stench of hypocrisy that underpinned such Establishment philanthropy.

Similar hypocrisy is still evident today, exercised most notably in Africa. I am physically sickened every time I listen to some vacuous pop star or actor prattling on about 'how they didn't realize things were so bad in Africa' after a visit to a new war zone's refugee camp. Often their solution to the beleaguered continent's problems is: adopt a black baby. Imbeciles! They completely miss the point that the reason why things are so bad is the legacy of colonialism and the intransigence of the International Monetary Fund. These twin evils make the nations beggars and their people paupers. You cannot draw lines on a map and make up the names of nations comprised of differing tribes. Suddenly these people are thrown together and are forced to compete for resources. The black people left in charge after the colonialists decamped to Blighty had been educated to be just like their departing white overlords, so how can any of us be surprised at the messy inheritance that remains in most African countries.

The periodic violent coups and deathly famines that beset the continent are seen by the developed world as evidence that black people are incapable of governing themselves. Well-fed celebrities flock around famine victims like brightly feathered vultures. They alight from helicopters and 4x4s to bask in the flashing cameras of half the world's press, eagerly maximizing their photo-ops amid the devastation so they can show the world how much they care. Sometimes they pluck some poor unfortunate child from the clutches of starvation and spirit them off to a life of plenty in palatial surroundings, never once thinking about the future consequences of their actions for the child. Most often, we mere mortals are tearfully exhorted to give, give, give while the IMF quietly takes, takes, takes. Enough. Saint Bob Geldof and Madonna eagerly campaigned in recent years to 'Make Poverty History', but surely the real aim should be to 'Make Wealth History'. Bet they wouldn't be so keen on that.

In the meantime, back to the 'buy one get one free' offer at the kiddies' supermarket. I do not wish to sound bitter about the good fortune of my adoption. I am grateful, to whom I don't know, but I am very grateful that I was chosen and taken home, however it happened. At that time, the alternative would have been an orphanage, probably the Dr Barnardo's Home in Dagenham. I've since met a few of the inmates who were in a similar position to me, and they are all damaged in their own ways, not from the Home per se, but from growing up in an institution as opposed to a loving home.

At first, my new parents fostered me with a 'view to adoption'. That phrase always made me laugh, whenever my mum said it. Fostering sounded like a first-floor window with a bright adoption vista on the horizon. The envelope that had been so meticulously written on by my real mother was registered, because it was used to send money to my mother for my upkeep each month. I was told that eventually the money dried up, so I was legally adopted at eighteen months old. I often wondered what happened in the intervening period. Did my mother visit me? The copy of *Treasure Island* that I had discovered suggests that she did. Did I pine for her? I would never know.

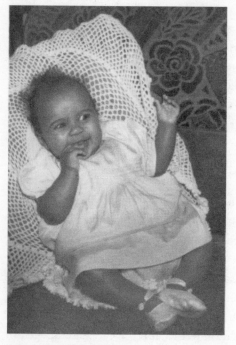

Me at eight months

I cannot say that I wasn't loved. I know I was. But I grew up feeling like a cuckoo in somebody else's nest. It's bad enough not looking like anybody in your family, but it is very confusing not being the same colour as them. Somehow it was like being doomed to play catch-up for the rest of your life. Nobody in

County of Essex
PETTY SESSIONAL DIVISION OF ROMFORD

E. TINSLEY.
SOLICITOR.
CLERK TO THE JUSTICES.

TELEPHONE: ROMFORD 915.

Court House,
South Street,
Romford.

Ref: ET/MM.

17th January 1955.

To: M: *&* M*rs* Vickers

Dear Sir/Madam,

Adoption

This matter will be dealt with at the Court House, South Street, Romford, on the 11th February at 3.5 p.m. Please attend and bring the child with you.

Yours faithfully,

Clerk to the Romford
Justices

---

the family had the language to deal with it. Nowadays, families are given instruction by social services about how to deal with the problems that might be thrown up by adopting mixed-race children, but no such checks and balances were in operation then. It was a case of 'suck it and see'. Unfortunately, my family didn't consider it a problem. Well, it wasn't for them.

When Mum told me that I was adopted, she had said that adopted people were 'special'. I have never figured out exactly what is special about being adopted. In common parlance, 'special' is used to describe a 'one of a kind' or something that is admired, precious or irreplaceable, but in reality it usually denotes something that is not acceptable, good or wanted, hence 'Special Olympics', 'Special Needs', where the word is used to denote a deficiency. Is it a deficiency to have too much melanin pigment?

Throughout my early childhood I longed to be special, just like my mother had promised; that was the biggest white lie of all, because I soon learnt that it is possible to be 'special' for all the wrong reasons.

TWO

'I'LL HAVE SOME OF THAT'

My dad, me and my mum

It began at age nine and it stopped in the summer of the same year that I passed my 11+ exam and changed school.

Opposite our house was a road full of small, well-kept front gardens and neat houses, a pleasant short cut that led to a subway under a busy dual carriageway. In 1962 a troll moved into the last but one house at the far end of the road. His name was George. His first wife had died and he had recently re-married. The new wife, Doris, was a good few years younger than he was.

George was a friend of Ken, my second oldest brother who, by now, worked in a furniture shop in Romford called Killwicks. George got him the job. Ken was a born salesman and since the newly introduced hire purchase had proved so popular with housewives, he made a good living. People loved Kenny, as he was affectionately known. He had an open face and a winning smile and could charm the birds from the trees when it came to selling something to somebody, whether they wanted it or not. What few people knew was that he was adopted too. However, he was white and about fourteen years older than me. I looked on him as a kind of role model after I found out about my own adoption. He seemed to have taken his lack of real parentage in his stride, so why shouldn't I?

George was also a friend of the family of Ken's wife, June. They were a typical cockney family from Dagenham. They would have family get-togethers, which seemed to involve their entire street descending on their house to smoke copious quantities of cigarettes and do some serious drinking. I hated their parties. My eyes would smart from the acrid smoke in the room. The adults wore colourful paper hats and after enough booze would start raucously singing music hall songs like 'Roll Out the Barrel' and 'If You Were the Only Girl in the World' at the tops of their voices, while I handed round plates of spam sandwiches and bowls of homemade pickled onions.

George would sit holding court on the sofa with a big smile on his face, chomping a cigar and being the life and soul of the party. When he saw me approaching with the sandwich platter he would wink at me and always say: 'I'll have some of that.'

It was his favourite catchphrase. People loved to hear him

Me aged nine

say it and some of them tried to copy him, but never with George's sense of comedic timing.

Everybody loved George, except Mum, who used to refer to him as looking like 'old Christie'. She meant that he resembled John Christie, the serial killer of 10 Rillington Place fame, who was hanged for his crimes a few months before my birth. And he did.

He had a large, domed head, with a few dark strands greasily trained across the leprous expanse of skin covering

43

his bony skull. Thick horn-rimmed spectacles completed the similarity to Christie, magnifying his steely gaze. He revelled in the notoriety that this resemblance gave him and delighted in telling anybody who would listen of how once a young woman ran out of the compartment on the Romford to Liverpool Street train when he got in the carriage, shouting: 'It's him, it's him. It's Christie.'

He would laugh when he told the story and he related it often. Even his friends told the story for him in his absence, if his name came up in conversation.

How it began, I don't know. All I know is that it did. I visited his comfortable house with its white, decorative shutters, situated on a corner plot overlooking the main Romford to London arterial road, every Sunday afternoon at his wife Doris's request, ostensibly to help out with their young child. This arrangement had been sorted out unbeknown to me, but probably Ken was used as a go-between.

The house had a long front garden and a small wall in front. It was semi-detached and had three bedrooms, as well as an upstairs bathroom, which I considered a luxury, because at that time our toilet was still outside. There was a spotless fitted kitchen just off the living room at the back and a sitting room at the front. Guests were entertained in the sitting room. It had a big TV with a wood surround, a three-piece suite in the deco style and a huge, carved dark mahogany sideboard that gave the room a funereal air. It was a big room, bigger than the rooms at our house, but maybe I just remember it as big because of the enormity of what happened there.

I liked to help his wife Doris with her year-old baby boy. I was never entrusted with the child, being considered too young then, but I was allowed to make myself useful, buttering bread for sandwiches and laying the table for tea, while she played with Junior. I had an ulterior motive in keeping myself busy at all times, because while I was doing useful chores, he couldn't touch me. I rarely stayed safe for long. Eventually he would think up some pretext for spiriting me away from Doris and I would find myself at his mercy again. He never worried about discovery.

Sometimes Doris would be out when I arrived, but he would always tell my mother, who usually delivered me to the house, that she was expected back shortly. These were the times I feared most. I wanted to scream at my mother not to leave me, but I never did. George assured her that they would drop me back home at 7 p.m. That gave him four hours to do things to me that I knew were wrong, but I didn't have the vocabulary to be able to explain what was happening.

■ ■ ■

I wasn't raped. I am eternally grateful for that. He enjoyed kissing and touching. I was nine and he was in his forties. Whenever an opportunity arose to indulge his passion, he attached himself to me like a leech and somehow he couldn't let go. Something would have to happen, like the creak of a door, a doorbell ring or a baby's cry before he felt impelled to stop what he was doing. The sorry business was executed silently.

I still cannot imagine why Doris didn't think that something was not quite right about her husband. His favourite trick was to insist that I help him put the baby to bed just before I went home. Doris was usually busy in the kitchen washing up, so she thought he was just being a helpful hubby. She lavished praise on him for his thoughtfulness.

As soon as Junior fell asleep, he would molest me next to the crib. In hindsight, such behaviour seems unbelievable, but

I didn't know how to go downstairs and start a conversation with his wife, which would begin: 'By the way, do you know that your husband...' Instinctively I knew she would not believe me. Probably nobody else would either.

When I hear the stories of other abuse sufferers I am always staggered by the everyday nature of the crime. It is not that you are captured in the street and dragged off into the undergrowth and raped, that would be bearable almost, because you could prove to everybody that a crime had been committed, but when an adult man French kisses and intimately touches a child, that is not something that leaves any tangible evidence. It is not something that a child can put a name to. That is the tragedy. The only evidence is the invisible mental scar. That is the crime.

When I finally got round to telling my parents, all hell broke loose. It had been a typical Sunday. I had walked to the house on my own, because I was nearly eleven now and I didn't need my mother to take me. Doris was not in when I knocked, only George. I knew what it would mean as soon as I set foot in the house. He would be on me. His hands would be on me, his mouth would be on me and I would submit, mainly because I didn't know what else I was supposed to do. I resigned myself to my fate.

He seemed to be wherever I went. He was always present at parties, wedding receptions and christenings that we went to; he would turn up to sports day with my brother Ken at Romford stadium, probably to ogle the girls in their gym knickers when we ran in the schools championships. Once he had mentioned that I shouldn't tell anybody about what he was doing because they wouldn't understand. I never thought to question why they wouldn't understand. His adult status lent him an authority that was beyond questioning by a mere child.

Parklands Junior School relay team at County
Championships, Romford stadium, winning the 440 yards
relay, me far left, aged ten

His behaviour didn't arouse suspicion in others. He held
down a good job; children came to play in his house; he had a
small baby and another one on the way; he drove a good car.
He was normal, therefore I tried to tell myself that what was
happening must be normal. While I was in the house, I was
the centre of attention. I was special. But I didn't want to be
that special. I just wanted it to stop.

Sometimes I would think that it had stopped. I was allowed
to spend a couple of hours unmolested, but eventually I
would be manoeuvred into a place where he could grab just a
few minutes with his hands on me.

On the fateful day that I finally spilled the beans, he had
plenty of time to do whatever he wished, but unfortunately
unlimited access to the sweet shop made him sick. He laid me
down on the floor and got astride me. Suddenly things went
too far, this was more than just touching. He was pushing
something hard against my leg and making grunting noises.

Then the doorbell rang. He jumped off me like a scalded cat and ran to the bay window. I heard him say: 'Shit, it's Doris. What's she doing here?'

As he hurriedly turned away from the window, I noticed that the front of his trousers was undone, revealing a fleeting glimpse of something pink and fleshy. What I saw frightened me. He must have seen where I was looking and hastily re-arranged himself, using the moment to bark: 'Get up off the floor and pull your dress down.'

Fortunately for him, his wife had forgotten her door key, otherwise he would have been caught in flagrante, with some serious explaining to do. As it was, just like 'Old Christie', he got away with it again, or so he thought.

He rushed to the front door and let in his wife and mother-in-law. They had come back early by car because somebody had given them a lift. Ordinarily they caught the Sunday service bus which took ages and was very unreliable. I often wonder what would have happened had they not come back when they did. If they had come back an hour later when they were supposed to, then I think that I would have been introduced to something more than underage heavy petting.

He was flustered for the rest of the afternoon. I was worried, because I knew that some invisible barrier had been breached, the Rubicon had been crossed and would be again unless I said something to somebody. But whom could I tell?

As the afternoon wore on, Doris sensed that something was amiss. She kept asking if anything was wrong.

'No,' I answered unconvincingly.

George looked worried, probably because he thought I might blurt something out that would stop his little game in its tracks. I just wanted out of the house as quickly as possible. Eventually I told them that I felt sick and wanted my mother to come and get me. Doris looked relieved when she realized that my quietness was due to illness. She could relate to that. She rang my mother and explained the situation and within fifteen minutes I was on my way home. As we left the house, I could tell from George's expression that he knew that he had gone too far this time and there was trouble ahead.

I went to bed early, because I had to keep up the pretence of feeling sick after I got home. I was sick, sick with worry, not sick in my stomach. I knew that you weren't supposed to see pink fleshy things at the tops of people's legs, and certainly not a man's legs.

I lay in bed for ages shaking with fear, until my mother came in to kiss me goodnight. She took one look at my face, which can be very expressive when it needs to be, and asked me what was wrong. I told her that something had happened that afternoon and I didn't know how to tell her. What do you mean? she asked.

Then I told her, I can't remember the exact words I used, but I remember saying between sobs: 'He laid me down on the floor, it was because he laid me down on the floor.'

I kept repeating those words, because that was what had been different from the countless times that he had handled me as though I was a doll completely at his disposal. Then I began to cry uncontrollably, begging her to believe me. I think she did, although the only thing I craved at that moment was a cuddle, which was not forthcoming. She just stood at the end of the bed staring at me, with a pensive expression on her lopsided face.

Dad poked his head around the bedroom door to see what all the fuss was about. Mum hustled him outside. I heard her say: 'George has been touching her.'

Dad's response was swift and decisive. Immediately he

wanted to confront George with his crime, but my mother said it was too late and besides Doris was pregnant, the shock would be too much for her. They went into their bedroom and shut the door. I listened to their low voices animatedly talking. Soon my mother came back into my bedroom and quizzed me again about what had happened. I answered her questions as truthfully as I could. Then she made me some cocoa and told me to go to sleep. How could I go to sleep, when I sensed that my tiny world was about to change for ever?

Early the next morning the house became a whirl of family comings and goings. Dad had not gone to work. My brother Ken arrived; he had not gone to work either. Dad and he paid George a visit first thing, before he had a chance to go to work. I do not know what they said, all I know is that Dad and Ken arrived back at the house after a short while with a nervous-looking Doris and George in tow. Junior had been left in the care of the mother-in-law.

They seated themselves on the three-piece suite in the sitting room. Then my mother came upstairs to fetch me. I began to realize the horror of the situation as she led me downstairs. I felt like a condemned prisoner. When I entered the room all eyes turned to me. It was like being led to slaughter. I was made to stand in the middle of the room and tell everybody what George had done to me for the past two years.

Under such intolerable pressure, I became completely tongue-tied. All I could hear above the thumping of my heart was my mother nervously repeating: 'Go on, tell him what you told me. Don't be scared.'

I cautiously lifted my eyes and stared directly into his. Seeing his discomfort strengthened my resolve. He looked like a gecko. His prominent eyes, made even larger by the thickness of his glasses, swivelled nervously around the room as if he was searching for a place to hide.

He was dressed smartly, white shirt and tie, pressed grey suit, highly polished shoes. He looked ready for battle and the picture of respectability, the illusion marred only by the large beads of sweat popping out on his upper lip. Doris sat beside him in her sensible coat and shoes, her right hand clasping his forearm protectively while her left hand balanced on her large pregnancy bump. Her face was expressionless.

I just wanted to get out of the room. I couldn't understand why my parents were making me see him again. They already knew what had happened. Why didn't they sort it out with George? Why did I feel like I was on trial? Then it dawned on me. Perhaps they thought I had made it up? Desperate to show that I hadn't, I blurted out enough words to explain what George had been doing. When I finished, it was as if the air in the room had been removed. The silence was complete.

Then Doris filled the vacuum by valiantly releasing a torrent of hot air in her husband's defence. Her words fell over each other in their haste to fill the yawning chasm that had opened up between the two families.

'She's making it up. Of course George wouldn't do such a thing,' said Doris heatedly. 'She's just a dirty little liar. Always wants to be the centre of attention. Always showing off. You'll have trouble with her, mark my words. You don't know what you're getting if a kid's not your own. Bad blood, that's what this is all about, bad blood.'

George told her to calm down. I think everybody in the room was scared that she was going to give birth right then and there. Simultaneously all the adults started shouting at each other. I was forgotten in the melee and began to cry. I kept thinking: 'Why did you tell, why did you tell? They don't believe you anyway.'

Eventually the shouting stopped and George and Doris left. They didn't leave voluntarily, Dad ordered them out of his house. The abuse was never mentioned again.

I had to pass his house every day on the way to my new school. Sometimes I saw him backing his car out of the drive. Occasionally, I had to wait while he backed right past me as his wife waved him off. She would slam the front door shut when she spotted me, as if to obliterate a bad memory. If she could have hit me with the same force that she unleashed on the door, then I'm sure that I would be dead. He pretended I was invisible. Soon I changed my route, preferring to walk over a mile out of my way rather than be subjected to this daily torture.

My parents never spoke to them again. Ken continued his relationship with them, albeit surreptitiously, I later discovered.

I felt betrayed.

The troll died in 2007.

THREE

'WHAT A WONDERFUL WORLD'

Me aged eleven – first day at senior school

The '60s were transitional times, both for the world and for me. Many countries were busy making the transition from being run by the British Empire to their own governance; from the children that colonialism had made of them to the fully fledged adulthood that only independence can bring. I, too, was busy making my own transition from child to teenager, moving from the hitherto omnipotence of the kitchen table to the freedom of my bedroom, that independent teenage fiefdom that must be defended at all costs.

Until my twelfth year, the kitchen table had been the hub of my family life. It was made of dark oak, with two hard-to-handle extending leaves, which were rarely used due to lack of space in the already cramped kitchen. It had large, swollen legs, like the oedema in the inflated ankles of old ladies. Diagonal wooden crossbars held the whole structure together. Two or three threadbare blankets, of pre-war origin, covered the tabletop, providing insulation from any heat sources. On top of these was a pungent-smelling, brightly patterned oilcloth, which was the tablecloth for weekdays, but on Sundays it was covered by a starched white cotton cloth for the ritualistic weekly roast dinner, which happened at about 2 p.m. or whenever my dad saw fit to return from the pub. The table occupied one side of the small rectangular kitchen. Only three mismatched wooden chairs surrounded it after my four brothers left home. When I was very small, Jock, an understandably grumpy, shaggy brown, crossbred terrier lived in a wooden box under the table until he died of distemper when I was eight. He was never replaced.

This table was the most versatile item of furniture in the house. On Mondays, the table was stripped bare except for the radio and used to sort out piles of dirty clothes into coloureds and whites. Then Reckett and Coleman's Robin starch powder was added to a large metal bucket of boiling water, which I stirred with a big wooden stick into a glutinous mess before going to school.

Some people think that 'cleanliness is next to Godliness', but this was not good enough for my mother; she considered that starchy stiffness was next to Godliness. All I can say is, I pity those poor angels if she is now working in Heaven's laundry room! My dad and I suffered sore necks from the amount of starch added to our white shirts, his for work and mine for school. The stiffened petticoats worn under dresses in the '50s were subjected to the same fate, before the advent of early '60s' fashions mercifully consigned them to jumble sales.

On Tuesday afternoons, the table was converted into a makeshift ironing board by rolling back the oilcloth and covering the blankets with a candy-striped winceyette sheet. My mother started ironing at precisely 2 p.m., when *Woman's Hour* began. I watched in awe as she worked her magic on the white starched meringues to make them at least recognisable items of clothing, if barely wearable.

The table was left idle on a Wednesday, apart from the daily late afternoon chore of peeling and preparing vegetables for tea. On Wednesdays my mother went shopping in the morning and visited friends or relatives in the early afternoon.

On Thursdays pastry was rolled out on it during the afternoon pie-baking session. Friday afternoons were reserved for mixing ingredients together in large Pyrex bowls to make lots of cakes for the weekend, just in case relatives unexpectedly arrived. Since this rarely happened, most of the cakes from these marathon baking sessions made their way into my dad's lunchbox for the rest of the week, much to his chagrin because he was not a sweet-toothed man.

Just before I started school, the table became a makeshift desk, where my mother taught me the alphabet and how to read, while she continued her housewifely chores alongside me. In return, when I was older, I would sit and read library books to her or write thank-you letters for her after school.

My cooking and cleaning skills were learned from observing her way of doing things for so many years, most of which are now redundant with the advent of labour-saving devices and ready-made meals, but I will always enjoy the taste of freshly prepared food and the smell of polished furniture in my home, in deference to my mother's way of doing things.

The table set my mother's agenda for every day and only illness or a death in the family caused a deviation in this schedule. It was privy to many a secret or family argument. This old wooden workhorse outlived both my parents and is probably alive and well today at the back of a junk shop somewhere in Essex.

In pride of place on the kitchen table, next to the wooden trays propped against the wall, which conveniently hid the flotsam and jetsam of old biros, bits of paper and buttons that washed up on its far shore, stood the radio.

In my early years, it was a wooden surround Ecko, with two big dials receiving long and medium waves and VHF. Every weekday, except Wednesday, my mother religiously tuned into two programmes, *Listen With Mother* at 1.45 p.m., followed by *Woman's Hour* at 2 p.m. I would sit at the table with my ear as close to the radio as possible, while she sewed lost buttons onto clothes or darned Dad's holey old socks. It was a ritual that we both enjoyed. I can still remember the frisson of childish excitement, as I heard the gentle melody of the 'Berceuse' from Fauré's *Dolly Suite* fade and then those immortal words, spoken in patrician tones by what sounded like a very elegant BBC lady presenter: 'Are you sitting comfortably? Then I'll begin.'

By the time I was twelve, the family radio had changed with the times, from the valve variety to one with transistors. Now, a new, shiny, beige plastic Bush radio with a red rotating dial and its own carrying handle brought the news to our household. My interest in pop music had suddenly flourished when I discovered the Tamla Motown artists and the Beatles. Immediately, I considered the radio my property, re-tuning it to the trendier sounds of Radio Luxembourg, instead of the Light or Home programmes favoured by my parents.

As I migrated from the companionship of the kitchen table to the seclusion of my bedroom with my new transistor radio in tow, I began a somewhat tortuous and confused journey towards adulthood. Most evenings I could be found sat at my desk doing my homework while listening to the radio, happily multi-tasking.

After bedtime at 9 p.m., I would huddle under the sheets, fiddling with the radio dial, trying to get Luxembourg's intermittent signal, but mainly hearing only white noise. I suspect that half the teenage population of Romford was similarly occupied, our future musical tastes honed by a small European Duchy.

Then I read in the newspaper about the new pirate station Radio Caroline that had recently started broadcasting the songs of the swinging '60s all day from a ship moored in the English Channel. Until then, and apart from Radio Luxembourg, there had only been a Sunday afternoon chart show on the BBC Light programme and maybe one other on a Saturday dealing with contemporary pop music. In 1965 another ship housing 'Radio London' entered the fray. It did the same job as Caroline, only better. Piracy on the high seas was fast becoming a winning formula for disseminating the new counterculture's pop sounds and simultaneously manipulating the innocent minds of the nation's youth.

At school the most popular bands were the Beatles and the Rolling Stones. Indeed, each pupil had to be a supporter of one or other of these bands. If you liked both then it transgressed some unwritten playground rule. Most of my friends loved

Romford Technical High School in the 1960s

the Beatles, particularly the girls who took the prettily insipid, puppy-dog-eyed Paul McCartney to their hearts. I couldn't see the attraction. As far as I was concerned the four mop tops from Liverpool looked cute in their matching suits and their songs were memorable in the same way that it was impossible to forget the words to nursery rhymes once heard, but for me nothing beat the raw power of the guitar-driven Stones. I adored Jagger's primal howl, seductive androgyny and energetic performance. He sounded black, but he wasn't; his facial features looked black, but he wasn't. Also the very sight of him wriggling his skinny torso suggestively while performing on TV was enough to enrage my mother, which was a prerequisite for me liking anything at the age of twelve. He was my perfect idol.

I loved many of the girl singers of the day too, Cilla Black and Sandie Shaw in particular, and even the mysterious French singer Françoise Hardy, who'd just entered the British charts. The only problem was that their images of long, poker-straight, parted-in-the-middle hair and thin, gamine bodies were totally unattainable for me. As I approached my teens my body had acquired womanly curves. Unfortunately in the early '60s girls with large breasts need not apply in the fashionable stakes, particularly if the twin orbs in question were always struggling to emerge from whatever cotton and elastic contraption held them in place. Just to clarify, I was hardly of Jordanesque proportions, but my blossoming bosom was a huge inconvenience for the style of uniform favoured at my school. Gymslips were de rigueur for us girls between eleven and thirteen. These old-fashioned garments suit only the flat-chested brigade; they are totally impractical for encasing rapidly expanding womanhood.

In among the teen angst and unrequited love stories that were the main fodder of the pop charts emerged an intriguing voice. When I heard Bob Dylan singing 'The Times They Are A-Changing' on a cold spring night underneath my yellow flowered eiderdown, I thought that he had penned the song just for me. His characteristic raw nasal voice, always seemingly in search of a packet of Lockets, roared a clarion call through the ether, imploring me to mount the barricades. Whose barricades didn't matter. Political ideas didn't mean too much to me at that age, but I was ready to follow him anywhere. His lyrics succinctly summed up my straitjacketed family life.

An awareness of another world beyond the sleepy, suburban confines of Romford took shape in my mind. Eager to be more familiar with this new world's styles, ideas and music, I started avidly watching *Ready Steady Go* every Friday. This innovative TV youth programme began with the immortal words 'The weekend starts here'. Unfortunately for me, that promise of an exciting weekend ahead finished with the closing credits. I had but one hour to enter this seductive alternative reality, where a magical audience full of young strutting peacocks dressed in hipster jeans and graphically designed clothes, their Vidal Sassoon precision haircuts elegantly swinging like weighted velvet curtains, bobbed their heads to the music, danced and cheered their new pop idols. I wanted to be one of that hallowed crew, but I was too young. I felt like Alice in Wonderland after she drank the potion that made her shrink – tiny and insignificant.

My chief problem was that I didn't have a natural peer group. All my friends were white and nothing is more imperative for a teenager than fitting in. What with the breasts and my skin colour, all I seemed to do was stick out. I'd also begun to notice that I was no longer treated as the cute little black girl by relatives or benevolent strangers. However irksome that status was, it was infinitely preferable to what I had recently begun to encounter when I went shopping alone in Romford town market, as I sometimes did when my mother was ill with a cold. Often, I found myself subjected to undisguised curiosity and rude remarks and deliberately ignored when it was my turn in a queue. I knew enough about the consequences of racial prejudice by now to know that such slights were intentional, but it was a profound discovery at first hand. In '60s Britain any black person, male or female, young or old, meant trouble to white people.

Hardly any black faces disturbed the milky white soup of humanity that inhabited this Essex backwater. It was a different story about fifteen miles further up the road towards London. My brother Tony and his wife had recently moved to Leytonstone. On the rare visits that my mother made with me to see them, I was amazed to see that the streets were filled with quite a few black faces. Some people were dressed in fancy African robes and some black men sported rakish trilbies, tight-fitting, buttoned-up, '60s-style suits like Malcolm X wore, and walked dragging one leg while still appearing to bounce on their toes.

When I first encountered such people, my mother grabbed my arm and told me not to stare, but I couldn't help it. Besides, these people were staring right back at me, particularly some of the men in trilbies. I suppose my mother and I must have made a rather odd couple. The sight of a black child and an older white woman was rare in those days and not always met with benign indifference.

I was old enough to read the newspapers and indeed had done so for quite a few years. My parents read the *Daily Mirror*, and at weekends, the *News of the World* and *Sunday Pictorial*. Hardly intellectually challenging, in-depth broadsheets, but it was all I had access to and I took a keen interest in what went on in the world.

It was during an English lesson at senior school that I first discovered the precisely drawn class boundaries that delineated Britain into the 'haves' and 'have nots'. I already knew that the 'haves' had loads of money and the 'have nots', like my family, didn't, but as yet the rigorous system's Oliver Twists, the 'please, sir, can I have some more' middle classes, remained undetermined. Our teacher, Mrs Morrell, thirtyish, dyed blonde and by far the most stylish member of her profession in school – she had once worn a mini-dress – asked us to write down what daily and Sunday newspapers our parents read. Then each of us had to read out our respective parents' choices in front of the whole class.

Immediately I discovered lots more newspaper names, some of which would be received by the teacher with a murmur of approval and others, mine in particular, by a slight pursing of the lips and eyebrows raised over the tops of her 'Marge Proops' spectacles. Apparently, it was considered good if your parents read *The Times*, *Sunday Times*, *Daily Telegraph* or the *Sunday Telegraph*. The *Guardian* and the *Observer* were met with grudging approval, but what could not be tolerated were the *Daily Sketch*, *Daily Mirror* and the *News of the World*. Why, I asked myself? Somebody usefully pointed out in the class that their parents thought that it was 'common' to read such newspapers. News to me.

After this lesson, I began taking a keener interest in the headlines of the different newspapers whenever I went to the newsagents for the Sunday papers with my dad. Our Sunday morning outings to Ramsey's, our local newsagent, were a ritual that we both enjoyed. I flipped through the pages of various newspapers while he chatted about cars with the shop owner, who he knew from the pub.

It struck me that the newspapers might be different in their views, but when it came to reporting anything to do with black people, they were usually united, depending on the story, in their condemnation or patronization. Even Cassius Clay, arguably the most famous black man on the planet in 1964, was subjected to vitriolic derision, not just for having the temerity to beat 'Our 'Enry', a popular white British boxer, in a controversial fight the previous year, but more importantly for changing his name to the profoundly foreign Muhammad Ali and embracing the Nation of Islam, a new militant black faith in America.

As soon as I became old enough to recognise Ali's extraordinary hubris and eloquence, coupled with an innate ability to antagonize grown-ups, I became his sole champion in our household. My dad reckoned he was a good fighter, but 'just too damn mouthy', whereas my mother refused to discuss him other than with a dismissive 'Tsk' whenever he appeared in the newspaper or on TV, which was often. Here was a young, strong black man to be proud of; anathema to my mother, particularly if her daughter took an interest in him. The spectre of Janet Sparks's demise hovered between us like Banquo's ghost.

But Ali's success was an exception, because the majority of black people I saw on the evening news were being savagely beaten or hosed down against a wall by uniformed men, just because they wanted to eat at the same lunch counter as their white counterparts. The images of four little black girls who'd been blown up by a bomb while attending their local church still haunted my memory. They were only a few years older than me. Whenever these kinds of news stories appeared, the newscaster automatically spoke about the fight for civil rights. Most of these fights took place in exotically named places like Mississippi or Alabama.

When I asked Mrs Morrell what exactly civil rights were, I was told that the people who demanded such things were just troublemakers. In her next breath: 'Can you spell Mississippi?' she demanded of the class. I didn't bother asking such questions again.

Similarly, African people were relegated to 'native' status in TV documentaries about the vast 'dark continent'. They were normally depicted as living in mud huts, scantily clad, with plates in their deformed lower lips or rings around their extended necks, herding scrawny, half-starved cattle or carrying skinny, fly-blown babies in a scrap of material tied around their waists.

The only exceptions to this depiction were the troublesome blacks in South Africa and Rhodesia. Occasionally I would overhear conversations among family members about work colleagues who had emigrated to one or other of these two countries for the chance of better working conditions and a higher standard of living. In letters back home, most of these émigrés upheld apartheid as a good thing. Even the lowliest white worker got a house with a pool and black servants. I even heard an elderly retired uncle, a former railway union rep, who fancied himself as a bit of a politician, and who had recently switched from voting Conservative to the National Front, say: 'They know how to keep their nig-nogs in their place. Pity we don't do that here.'

My cheeks flamed when I heard what he said, but I was still some way off identifying personally with the 'nig-nogs' in question. Silently, I watched world events unfold. I listened and attempted to learn, but any sense of a deepening black consciousness on my part was embryonic. However, it was beginning to develop. Indeed perhaps it had been developing since 22 November 1963; I just hadn't realized it.

Then I had been ten years old, having a weekly piano lesson with my arthritic teacher, the extravagantly named Victoria Maude Bannock, who lived across the road from our family home. My half-hour lesson was almost finished. The next pupil was already ensconced on one of the two uncomfortable wooden chairs which were exclusively for the use of waiting children in Mrs Bannock's cluttered, antiquated front room. I had long suspected that she used this music room solely for storage, because the rest of the house was completely full. Even the upright piano's top was chock full of boxes, containing old musical scores, precariously towering up towards the ceiling. For such an immaculately turned-out lady, her housekeeping skills left much to be desired.

Her long-suffering husband could often be overheard in the back room shuffling about in his tartan slippers making cups of tea for her and answering the telephone. They were an odd couple: Mr Bannock was a retired pen pusher for the Shell Oil company and Mrs Bannock supplemented his meagre pension by carrying on her lifelong role as a mediocre piano teacher to barely interested pupils after school hours.

The door burst open and Mr Bannock, who was usually heard but never seen, suddenly appeared. This was worthy of comment in itself, let alone what he had to relate: 'They've shot the President, Vic, they've shot the President,' he shouted in his heavy Scottish brogue, his normally rheumy eyes startled into horror.

Mrs Bannock leapt up and rushed out of the room with him, leaving me with the next pupil, a boy who attended the Royal Liberty School, a local all-boys independent school, alone in the room. We stared at each other, unable to comment on such a turn of events.

After a few minutes, a red-eyed Mrs Bannock reappeared, with tears coursing down her wrinkled cheeks. This was another first, because Mrs Bannock was from another era – emotion was never shown; she wasn't named Victoria for nothing. She demanded that we accompany her into the back room where we were invited to sit on the sofa and watch the whole sorry saga of the assassination unfold.

When our respective mothers arrived to collect us, they were invited in too. Soon the back room was awash with people, all transfixed by the shocking images on the TV screen. People who lived through these tragic events often know exactly where they were on this unfortunate day. For me, the mournful first movement of Beethoven's *Moonlight Sonata* is inextricably linked with the death of President Kennedy, because that is what I had been playing when Mr Bannock burst into the music room.

For a ten-year-old these were shocking events. It was my first experience of violence being meted out to a leader of the western world. The one word on everybody's lips when discussing the President's assassination was 'Why?'

I devoured the coverage of the horrific events in the newspapers and on the nightly television news. I particularly paid attention when it was said that President Kennedy was a good guy when it came to helping black people. Pundit after pundit said he was on the side of Dr Martin Luther King, who was also considered to be an all-round good guy, because he believed in getting laws changed by peacefully marching for justice, despite the violence meted out to the marchers.

This concept of non-violent demonstration captured my imagination. In the aftermath of the President's assassination, much was made of Dr King's iconic 'I have a dream' speech, which had been delivered just a few months before Kennedy's fateful journey to Texas. Throughout my teenage years I wondered when 'little black boys and black girls would walk hand in hand with little white boys and girls' as predicted by Dr King. Did some parallel universe exist where cruelty and inhumanity to American blacks was absent? Even though they were on another continent, separated by thousands of miles of ocean, these were 'my people' who were maligned, spat on and ridiculed and somehow I wanted to put that injustice right, but I wasn't sure how – yet.

I had nobody with whom I could discuss this discovery. My peers at school were not interested and, indeed, why should they have been? They were far too busy discussing the latest hairstyles, skirt lengths and boys. I rarely spoke to any of the boys at school. They only seemed interested in football and cars. If we did speak, it was to discuss music, youth's international language.

In 1965, as if to miraculously further that musical discussion, *Ready Steady Go* broadcast a Motown Special presented by Dusty Springfield. I don't remember too much detail about the programme, but I do remember the first time I saw the Supremes sing 'Baby Love'. Dressed in spotless white shift dresses, with shiny, lipsticked mouths and swathes of straight, styled, black hair on their beautiful heads, the three young women shimmied and swayed in time to the music in a discreet spotlight. I'd heard Diana Ross sing on the radio, but nothing prepared me for the sophistication and precision of her performance. I spent hours that night trying to straighten my hair with the aid of a hairbrush and quantities of water. All I got for my efforts was a bad cold, because I'd gone to sleep with slicked-back wet hair, convinced that I would wake up with it straight, only to find it had reverted to its usual fluffiness by morning.

A few of my schoolfriends had seen the programme, but weren't inclined to join me in a discussion about it the following day, although a few of the boys enjoyed lampooning Little Stevie Wonder's harmonica playing, closing their eyes and shaking their heads from side to side while grinning impossibly wide. I felt cheated. I wanted them to talk about the Tamla Motown sound in the same way that they enthusiastically discussed the Liverpool sound but, just as I found it hard to identify with Cilla Black, they didn't want to look like Diana Ross. My friends were quintessentially English, whereas I felt my lodestone weighted with a black American sensibility, because for me, 'That's where the black people were at.' Maybe if I'd lived in London I might have felt differently, because I would have come into contact with West Indian and African immigrants, but they were not present in Essex, so I could indulge my American fantasies any which way I chose.

The monotony of family routine and my adolescent angst were relieved between the ages of twelve and fifteen with a week-long annual holiday in North Wales. My youngest brother Roger had flown the coop and my parents could now leave the house without worrying about what he was doing at home while they were away.

Llandudno was my dad's choice of holiday resort. In between working as a coalman and his present mechanic's job, he had been a long-distance lorry driver. Many of his deliveries were in North Wales and he had grown to love the dramatic scenery. He had often stayed overnight in this seaside town, which nestled in a bay between the rocky outcroppings of the Great Orme and the Little Orme. On first sight, I shared his enthusiasm. I kidded myself that Wales was a foreign country. It was here that I first performed in public, playing the piano in a kids' talent contest in Happy Valley, a pleasure park on the Great Orme. I never won.

We stayed in a family hotel. I had to share the room with my parents, which probably wasn't much of a holiday for them. My mother and I generally spent the day on the beach or wandering around the shops while my dad spent lunchtimes and evenings in the pub. He loved to eat whelks, but I think he was probably allergic to them. When he was the worse for drink he would forget about his allergy and down a few pots of jellied eels and whelks, which meant that he would be up half the night puking into the sink in our room with great heaving retches.

A favourite haunt of ours was an octagonal camera obscura on the Great Orme, an unassuming little building housing an ingenious arrangement of mirrors that offered panoramic views of the town. My mother and I watched enthralled as this magic eye zeroed in on areas of Llandudno Bay. Once we spotted my dad lurching out of a pub on a Friday afternoon and making a beeline for the whelk stall on the promenade.

'Look, there's Dad,' I blurted out, much to the mirth of our fellow viewers, whereupon Mum grabbed my arm and dashed out of the round hut, running down the narrow roads that wound their way up the Orme, to try and intercept him before he downed too many of the offending sea creatures. Needless to say, he began throwing up approximately two hours later. He was hospitalized on that occasion.

I had decided long ago that my best ticket out of Romford was to study hard and go to university. I was in the express stream at Romford Technical High School, which meant that I got the chance to take the nine 'O' levels that I had been entered for a year earlier than designated for my age. In my quest for the freedom that higher education offered, I turned my bedroom into a study haven.

Just lately, it had felt as if I had very little to talk to my parents about any more. A discussion about the assassination of Malcolm X wasn't exactly suitable fodder for an after-dinner chat on a Sunday afternoon. For much of the time I felt isolated and unhappy, but to be fair, feeling confined and at odds with one's parent's chosen lifestyle is almost a rite of passage for any teenager. I fervently wished that I had more friends, but my troubled thoughts about inequality and racism in the wider world preoccupied me and turned me into a loner. I tried to use my self-imposed exile wisely and studied at the local library for an hour after school every day so that I could read more informative newspapers and books.

Slowly I began to understand the problems of the black diaspora. I discovered a horrendous catalogue of injustices against American blacks throughout the continent's comparatively short history. The Deep South had even denied black people the vote until recent years. Such knowledge filled me with a deep anger and resentment. These feelings were made worse by the arrival in Romford of organized racism when I was thirteen. The National Front had begun to sell their newspaper and actively recruit within the newly built shopping precinct. On Saturdays while out shopping with my mother, I made it my business to stare at them very hard and with a hateful expression that I had perfected in my bedroom mirror. How could they peddle such vitriol without anybody complaining? From the activity at their stall, it looked as though many passers-by welcomed the new NF presence on the street. Far from being a problem, they were treated as part of the solution. My Uncle Will, Aunt Vi's husband, often said, 'The NF's got the right idea.' He was an irascible old fool.

One hot summer night in 1967, while listening to Radio Caroline underneath the bedclothes, I heard Aretha Franklin sing 'Respect'. I was instantly bowled over by the energy with which she asked the questions: 'What you want? Baby, I got it. What you need? You know I got it' – questions that were followed by the ultimate statement: 'All I'm asking is a little respect…yeah…Just a little bit!' In the hands of a lesser artist, the song might just have been dismissed as yet another wronged woman's rant against her errant lover, but Aretha Franklin's visceral vocal inhabited the lyric and music so totally that it transcended the obvious unrequited love lament and became a future clarion call for unempowered people everywhere.

As soon as the song finished I wanted to know more about this woman. Instinctively I knew she was saying something profound that would affect me for the rest of my life. By the time I got to see her filmed performance of the song on *Top Of The Pops*, I was a fully paid-up devotee. The sight of this proud black woman, with her unprocessed hair in a natural Afro, walking down the street like a modern-day African Queen, singing such a simple powerful truth, made my heart swell with pride – this new black pride that was increasingly being talked about. Recently, slogans like 'black consciousness' and 'black is beautiful' regularly appeared in the media. I had reached the age where I needed to hear that from somebody.

I had begun to buy make-up like all the other girls at school, but brown foundation creams had yet to be invented at British beauty counters, which were awash with chalky, rose-tinted concoctions designed to aggravate teenage spots and acne. My mother's response to how I looked after a lengthy session applying it said it all: 'You look as though you've dipped your face in a flour bin.'

Even buying a pair of tights was fraught with danger. My legs, encased in the unflattering burnt umber hues of 'American Tan', looked as though they belonged to some other person. It was as if black people didn't exist on the high street and, in terms of spending power, they didn't.

Until then it had never occurred to me that how I wore my hair was a political decision. Articles began appearing in newspapers and magazines, not many but enough, talking about the new Afro hairstyle being worn by black women in America. No more 'processed hair', trumpeted the headlines. I didn't even know what 'processed hair' was. I thought it was some kind of wig. Hot combs, relaxers and the concept of 'conking' were unknown to me. I naively – and in retrospect, laughably – thought that Diana Ross's impossibly high, elaborately tonged, glossy, straight black hair was real!

Also, the word 'black' had begun to be used; not negro or coloured, but telling it like it is, black. And not just the word black, but Black with a capital B. I loved this new word and began referring to myself as Black at every available opportunity, much to the consternation of my mother, who argued: 'You are not black. Don't keep saying that. You are coloured!'

Such a response was like a red rag to a bull. By 1968 war was declared in the house. My *raison d'être* was to defend 'blackness' no matter the cost to familial relations.

The year began with Louis Armstrong releasing, or rather unleashing, the song 'What a Wonderful World' on the British public on New Year's Day. It instantly went to No. 1, even though everything in the world was decidedly not wonderful. It's interesting that it was also released in the USA where it bombed dismally. The contradiction between the reality of the American homeland and the song's fantasy universe was too stark to fool the public.

I hated the song. I consigned Louis Armstrong – in retrospect totally unfairly – to 'Uncle Tom' Siberia. I loathed it that white people loved the way he sang the trite lyrics. He was the acceptable face of 'coloured' and I was having none of it.

'Oh, he sings that lovely,' my mother opined every time it came on the radio. 'Such a shame he sweats so much.' Why Louis Armstrong's sweating habits should matter is something that only my mother would be able to explain.

Ironically, 'What a Wonderful World' kicked off the year that informed my thinking for the rest of my life. It was the year when everybody got to see the mess that was happening. It was the year that the revolutionary funkster James Brown would name a people, not just in his country, but worldwide, with the famous slogan 'Say It Loud, I'm Black and I'm Proud'. It was the year that two black athletes, Tommie Smith and John Carlos, raised black-gloved fists at the Mexico City Summer

Olympics and symbolized the dissatisfaction of a people for ever. It was the year that the magical whirling dervish Jimi Hendrix recorded 'Voodoo Chile' with the opening lyric of 'Stand up next to a mountain, chop it down with the back of my hand' – the best lyrical indictment against racism coupled with a call to arms that I have ever heard. The sense of empowerment for blacks was palpable.

And yet that same summer, Dr Martin Luther King was gunned down by a single bullet on the Lorraine Motel balcony in Memphis in April and a few months after, Robert Kennedy, the Democratic presidential nominee, was gunned down in a dirty kitchen passageway at the Ambassador Hotel, Los Angeles, after delivering a victory speech in the wake of winning the Californian primary.

So much for civil rights legislation! It was 'open season', not just on blacks but on white liberals too. I watched in awe as the world unravelled. Suddenly young people, particularly students, were on the march. American blacks were rioting in most major cities; all seemingly wanted their pound of white flesh as indignity was piled on indignity until only burning hatred prevailed. The world was crumbling and yet in Romford nobody seemed to notice. I had to get out of there.

■ ■ ■

But what could I do? How could I make any kind of definitive statement from such suburban solitude? Then I hit upon an idea. It was late October 1968 and the newspapers were eagerly promoting a new musical that had just hit Britain, *Hair*.

Hair was Broadway's groundbreaking rock musical. The Vietnam war was escalating, so *Hair*'s plot about a New York street kid and his friends deciding if he should burn his draft card was very topical indeed. The original London cast even included such present-day theatre stalwarts as Tim Curry, Paul Nicholas and Elaine Paige. The songs about sex, drugs, race and personal liberation were controversial, and the musical caught the Zeitgeist of the time. The biggest stir happened at the moment before the interval when the entire cast appeared naked under a dim blue light. How typical that England should be more preoccupied with the concept of nudity than with the concerns of humanity.

Even more ironic was the fact that the cast member who garnered most publicity – even though she had only two lines of dialogue – was a nineteen-year-old American, Marsha Hunt. This Afro-haired piece of gorgeousness became the first black woman to appear on an up-market magazine, *Queen*. She dated Mick Jagger, signed to Track records (also Jimi Hendrix's record company), and appeared on *Top of the Pops*, singing a hit single, all within a matter of months.

I was knocked out. She was indeed the 'sweet black angel' that Jagger would sing about on 'Exile on Main Street', and her achievement offered a much-needed way forward for me. If she could succeed with her chosen goal, despite being labelled black in a white society, then so could I. She looked wild in her fringed buckskin outfits and hippie-ish ensembles, completely at odds with the manufactured, manicured sophistication of Diana Ross. Her innate originality made me want to be her, but since this was impossible, I settled for the next best thing: I wanted her hair!

My hair, or perhaps I should say the lack of it, became a singular preoccupation. I normally regarded it as an inconvenience on top of my head, something that was rarely remarked upon with any civility, constantly described as frizzy or woolly and apparently longing to have white hands reach out and touch it at every opportunity. That was the main trouble: in those days white folks just loved to touch your hair or your skin. They always expressed surprise after a casual feel, usually saying: 'Ooh, I thought your skin would be leathery,' or another favourite, ' Ooh, your hair's really soft, well, I never.'

Such treatment had led me to be very mistrustful of people and their prying hands. Prior to Ms Hunt arriving on the scene, I yearned to have the poker-straight, shoulder-length tresses of my white girlfriends either with a heavy fringe or parted in the middle. Such hairstyles were the epitome of the '60s 'cool' generation. Therefore a curly mop of hair on top of my head, in a fashion world ruled by Marianne Faithfull, Twiggy, Jean Shrimpton and Penelope Tree, seemed like God's cruel joke for an over-sensitive teenager.

The role models that existed had hair creations that seemed to defy gravity, humidity and credibility. I studied photos of the girl groups on the Motown label or some of the ladies that graced the Stax label for some kind of clue as to how they successfully managed to coax their hair into the semblance of a Mr Whippy ice-cream cone, but I'd never heard of straightening combs or flat irons, the gothic horror tools that got the job done. I didn't know that 'black hairdressers' existed. My mother cut my hair and didn't have the faintest idea how to do it. Her idea of styling was dangerously close to trimming an unruly hedge.

I had found my perfect role model in the wilful goddess, Ms Marsha Hunt. Little did I know at fifteen that in eleven years' time we would meet under wholly different circumstances in Los Angeles, with me as the pop star and her as a working single mother.

But, for now, here was somebody who had a head of hair that I could aspire to. Marsha Hunt was hard not to notice.

She cropped up everywhere in the papers, magazines and television. I followed her progress with interest, and a huge amount of glee. I cut out any photo of her that I could find and pinned it on my wall.

My new fascination didn't escape the notice of my mother, who made it quite clear that she did not approve of my new heroine. My mother's ideas of suitable black females to emulate were Winifred Atwell, a rotund, jolly black Caribbean piano player on the odious *Billy Cotton Band Show*, or, diva of all divas, Shirley Bassey. Much to my mother's horror, I nicknamed Ms Bassey 'Burly Chassis'. I loathed her stentorian singing style, her revealing sequined gowns and her cheesy perma-grin. She was not the role model I craved even if she was homegrown talent and came from Tiger Bay in Cardiff. As far as I was concerned, both of these women belonged to another age, an age of 'knowing your place'. Marsha Hunt represented the 'shock of the new'. Black people were on the rise.

In order to incense my mother further, I painted 'Say It Loud, I'm Black and I'm Proud' on a large piece of cardboard in black paint, with a clumsily designed clenched black fist beside it. This huge statement now hung on my bedroom wall, directly opposite the door she entered every morning to give me my wake-up call. She would mutter under her breath, 'This sort of thing is turning your mind,' and 'No good will come of it, you know.'

'How wrong can you be,' I thought, pretending to be asleep. 'You'll see.'

In 1969 I became aware of the Black Panther Party in America who were championing a radical new concept, 'Black Power'. Everything about the Panthers was provocative: their Maoist-inspired political slogans, their ubiquitous black berets and leather jackets, their clenched-fist Black Power salute, their big Afro hairstyles, their practice of openly bearing firearms, and their disciplined militancy and revolutionary political vision. The Black Panthers not only fired the imagination of their generation but also shifted the strategy of the African-American struggle and all movements for justice and social change in the United States by seeking solutions rooted in a basic redistribution of power.

That's all I needed to know. My imagination was captured, even though it was more hook, line and blinkered, rather than sinker. I would be an English outpost. As the only raw recruit in Romford, I needed to get a black beret from somewhere and a big Afro, not necessarily in that order and never mind that trying to fit an Afro under a beret defeated the object of the Afro in the first place.

Obtaining a black beret was the first hurdle. I decided to eschew pocket money expense and settle for my school beret, which was actually navy blue, but the next best thing to black given my meagre resources. I hid the school badge by wearing it back to front.

I began to grow my hair from the tiny patted-down-with-water growth of curls that it was, into a full-bodied, proud Afro. Anyone who has ever tried to grow an Afro quickly soon realizes that this can take a few months. During this interminable growth period I sat and passed eleven GCE 'O' levels. I was pleased that my after-school revision stints in the library had paid off, but I could have done with a bit of help during the next step, deciding what to study at 'A' level. My parents didn't really know what I had achieved, but just that the number of subjects seemed a lot. I recently read that a distinguished Harvard economist, Martin Fryer, asserted that mixed-race adolescents '– not having a natural peer group – need to engage in risky behaviour to be accepted'. I'm not sure if he is generally correct or what he bases his evidence on, but in my case he was spot on. At this point in my life I opted for the riskiest behaviour possible: I chose to study biology, chemistry and physics at 'A' Level, instead of English literature, French and history, in which I had got top grades. Perhaps I felt I needed the challenge? I don't know, but I sometimes wonder how my life would have turned out had I not gone down the road less travelled. Maybe it was just a cunning plan to have a class full of boys at my disposal without any female competition gumming up the works. Who knows?

At the beginning of the new sixth-form term, I was ready to embark on my first covert black guerrilla mission at Romford Technical High. This took the form of a meticulously planned assault on my 'A' level physics class. I got up early that morning and prepared my hair by 'freaking' the whole thing out with the aid of an Afro comb, a newly acquired piece of kit sourced in the local Woolworths for my covert arsenal. No holes or bits of fluff were allowed in a perfect Afro. The illusion of a faultless sphere was paramount. Easier said than done, it usually took half an hour of painstaking teasing to get the desired effect. I stared at my reflection in the mirror when I had finished, completely awestruck. For the first time in my young life, I thought I looked that indefinable thing – cool.

I smugly went downstairs to the kitchen to eat my breakfast, but even before I sat down at the table, my mother took one look at me and screamed: 'You look like a bloody golliwog. Go upstairs and pat it down with some water right now. You needn't think you're walking down the road looking like that and making a show of yourself to the neighbours.'

'No!' I shouted back as I grabbed my satchel and flew out the door.

That 'no' was my entry into adulthood. Of all the words that she could have used, she used the word 'golliwog', malevolent little beasties still much prized in some Nazi circles today. Even though I had unknowingly cherished a golliwog that Aunt Rose had seen fit to give me for my first birthday, it had been consigned to the bin when I became conversant with the political notion of black racial pride. Now I hated the little fuckers in their stripy pants and blue jackets, with their red-lipped grins – racist icons perniciously masquerading as children's cuddly toys. My library research had even revealed that golliwogs had female counterparts, pollywogs. Not a lot of people know that.

My Afro was huge. Look at me, the Afro screamed, as it bobbed along on my head, oblivious to the stares of passers-by; it was as if it had a life of its own. It was wearing me, not the other way around. It bounced contentedly while surveying the world from a lofty height and, by comparison with its very hipness, everything else looked outdated, outmoded and, dare I say it, plain lame.

My first class that morning was physics. I hoped there would be many of the same stupid boys in attendance who had jeered at me behind the teacher's back during a practical class about thermodynamic law in my 'O' level year. 'Hot stuff', the ringleader of the most troublesome group had shout-whispered at me while simulating masturbation. I had wanted to scream back at them, 'Black body radiation,' ha bloody ha, 'so black bodies absorb heat and light, big deal, get over it.' But I couldn't.

I wasn't sure if it was the implied sexual connotation that upset me so much or just the mere fact that white bodies reflecting heat and light sounded much more ideal. Call me over-sensitive but, believe me, simple little things like this reinforce that hoary old homily that black is bad and white is good. So fucking stupid, but so fucking all-pervasive. It was difficult to cope with such boyish nonsense. I had already discovered that answering back usually led to more embarrassment rather than less, but not answering back left me vulnerable and easy prey; I hated that.

This was the first day with a new physics teacher, a recent postgrad, who had only started at our school the previous term. He was not only comparatively young, but also quite hip, meaning that he wore jazzily patterned ties and cool specs. I hoped he would be more on the ball when it came to maintaining discipline than the profoundly deaf and arthritic former physics master that he had replaced.

Our new sixth-form status meant that we had graduated from the classroom to a lecture theatre situated in a purpose-built science block on the other side of the road opposite the main school. The lecture theatre had serried ranks of desks rising upwards from the floor. Their stacked splendour looked very grown-up, reinforcing the fact that we had lectures now and not lessons. The room had no natural light, only the sickly glow of fluorescent strips in the ceiling, which made white flesh look particularly leprous and fish-like. The ventilation was scant too, emphasizing the fact that boys paid little attention to their body odour.

When I marched into the room sporting my new hairdo, the entire class shut up, simultaneously relaxed their lower jaws, and stared at me like dead fish. I stared right back, or perhaps I should say my new hair creation defiantly stared back. Even the teacher raised his eyebrows. I sat down in the middle of the third row – the first three rows were always left vacant – and just stared ahead. I thought I would give them the best view of the 'do'. Twenty pairs of eyes bored into my back. Result: 'That made you sit up and notice,' I silently murmured to myself. 'One small Afro for Pauline, one giant poke-in-the-eye for schoolboykind.'

I'm not sure what I was trying to achieve by this simple defiant act. Perhaps it was just a cry to be noticed, or perhaps everybody, despite their circumstances or colour, has to define their youthful self with a flash of self-identity. But it must have worked because nobody took the piss out of me again. For once I had pushed the agenda. I was no longer in thrall to the poker-straight, lemon-haired brigade who swung their long tresses between their bony shoulder blades as they walked along the road for every building worker to whistle at. My Afro was at war with their Englishness and I loved every minute of it.

However, due to this new all-consuming preoccupation with running my mini-Black Panther Party from the confines of my bedroom, I began to neglect my studies. I did the barest minimum because quite frankly pure sciences began to bore me. By this time I had been provisionally accepted for a place at Birmingham Medical School to study medicine, but the 'A' level grades that I had to achieve were way beyond what I was presently capable of, particularly if I carried on working in such a lacklustre way.

My favourite haunt was Romford Town library. I went there after school, ostensibly to study and finish homework, but secretly I scoured the well-stocked shelves for information about the emergent radical black politics. I began with Malcolm X's autobiography and then moved on to the 'hard stuff', the Black Power movement.

I memorized whole swathes of some of the less incendiary thoughts of Malcolm X. Little nuggets of wisdom like: 'The earth's most expensive and pernicious evil is racism, the inability of God's creatures to live as one, especially in the western world,' and 'We didn't land on Plymouth Rock, Plymouth Rock landed on us.'

These words tripped lightly from my tongue when relatives came to call. Such utterances were met with a stony-faced silence, or my mother's urgent need to rush to the kitchen to make yet more tea for the guests. Accusations of racism go better with tea, ask any PG Tips advertising chimp!

I don't know who was responsible for ordering books at Romford Town library in the late '60s, but I remain eternally grateful to them for providing me with the information that I required at sixteen. Stokely Carmichael's *Black Power: The Politics of Liberation*, Eldridge Cleaver's disturbing collection of essays, *Soul on Ice*, books like these were grist to my mill. I had no real idea of the enormity of the struggles that these new heroes of mine were engaged in, or in retrospect their muddle-headedness and in some cases sheer hatred and criminality, but it was exciting, new, underground and, most of all, my discovery.

If my parents had known that I was reading such stuff, instead of teen magazine fodder like *Jackie* and *Petticoat*, they probably would have raided my bedroom and instigated a book-burning. While my peers were out enjoying illicit drinks at The Lamb pub in Romford market, I was in the library reading Eldridge Cleaver's litanies about how raping white women was a 'political act and duty' of all black men – not an idea that can be casually tossed into conversations with other sixteen-year-olds, whose main preoccupations are bad skin and whether to indulge in heavy petting.

For me to suggest that reading such material as a teenager was conducive to growing into a balanced adult is probably misleading. It wasn't. If I'm honest, I was growing into a sexually confused, racially intolerant loner who had no outlet for her teenage angst. Perhaps it's a good job that Internet access didn't exist in those days, because I might have hooked up with similarly motivated individuals who favoured a more 'Columbine' approach to sorting out their problems. Me, I just festered privately in my bedroom.

The real killer for me was the fact that my girlfriends were dating boys. They went to the cinema, dances and fairs, on the backs of their mopeds, scooters, or in the case of a particularly incorrigible girl nicknamed 'Haystack' (due to a perilously high blonde beehive style that she back-combed at every available opportunity), motorbikes. Unfortunately, boys just weren't interested in me. After all, how could you invite a black girl home, or even admit to going out with a black girl without getting ridicule heaped upon you? It was just not a sane option for a nice Essex boy.

I had friends. That wasn't the problem. We discussed the latest music, new books or interesting avant-garde TV programmes like *Monty Python*, *That Was The Week That Was* and *Rowan and Martin's Laugh-In*. I prided myself for knowing what was going on the world, but none of this was a substitute for being snogged in the sixth-form common room.

I had known that I would have a dating problem ever since the school's end-of-term dance in 1968, when I had had my first brush with black men. The Foundations, a multi-racial pop group, had already had a hit with 'Baby, Now that I Found You', but had fallen on harder times when their follow-up single bombed. Consequently, they had been booked to do our school dance, probably to reach out to a younger audience again. They must have been pretty desperate to turn up at our school.

For the first time in my teenage life, I was allowed to go to the school dance. Perhaps I was just adamant about it and my mother didn't fancy an argument. I went dressed in a short red dress, white tights and red character shoes. The other girls were dressed in much more revealing outfits than mine, but I knew I looked good.

The band came on and did a short set, then retired to the dressing room/classroom for a twenty-minute break before concluding their performance with another short set. I had never heard a live band before. It was a totally new experience. The guys were all tall and sported mini Afros. The rest of the kids seemed to know their songs and I wondered why I didn't; they were homegrown talent after all. Perhaps I spent far too long checking out black American talent, when it appeared that I could find the same thing closer to home. I knew there were lots of black folk in London but the spectre of Janet Sparks still loomed large in my mind and I wasn't yet ready to take on that particular shibboleth.

I danced down at the front with a couple of my girl friends. The boys were grouped round the sides of the dance floor looking greasy and sweaty in various garbs. There were three main groups: the hippie fraternity sported flowery shirts and flared trousers; the greaser fraternity wore black leather jackets and jeans with turn-ups; and then there was a small skinhead contingent dressed in three-button tonic suits, sporting black or brown loafers on their feet. Each of the skinhead boys had girlfriends with characteristic feather-cut hairstyles, heavy make-up, tonic skirt suits, white socks worn over black fishnet stockings and black penny loafers. The hippie lot thought they were cool, the greasers hoped they were cool, but the skinheads knew they were cool.

The skinheads at our school mainly came from Dagenham. They loved to listen to ska, reggae and bluebeat. Pupils who made it into the fifth form and beyond were allowed access to two common rooms which occupied old converted stables on the other side of the road to the main school buildings. Outside the windows was a small lake divided into two smaller pools by a dilapidated wooden bridge. Mature horse chestnut and willow trees grew around the water's edge.

When revising for exams we would congregate outside the common room, watching the school tennis team play or just idling away the lunchtime by staring at the clouds and playing transistor radios. Every now and again the skinhead lot would commandeer the red Dansette record player in the common room and start playing songs that had a choppy rhythm and indecipherable lyrics. This made a welcome change from the usual fodder that the hippie fraternity liked to play. I lost count of the number of times I was forced to listen to the sickly sweet 'California Girls' or 'Sloop John B'.

The first ska record I heard was 'Long Shot (Kick de Bucket)' by the Pioneers. The melody chugged its way out of the open windows and floated on the breeze across to the lakeside where I was sitting with some of my hippie friends. The rhythm instantly felt natural, as though I'd been listening to this kind of music all my life. I got up and went up the rickety wooden staircase to the common room and saw about five girls in loafers, short white socks, skirts hiked up a good two inches above their knees and all with a strange haircut, short on top with carefully combed longer pieces falling on either side of their heads, doing the sexiest dance I had ever seen. One of them, Janice, caught me staring and asked me to join in. Reluctantly I did, but soon found the rhythm easy to move to. It was new and exciting all at the same time.

I asked them what this music was called which, when you stop to think about it, is really ironic – a bunch of white skinhead girls turned the only black kid in school on to ska music, but that's how it was. Then the skinhead boys turned up and looked at me in a strange way, but didn't say anything. I felt uncomfortable with them around, so I slipped away and in future listened to the music from afar, but I was always secretly proud when they wrested the Dansette from the hippie contingent in the school. The world became a much brighter place.

The skinheads liked The Foundations even though they didn't play ska. By the end of the band's first set that night, they were applauding and cheering wildly. I had gravitated nearer the front just to watch the skinhead girls dancing. They looked so smart and elegant compared with the hippie girls, who flailed their arms around to the beat and had a ubiquitous 'lost in the cosmos' look in their eyes. The DJ started playing pop chart records in the interval, while everybody stocked up on soft drinks being served at the back of the hall.

Suddenly three tall black guys appeared out of the door that led to the backstage area. They made a beeline for me and surrounded me. I could smell their sweat mixed with a sweeter smell, which I later found out was a mixture of Dixie Peach hair pomade and Palmer's Cocoa Butter Cream. One of them started talking to me from his lofty height in a language that I didn't understand. Patois was lost on me. The whole experience was surreal and slightly intimidating. The irony was that I had spent the whole evening wishing that some boy, any boy, would ask me to dance and now that I was the sole interest of the band, I was too scared to speak or move.

I fled into the night. Janet Sparks cast a long shadow over the evening. The real world of black folk and the Pantheresque fantasy world that I had built for myself were at war with each other in my mind. There was no 'Wonderful World', only a scary world into which I didn't fit. It would be many years before I resolved the contradiction.

FOUR

A LOST GLOVE

Coventry city: some people are born here, some get sent here and some choose to come here. I chose Coventry, or at least I think I did, but perhaps it chose me.

Initially, I came here to further my studies. I liked the idea that Coventry was in the middle of England. I wanted to be in the middle of things. I was tired of being an outsider, so I thought that if I placed myself at the centre geographically, then the rest, whatever that was, would follow. Also, Coventry was only one hundred miles away from Romford, so it was near enough to go home in an emergency, but not so close that I would have to endure a visit from my parents every week.

The real clincher was when my dad got really animated and excited about my suggestion that perhaps I should consider studying at Lanchester Polytechnic in Coventry. For a man who was normally short on talk, some might even say monosyllabic most of the time, a misty look came into his eye as he repeated the names of car manufacturers with the solemn gravity of a Latin Mass: Armstrong Siddeley, Lanchester, Rolls-Royce, Daimler, Standard, Triumph, Jaguar, Alvis, Lea Austin, Ford, Vauxhall. I had never heard him say so much in one go. There was even a branch of Silcock and Collings, the company he worked for in Dagenham, at the motorway end

1972 student days at Lanchester Poly, with an Afro and fur coat

of the Foleshill Road in Coventry. So serendipity had a lot to do with my decision to fetch up in Coventry.

But if I'm being brutally honest, the fact that I ended up there to further my studies was a necessary compromise rather than part of some well thought-out master plan. As expected, given my minimal revision, my 'A' level grades were not good enough to take up the place I had been offered at

Birmingham Medical School. It was my own fault. Once upon a time, I had avidly read about the world's first woman doctor, Elizabeth Garrett Anderson, fervently wishing to follow in her footsteps. Now I wanted to know all about the Black Power Movement's intelligent left-wing pin-up girl, Angela Davis. As my mother had predicted: 'No good will come of it.'

I had been left with two options: stay on at school for an extra year and re-take the exams to get better grades, or use what I had and settle for a polytechnic instead. Not wanting to remain one hour longer in Romford than I had to, I opted for my second choice.

I entered my comparatively woeful results into the UCCA clearing-house system and was invited for an interview at Lanchester Polytechnic with the head of the Science faculty. My mother insisted on accompanying me to Coventry. She wore her beaver-lamb fur coat, which she thought made her look posh, but in the sweltering heat of an early September heatwave, made her look not only sweaty but decidedly crazy. As usual, we made an incongruous couple.

There was a Lyons coffee house in Broadgate, near the old Coventry cathedral ruins, which captivated my mother. 'You can have your dinner here every day, dear. I feel much better about you coming here, now I know that there is a Lyons just around the corner.'

You have to remember that 'dinner' meant 'lunch' to my mother and she had no idea that the polytechnic had two lunchtime refectories and three coffee bars. My mother liked the safety of a good brand name.

The Poly's proximity to Coventry Cathedral was also a big plus for her. In her opinion, any college next to such 'Godliness' must be a good thing. She wouldn't have been so enthusiastic if she'd known that two years previously John Lennon and Yoko Ono had planted two acorns in the Cathedral gardens. The acorns were planted in easterly and westerly positions, symbolizing the meeting of the couple and the union of their two cultures. They followed the planting by sending acorns to world leaders in the hope that they would plant oak trees in their gardens. It was supposed to promote world peace. Unfortunately, such promotion worked neither on the world leaders nor on my mother, who considered John Lennon the anti-Christ for having the temerity to say that he thought the Beatles were more famous than Jesus.

My parents rarely enquired about my educational path. They were happy to let me organize my studies. It was tacitly understood between the three of us that if you were black, then working in a hospital was an obvious choice; it was one of the few places where a black skin was no barrier. I had been steered in this direction from an early age. Nobody had expected that I would make it on to a degree course. So anything above nurse status was considered a result. Even the fact that I had lost my place at medical school didn't upset them as much as it did me. As long as they could say that I was at college they were happy.

A week later an official letter arrived at home offering me a place on the Combined Science B.Sc. course. I immediately accepted. My mother would have preferred it if I had gone to a college nearer home because then they wouldn't have to fund my living expenses. Unfortunately, my dad couldn't afford the rent for me to stay in the hall of residence, so she organized an affordable place from the list supplied by the Polytechnic's accommodations officer. As I suspected, she picked a room in an elderly couple's house, the Woodbridges. Her choice was a total disaster. It was worse than being at home.

The Woodbridges lived three miles out of town, on the Binley Woods Estate. The designated room was poky, with laminate furniture, a saggy single bed, purple shag pile carpet and cardboard-like walls, not a winner when the other inhabitants snored like hooting ships on a foggy night.

Mrs Woodbridge, a rumpled bed of a woman, provided me with a greasy-spoon breakfast and a mountainous evening meal, invariably consisting of soggy chips and over-cooked, gelatinous cabbage served on a small table covered in knick-knacks in a corner of the living room. Meanwhile, Mr Woodbridge, a short, ruddy-faced Welshman, sat on the sofa belching and farting his way through the six o'clock evening news. She watched me eat until I cleared my plate, occasionally engaging me in small talk about her grown-up children and grandchildren, in which I was not the least bit interested.

After dinner, I was expected to sit with them, usually in silence, and watch 'soaps' such as *Coronation Street* and *Crossroads* until they went to bed at 9 p.m. At which time, I would retire to my room and cry. It was awful.

On Saturday afternoons Mr Woodbridge donned his blue and white Coventry City scarf, sat in his favourite brown and orange upholstered armchair immediately opposite the television and checked the football results, his pools coupon in one hand, pint of beer in the other and usually much cursing on his lips. He drank his way through a couple of crates of beer most weekends, which were conveniently delivered to his door by the 'pop man' on Friday evening. As he guzzled his way through his 'pop', all I thought about was how to get some 'pot'.

I had discovered that most of the interesting students at college were smoking marijuana, living in fascinatingly decorated student houses, their walls adorned with posters and photos of their Indian holiday exploits. I'd only ever been to Llandudno and didn't think that qualified as a foreign country.

What to do? Stay out all night and see what happened. The first time I did this, my mother was on the train to Coventry the following morning. The Woodbridges had taken it upon themselves to phone my parents just before midnight on the day of the felony and inform them of what they suspected, namely that I was having sex and smoking dope. This was thoroughly perceptive of them and correct on both counts, although not necessarily in that order.

'You'll end up like Janet Sparks,' she said as soon as she stepped off the train at Coventry station. 'After all we've done for you, this is how you repay us.'

She had brought an overnight bag, so I knew our struggle would be a fight to the death, particularly if I wanted her to leave on the evening train.

I let her blow herself out with her list of recriminations, before adamantly saying: 'Either let me move out of the Woodbridges' house or I will do it anyway. I refuse to spend a moment longer with them.'

People usually know when I mean business and my mother was no exception. In the few short weeks that I had been in Coventry, I had changed. The young people I mixed with showed no prejudice. Indeed I began to realize that being black was a positive advantage if those around you thought that Jimi Hendrix was the second coming. I had no shortage of male admirers either; sex with a black girl was permissible while away from home, even mandatory for the real thrill-seekers eager to slough off the provinciality of their upbringing. Thus I had developed a self-confidence that made it less easy for my mother to dictate what I should do. We returned to the Woodbridges' where my mother and Mrs Woodbridge clucked like eggless hens in the kitchen while I packed my bags, dragged them downstairs into a waiting taxi and in a rather ill-mannered way took leave of the house, while my mother attempted to smooth things over with: 'I'll write and let you know how things are getting on.'

She did too. She even holidayed with them.

I had arranged in advance to leave my bags with two other girl students that I had recently got to know, who lived in a house in Gordon Street, Earlsdon, the student area of the city. It was a compact, less than bijou two-up two-down with an attic space masquerading as a third room, that backed on to the local abattoir. The stench from this animal funeral parlour was nearly a deal-breaker, but the rent was cheap, so my mother immediately warmed to the idea.

My two new acquaintances, Helen and Alison, were studying the considerably more trendy subjects of social science and economics respectively. Whereas they were fashionable and had boyfriends, I was still running around in the clothes that I wore to sixth-form parties – mini-dresses and sensible shoes. They were wearing loons, long skirts, cheesecloth tops, Afghan coats and fringed bags bought at those twin hippie Meccas, Biba and South Kensington market in London. They listened to Joni Mitchell and Joan Baez and Janis Joplin. All the new female artists seemed to have names that began with J in those days. I still liked Cilla Black, Diana Ross and Sandie Shaw. Even name-dropping Marsha Hunt was met with derision, because she had appeared on *Top of the Pops*, which apparently meant that the artist had 'sold out'!

Through them and their friends, I was exposed to the music of Jimi Hendrix, Hawkwind, Led Zeppelin, Soft Machine and

Eric Clapton. I thought they were all shit except for Hendrix, but in those days I kept my opinions to myself. All I wanted to do was to fit in.

■ ■ ■

I acquired another two 'must-haves' for the 1971 autumn term: a pinkish-beige, moth-eaten fur coat and a totally inappropriate boyfriend, Ken Harker, whose father was a squadron leader who lived somewhere in Lincolnshire. Ken was twenty-four, much too old and knowledgeable for me. He'd spent a couple of years backpacking around that holy of holies, India, which added to his allure, but rather than expanding his horizons, these adventures had narrowed them down to the tiny airless room that only the hopeless drug taker with serious depressive issues occupied.

He had shoulder-length blond hair, a blond roué's moustache set in a hawk-like face, and one blue eye, the other having been traumatically removed in an accident that I think involved a hand grenade. When he was stoned, a favourite party trick involved the removal of the glass eye, which was held aloft for a quick look around and sometimes thrown into the lap of some similarly stoned individual, much to the macabre delight of his student friends. We were both outsiders compared with the rest of the Fresher students; perhaps that is why we were attracted to each other. Who knows? All I know is that he was my first boyfriend, my first fuck and my first suicide all wrapped up in a neat package.

What he did have was style, which was sadly lacking in most of his contemporaries on the social studies course, who were the usual plethora of spotty, emotionally challenged boys in their late teens, their ungainly arms and legs suffering the nightly vicissitudes of hormonal growth spurts. Ken wore a brown nurse's cape, which swished and swirled around him, just like Dracula's. His eccentric dress style was all his own and made him appear confident and self-assured. In my limited experience, he was so 'far out' as to be off-planet. He introduced me to salt on my porridge, marijuana and 'interesting' sex, in that order. He was well read, if you consider a penchant for the Marquis de Sade's works useful, and very adventurous when it came to drug taking.

Within a few weeks of moving out of the Woodbridges', I was walking barefooted around the concrete jungle that is Coventry city, dressed in an Indian kaftan while twanging a Jew's harp between my teeth. With Ken a whole new musical world opened up. We saw MC5, Fairport Convention, Arthur Brown, Pentangle and many more perform in the Lanchester Main Hall. I had no idea that within eight years I would be playing to a packed hall on the same stage.

By now my Afro was way bigger than the head it used as a vehicle and although that made me look like quite the coolest black 'chick' in the Poly, I was overwhelmingly aware that was due to my being the only black girl there. I'd made inroads into realizing my student fantasy life. I had friends, admittedly druggie ones, but friends nonetheless. I had a boyfriend, unsuitable maybe, but I no longer wallowed in the virginal frustration of my sixth-form years. For the first time in my life I was choosing how I wished to live, how to present myself to others and absorbing the many new lifestyle ideas on offer – all infinitely better than the closeted unreality of waging guerrilla warfare in the confines of my Romford bedroom. But, and it was a big but, I still didn't know any black people.

I soon learned that there was 'student' life and 'townie' life. Student life happened in the little bubble that existed between the Art School campus near Far Gosford Street and the Students Union and administration block that faced Coventry Cathedral. Townie life happened everywhere else. Townies were the young folk who tried to get into the student bar in the evenings for the cheap drinks or to see famous bands in the Main Hall for considerably cheaper prices than at the local Locarno. Student jobsworths made it their business to discourage such unnatural mixing. There seemed little chance of ever meeting black people with such a draconian policy. So I pushed such thoughts to the back of my mind and got on with the serious business of pretending to be an interesting amalgam of Marsha Hunt and Angela Davis around college.

Ken and I spent a lot of time at the dilapidated three-storey 'Hawkwind House', presumably named in homage to the band, in Hillfields, an area that the Woodbridges had derogatorily referred to as 'Little India'. This rabbit warren of rooms was home to a variety of students whose main occupation was drug taking. It had no electricity, discernible plumbing or heating. It was like entering a 'Furry Freaks Brothers' cartoon.

Ken struck up a friendship with a town-planning student, Duncan, who lived there for a while in hedonistic squalor. This young, hairy-headed and hairy-chinned man, with fathomless brown eyes, had a deep passion for playing the crumhorn, a medieval instrument that turned up at the end in an insouciant curve. Ken often accompanied him on treble recorder after long marijuana-smoking sessions, their discordant duet sounding like Igor's unearthly lament for Frankenstein's monster.

Soon my social life became more interesting than my studies. Nobody realized that Ken was my first boyfriend. I

Ken and Duncan harmonizing on recorders and crumbhorn at Hawkwind House, 1971

thought I was in love. So much so, that I tentatively suggested, after a particularly drug-fuelled day in London, mainly spent rampaging around Hamleys toy store and making out behind some bushes in Hyde Park, that he come home to Romford with me to meet my parents. I think he was too stoned to refuse.

During the train journey to Romford, some clarity must have entered my foggy senses, because I suddenly became aware of how our outlandish appearance would appear to my parents. But it was too late to abandon the journey and besides Ken was oblivious to my dilemma and I wanted to keep it that way. By the time I knocked on my parents' front door I was a nervous wreck. I knew I had made a very bad decision. I even went so far as to suggest to Ken that he wait by the gate until I managed to explain away his less than sartorial appearance to my mother. This probably sounds like crazy behaviour, but now I was home, my confidence evaporated in the face of my mother as she opened the front door. 'What are you doing here?' she asked suspiciously.

'It's all right,' I said nervously, 'I've just popped home so that you can both meet my new boyfriend.'

Her eyes narrowed as she looked me up and down. Her gaze rested on my belly, hidden underneath the new smock-style top that was all the rage – a style that looked good on flat-chested girls, but my hourglass figure gave the illusion of a maternity smock.

Then she started hysterically shouting. 'You're in trouble, aren't you? Where is he then?'

Instantly I knew our conversation was about to take a turn for the worse: 'You're in trouble' was Mother-speak for 'You're pregnant'.

Having made this quantum leap in her mind, her thought processes reached warp speed. Before I'd even had a chance to put her mind at rest or introduce Ken, she jumped to the only conclusion that would satisfy her. 'He's black, isn't he? That's why he's hiding. I knew this would happen,' she yelled.

We were both yelling by now. 'No, no. He isn't. You've got it all wrong.'

'You're lying, you're lying. I always know when you're lying.'

'Besides, what if he is?' I was screaming by now.

God knows what Ken, who was within earshot, thought about this extraordinary scene. I glanced towards the gate where I could just make out his shape in the dim twilight. He appeared to be engrossed in looking down the end of a toy kaleidoscope that he had nicked from Hamleys. Since he had only one good eye, such a practice rendered his peripheral vision almost blind. At that moment I fervently wished he was deaf too. Fortunately Dad, wondering what all the commotion was about, intervened and told her to get out of the way of the door, whereupon she started loudly exclaiming: 'He's not coming in here, you needn't think he is. I'm not having him in my house.'

'Shut up, woman. I don't care what bloody colour he is, just so long as he's treating my girl right.'

I'd had enough. In my heart I secretly thanked my dad for his words, but all I could think about was getting as far away as possible. I grabbed Ken by the hand and we ran all the way to the bus stop, a quarter of a mile away. There was still time to get to London and catch a train back to Coventry.

My relationship with Ken was irreparably traumatised. The whole episode was made worse because he had been tripping on LSD throughout that day. A week later, at the end of term, he unceremoniously dumped me, saying that he was too old for me. I blamed my mother.

I spent most of the following term trying to get him back, but to no avail, until he unexpectedly attended an end-of-term party just before the Easter vacation at the 'abattoir' house. Within an hour, we were on our way back to his flat. That was the last night we ever saw each other. The following day I went home for the holidays.

During the afternoon of my first day back at college, while in the middle of a particularly difficult chemistry experiment, I was summoned to the administration block. I thought nothing of it. I assumed that the admissions office had discovered some problem with my grant payment. On arrival, a secretary ushered me into a room where several be-suited men waited. One of them asked me in a hushed, kindly tone if I knew Ken Harker. I said that I did. The other men tried hard not to make eye contact as I looked from one to the other. I was told that he had been found that morning by the head porter, swinging by a length of washing line from the railings outside the Students Union building. He was dead. Of course.

I think I cried, but I can't be sure. The men were duly solicitous and told me to go home and not to come back to college until I recovered. But where was home? The news had gone round the students like wildfire. People looked away when I entered the coffee bar in search of my friends.

Suicide among one's contemporaries is an unsettling business. Why? That is the only question that screams at the back of your mind. Why? I still don't know why, but then I didn't really know anything about him anyway. The gossip was that he took rather more belladonna than was good for him, which spiralled him into a depression so deep that there was no way back. The coroner reached a verdict of death by suicide.

I hardly remember Ken's funeral. I was not introduced to any of his family. Afterwards I grieved for weeks. Fleetingly I contemplated suicide too, in that copycat way that many recently bereaved people do. I don't think I was ever particularly serious about it, because I loved life far too much to want to leave it. I struggled through to the end of term and then flunked my exams at the end of the year. To go back to Romford would have been like admitting defeat. I wanted to stay in Coventry, but how?

Some months before Ken's death, he had introduced me to a young couple, Jerry and Pip, who had three children below the age of five. They affected a bohemian lifestyle in a small semi-detached in Radford, an area of Coventry about two miles from the city centre. Pip was the spitting image of John Lennon. Jerry was a blonde hippie-ish earth mother, much like the future Mrs Linda McCartney. They were older than us but very cool. They ran Gestalt Therapy evening classes at Lanchester Poly, which Ken often attended. The sessions were very popular with students and a big audience was guaranteed. I went along to one with him and was amazed that this huge group of strangers were quite prepared to sit down and talk about their personal problems with each other. This pre-dated all the touchy-feely stuff that is currently seen on morning television.

Jerry ran the group while her husband offered practical assistance when required. She had a beautifully soft, lyrical voice, which coaxed all manner of painful confessions from people. Her calming presence pervaded the room. I had never met anybody like her. So, naturally in my time of trouble I sought her out. Instinctively I knew it was the right thing to do.

I only vaguely remembered where she lived, but I searched the streets of Radford on foot until I found her playing in the front garden with two of her children. She took me in her arms when she saw me standing at her front gate and let me sob until I was completely cried out. Then she invited me to join a weekly meeting of people at their house that evening. It was called an encounter group.

At 8 p.m., after the children went to bed, a steady stream of people arrived on the doorstep. They all seemed friendly and open. When the room was full enough Jerry began laying out the rules of engagement: no swearing, no physical violence, only love and understanding. Some people, like me, were new to the group, but others were stalwarts and launched straight into discussing what had happened in their lives since the previous meeting. I sat in the circle that we made, astonished that everybody sounded so self-absorbed. The smallness of the group made it much more intimidating than the huge group that I'd attended with Ken. So I just listened. Then I noticed that another member hardly said a word, but Jerry spoke to him by name, so this wasn't his first time. His name was Terry.

He was slight, well-muscled, with shoulder-length hair and a face like a Cherokee, a large square jaw and high cheekbones, slender nose and wide mouth. From some angles he bore an uncanny resemblance to Charlie Watts, the drummer in the Rolling Stones. When he did offer an opinion, he spoke with an urgency that suggested he was there on serious business, not in a 'go-see' capacity. He dressed in the fashion of the day: flares, black shirt with two embroidered red dragons on either side of the buttons, black leather jacket and black Chelsea boots. I was instantly attracted to him.

We struck up a relationship within a few months of attending the group. Terry wasn't like the others, probably because he wasn't a student. He worked as a production engineer at Rolls-Royce aero engine division in Coventry, having relocated after being made redundant at the same company in Derby. Eventually, we outgrew the encounter group and decided to discuss our problems only with each other.

I struggled on with my studies. I was exempted from first-year exams after the trauma of Ken's death. I opted to repeat my first year, but within a few months I knew I had made a mistake; I no longer seemed to have any interest in my science course. In 1973 student life was still the province of middle-class white kids, who fancied a few years out of the rat race before succumbing to the inevitable – a job. These kids, with big allowances provided by their parents, had the most fun. They were free to experiment with hair, clothes, music, politics, attitudes and food. Exams were considered a nuisance, but a necessary evil. I remember one of them telling me that it didn't really matter whether he got a degree or not because employers just wanted to see that you had survived three years of drug taking and listening to rock music! Such hippie ideals were on the wane, the 'summer of love' was forgotten history. Change was in the air again. I began to realize that this laissez-faire lifestyle that my friends and I had enjoyed as Freshers wasn't for me. I badly needed some structure to my life, but more importantly I needed my own money.

Terry and me, 1974

I decided to call it a day with my academic career after I flunked my exams for the second time. Terry suggested that I get an interim job while I figured out what to do with my life. He had a friend who was a social worker at the Central Hospital, locally known as Hatton, a psychiatric institution on the outskirts of Coventry near Warwick. This friend recommended me for an unskilled job as a temporary nursing assistant for three months. The hours were long, forty hours spread over three and a half day shifts. The pay was even worse, twelve pounds a week. But for the first time in Coventry I got to see where all the black people were at!

Most of the untrained staff, nursing assistants, porters and domestics in this sprawling Victorian eyesore were black Caribbeans. At first they treated me with suspicion, particularly because of the way I talked, which was very English. My knowledge of patois, their favoured means of on-duty communication, was non-existent. The only time they spoke recognisable English was when they were talking to a nursing sister or doctor, who were universally white. I envied this useful bilingual capability. But they were not unfriendly, quite the opposite. When they discovered that I was quite prepared to do my share of the work, they soon took me under their wing and showed me the ropes, even relaxing their patois so that I could understand what they were telling me to do. A twelve-hour shift spent with psycho-geriatrics is a character-forming experience. Many of my new acquaintances had been doing these shifts and bringing up a family, often single-handedly, for years. I was a complete novice and rapidly formed a huge respect for these ladies who downed tools at precisely 7.30 p.m., grabbed their hats and coats and ran for the utilitarian grey bus that shipped them ten miles back to Coventry and their hungry families, only to return again the next morning at 7 a.m. My life was a doddle by comparison.

It was draining work, but I enjoyed the responsibility. Armed with a new resolve, I decided to further my studies with hospital work in mind. In those days, I was over-qualified for nursing, but a friendly staff nurse suggested that I try a vocational course like radiography or physiotherapy. I took her advice and applied to Coventry School of Radiography. After a lengthy interview, I was accepted. I began my course in September 1973. I had been in Coventry for two years.

Perhaps I should have given the future course of my life more serious thought. Suffice to say that I hadn't. Would it have made any difference back then? I doubt it. Radiography suited me. It was practically based with an easily assimilated theory, plus I got paid while studying. It was hard work, but a thoroughly good training. For the first time in a long time, I had to be disciplined. Work began at 9 a.m. sharp every weekday. More importantly, I worked in a variety of hospitals with other black people, many Caribbean nurses, Ugandan and Kenyan Asian technicians, and Nigerian or Egyptian doctors. I belonged.

Graduation day as a fully fledged radiographer, summer 1976

I was walking to work one morning, not long after I started my new job, when I saw a lost glove lying on the pavement. It looked so lonely. I knew it would remain there until either the owner found it again or, more than likely, a road sweeper deposited it in a dustcart, before its final journey to the local tip. Suddenly tears pricked my eyes. In that moment I remembered how I had felt so abruptly and hopelessly abandoned after Ken had died – just like the glove.

Terry had been in a similar situation after relocating to Coventry, having been made redundant from the draughtsman's job that he had loved, staring at the job scrap heap – just another lost glove. By chance we had found each other. Together we made a pair, albeit mismatched, but who said that was important? After all, the primary function of a pair of gloves is to keep the hands warm in cold weather. We have been keeping each other warm for the past thirty-eight years.

FIVE

'DO YOU WANNA BE IN MY GANG?'

My singing career began in 1976, a few months after my adoptive dad died of lung cancer. His death was no great surprise. He had smoked an ounce of Old Holborn a day in Rizla'd rollies for most of his adult life. Let's face it, eventually that's going to kill you.

Ever since I knew him, a skinny rollie would be clamped in the left-hand side of his mouth, in a ready prepared groove in his lip, which had an unsightly slick of tar adhering to it most of the time. Each cigarette pushed the tar further and further into his airways until it caused an abnormal cell to reproduce. Within six months these cells had spread all over his body, including his brain. Nonetheless, he invariably had a smile on his face, even though his sense of reality was severely warped due to all the morphine he was given. He once told me, with a giggle in his voice, that the Tiller Girls had just got out of the television during a popular Saturday night family entertainment programme and danced round his bedroom. It was good to hear this flight of fancy because I knew someone was still at home in his shrunken head and emaciated body. Eventually his skin and bones clung to life by a yellowed fingernail. Soon he was gone. I missed him desperately. He had always been there for me, unconditionally. Nobody could replace that kind of love.

After the funeral my mother moved into sheltered accommodation because she said that the family house reminded her too much of Dad. I returned to Coventry and poured my grief into my new hobby, singing.

Terry and I had been together for four years when my dad died. At first, we had rented a tiny detached bungalow in Kenilworth, near Leamington Spa. The layout comprised a quarry-tiled corridor with five rooms leading from it: two bedrooms, a sparsely furnished living room at the front of the house and a large, ill-equipped kitchen and tiny shower room at the back.

Among Terry's meagre belongings was a Spanish guitar that lay neglected in a cardboard box in the front room. His intention was to learn to play it. He had bought a 'Play In A Day' manual, but at the age of thirty-eight, he lacked the perseverance required to master a musical instrument. I, on the other hand, with the over-arching chutzpah of youth, taught myself to play in a few weeks. Before I knew it I could sing and play most of *Leonard Cohen's Songbook*. You can tell I was depressed.

All I wanted at this point in my life was normality. Living with Terry provided it. He taught me a work ethic. He was a member of the Socialist Labour League when I met him. By the time I joined it had become the Workers Revolutionary Party.

Together we formed a branch of the organization in Leamington Spa. If you know this town, then you will realize that bringing Marxist politics to the attention of the masses in this spa idyll was a tough call. We valiantly aligned ourselves with folk who were getting community-based projects together in the Bath Place area of town, but our branch never amounted to many more than six people trying to sell the

Workers Press, our daily paper, outside the Potterton factory when the shift changed in the early morning or organizing Young Socialist discos and five-a-side football matches every week. Needless to say, it was a hard slog. I valiantly threw myself into learning about Marx, Engels, Lenin and Trotsky but, if I'm honest, I was still more concerned with solving the black-white divide in society than I was with workers' power.

Just as the party membership began to wane in Leamington, our landlady asked us to move to a house that she owned in Earlsdon, Coventry. We were glad to be back in the city, because the daily commute to work was a strain and Kenilworth was an unfriendly place to live as a mixed-race couple. If we went for a drink in a pub, our arrival could cause a lengthy silence among the punters until we had been served. Coventry pubs were much more forgiving. As a bit of light relief from our political rigours, Terry and I recharged our batteries at our new local every Sunday afternoon and evening.

The Old Dyers Arms in Spon End was run by Mavis, ably assisted by her long-suffering husband Barry. Mavis was a Yorkshirewoman of ample girth, whose backcombed beehive stood up as proud as the foam head on her pints. She ruled her clientele with an iron fist and pulled the pints with the muscular dexterity of a wrestler, but most of all she was fun. Mavis and Barry were an entertaining double act, just like the sitcom characters George and Mildred.

Often a couple of the Fureys, a famous radical Irish band, would turn up in the back room for the Sunday afternoon folk session and wow everybody with their pro-republican songs. Mavis always allowed a drinking 'stayback' when they played, because invariably the room would be heaving with Guinness drinkers, which meant more money in her till. It was an exciting place to be in the mid-'70s.

The bloke who ran the backroom folk club was Dave Bennett. He was an excellent guitar player, with a penchant for John Martyn songs. During one Sunday evening session, he asked his girlfriend, who sported a blonde, pudding-bowl hairdo reminiscent of comedienne Victoria Wood, to sing. She chose a Donovan song, 'Yellow is the Colour of My True Love's Hair'. As soon as she began, I knew I could sing as well as her, if not better. The blokes in the pub lapped it up. I decided then and there that the following week I would attempt a song at the Sunday afternoon session. Probably a surfeit of bitter shandy influenced my decision. I spent the following week practising singing while accompanying myself on guitar. Terry wasn't too happy about my decision to perform, but I ignored him.

The first song I sang in public was Bob Dylan's 'Blowing in the Wind'. I had typed the words out on a piece of paper and written in the relevant guitar chord changes. My hands shook and my voice wobbled for the opening stanzas, but then I just forgot that the audience was there and performed. I loved it. Polite applause greeted my rendition, but I could see that I'd impressed Dave Bennett and Terry. I didn't much care about the others in the room.

The following week I turned up to the session again. Dave Bennett smiled knowingly at me and said: 'Bang one out, Pauline.'

I'd chosen Bob Dylan's 'Girl from the North Country', complete with complicated finger picking. Dave winked at me after I'd finished and said the immortal words: 'Yeah, you can stay.'

My musical career began with those four words.

Soon after my debut, I got to know another male singer who had an anarchic streak to his performance that I found captivating. His name was Tim Crowe. His after-hours party piece was a mean version of 'Brown Sugar'; little did I know that he was also smoking it. Tim had an idiosyncratic style of playing and singing that was beautiful to listen to. He had that knack of the best performers, the unique ability to take a song and make it their own. His version of 'Leopard Skin Pillbox Hat' easily rivalled that of Dylan. I liked him. He was a maverick. Musically we supported each other. Sometimes he became so raucous that he would get thrown out of the pub. On those occasions I would leave too in solidarity and take him back to our house, where we would sit up half the night rolling joints, drinking Terry's home-made wine and singing and playing guitar. Terry would record everything we did on an old Akai reel-to-reel machine.

Unfortunately, Tim was an uncompromising fellow and within a few short years died of cirrhosis of the liver in Walsgrave Hospital. I only found out about his demise much later. I left him behind, as I did many others, but he is often in my thoughts. I knew nothing about his personal life, just his music. I don't even know where he is buried.

By the end of 1977, I outgrew the Dyers Arms. I was offered a gig in a folk club at The Golden Cup on Far Gosford Street. They needed a support act quickly, because somebody else had cancelled. I think I was chosen out of desperation, because nobody else was available. I wasn't sure what was expected of me, until the guy who ran the evening and booked the acts said that ten songs would be enough and would I accept £10 for the performance? Ten songs! For ten pounds! A pound a song, what a result.

Ever the optimist, I dug out my songbook and settled on my first set list: a few of mine, a couple of Joni Mitchell, some Bob Dylan and some Joan Armatrading. Most of them were

Singing in the Old Dyers Arms, Spon End, 1978

far beyond my capabilities, but I carried on, oblivious to any technical deficiencies that I had.

My self-confidence knew no bounds. I led a double life. By day I was mild-mannered Pauline, the hospital radiographer, in a fetching white uniform and matching clogs, and by night I was Pauline the singer/guitarist, clad in a yellow linen shirt and brown corduroy dungarees, performing at any folk club that gave me a gig. I didn't try too hard to be anything very much. I just enjoyed myself.

I can't remember exactly how that first gig went, mainly because I was so nervous. There wasn't any PA system, so no enhancement was offered to my vocals or guitar playing. About thirty people sat quietly and dutifully applauded when I finished each song. What I hadn't reckoned on was what you're meant to say between songs during the set. I had never played a whole set before. I had been so intent on rehearsing the songs that I had forgotten about how I was going to introduce them. The slick patter of a professional was replaced with innumerable 'ums' and 'aahs', while every introduction began with the words: 'This song is about…' I remember wishing that I had taken more notice of an old stalwart folkie who had once advised me after a performance: 'You should learn a few jokes, lovey, breaks the ice.'

Probably my novice level of stagecraft became very monotonous after the third song. But if it did nobody complained. To be honest, the audience was waiting for the main attraction, the rather more famous singer/guitarist Bert Jansch.

The pièce de résistance of my set was a bleak, self-penned song entitled 'A Whore's Life', about the dreadful spate of killings in and around Bradford, perpetrated by a man dubbed 'The Yorkshire Ripper'. At the time, the killer's name was unknown. The song was written from the perspective of a young prostitute on the streets and dealt with the fear she felt every night.

> *In Bradford City, on the wrong side of town*
> *Mary used to be pretty, when she first came around*
> *Now she's waiting for the man with the knife*
> *Waiting to be reborn.*

Macabre indeed.

As I was packing away my guitar, a young, bespectacled, clean-cut black man bearing a strong resemblance to Malcolm X approached me. He shook my hand and said that he had enjoyed my performance. His name was Lawton Brown, and he was a politics student at Warwick University.

He must have impressed me because we instantly fell into

Performing in the downstairs bar at Lanchester Poly

a discussion about music, our likes and dislikes, and then on to the much thornier subject, black politics. He liked the fact that I had tried out a couple of my own songs, which were even then about the dispossessed: young mums, prostitutes and dead black people. I pricked up my ears when he told me that he was a guitarist and songwriter too. He wanted to know if I had listened to much reggae music?

I'd listened to a few Bob Marley albums at a friend's house, but I thought that was probably too mainstream for his more sophisticated and knowledgeable tastes. So I said no. He looked surprised and suggested that I needed an immediate black musical education. I agreed. He invited me round to his flat the following day. In retrospect I think he was just chatting me up, but I took him at his word and, much to his amazement, turned up on his doorstep the following evening.

He played me Third World's legendary album *96 Degrees in the Shade*. The only other sound in the room was the gentle rustle of Rizla papers as he built one spliff after another with generous amounts of Sensimilla. Until then I'd only smoked Moroccan or Afghan Black. Sensi was an altogether much more enlightening, almost mystical experience. There was no need for conversation, because the song lyrics spoke for us.

Next he played Bunny Wailer's *Blackheart Man*, then Culture's *Two Sevens Clash*. This music was special. Conscious lyrics coupled with righteous music. What a combination. Lastly, he played his trump card, a tape recording of the Last Poets' 'Wake Up Niggers'. This tension-filled rhythmic rap artfully used rhyming couplets to describe the inner-city predicament of blacks, imploring them to 'stop drowning in the white man's spit'. It is almost hip-hop, but preceded that particular music genre by more than a decade. The chanted refrain, 'Wake Up Niggers or You're All Through', built in intensity as the song progressed, like an orgasm waiting to happen during particularly good sex. The relief I felt when it finished only made me want to hear it again. Lawton's eyes twinkled behind his gold-rimmed glasses.

'Who are they?' I blurted out, eager to know who penned these kinds of lyrics. He patiently explained that the Last Poets were a group of American poets and musicians claiming to be black nationalists within the civil rights movement. Their name came from a poem by a South African revolutionary poet, Keorapetse Kgositsile, who believed he was in the last era of poetry before guns would take over. 'An interesting concept,' I replied. 'Got any more?'

From that moment on I was hooked. This music went way beyond the mere protest song. It was a clarion call to the uninitiated. An epiphany. 'Wake up nigger!' I silently told myself. I was eager to write songs as forthright as this.

'Well, perhaps you can help me with this,' Lawton responded, handing me a yellow sheet of lined paper with a few lines of lyrics written in his sprawling handwriting. *'They use their fancy words to control your mind, but since I never did no elocution rhymes, made me think that everything they said was fine.'*

He played a few chords on his guitar and sang the words to show me the melody. Immediately we finished the verse and came up with a chorus. Before I left an hour later I'd written the words to a second verse and we had a complete song. Thus began our writing partnership. The song 'They Make Me Mad' later found its way onto the first Selecter album, *Too Much Pressure*.

Lawton shared the house on the Foleshill Road, near the Wheatsheaf pub, with a short, stocky musician-cum-painter and decorator, 'Aitch', aka Charles Bembridge. It was a typical student house, a couple of bedsits with a communal bathroom and kitchen. The downstairs space was piled high with musical equipment and sound-system paraphernalia. The smell of spliff and sweaty socks pervaded the house.

Lawton was my conduit into Coventry's black community. He took me to see a show of Coventry's premier reggae band, Hardtop 22, at Sydney Stringer School in Hillfields. I was surprised to see Aitch among the raggle-taggle bunch of musicians on stage. Lyrically they were hardly the Last Poets, but I enjoyed the relaxed sound they made.

The bandleader, Charley Anderson, was the big cheese on the Coventry black music scene in those days. He was tall and rangy with a head full of red Rasta locks, which usually remained hidden beneath a variety of high-brimmed hats. He had obviously modelled his appearance on that of Bob Marley, but couldn't yet produce the quality of his idol's authentic Jamaican reggae sound, whose music was successfully spreading throughout Britain and the rest of the world. When Charley smiled it was like staring at rows of marble tombstones on a full moon.

After a while, a band began to coalesce around our song-writing efforts. Aitch became interested in our songs, probably because he was forced to listen to us singing them every Sunday morning. Sometimes he would jam along with whatever instrument was to hand. He was a versatile musician and could play Hammond, bass and guitar, and offer sweet harmonies to any newly penned tune.

The band that was coming together remained nameless. Aitch took on bass duties and new member Silverton Hutchinson on drums completed the rhythm section. Silverton was still sore about being kicked out of the Specials and replaced by John Bradbury, so he wanted to prove his worth in a new band. I thought he was a really good drummer. Some people said that he had a bit of an attitude problem, but I didn't see any signs of it. In those days, most white people, musicians or not, thought you had an attitude problem if you were black and complained about something. Often I've heard the position advanced that 2-Tone got whiter and whiter in choice of personnel, as time went on. I guess that's one way of eliminating potential troublespots!

At some point in the band's growth, Aitch's friend Desmond turned up to rehearsal. He was a huge bear of a man with some of the most obtuse turns of phrase I'd ever heard. When I told him that I didn't understand what he meant he would do a little jig on one leg, turning his large frame round and round, while laughing to himself. He was a strange man, but his fearsome Hammond playing more than made up for his oddities. He had that indefinable thing called 'touch' which only the finest keyboardists master. His musical ideas were always understandable, even though he spoke for the most part in riddles.

Our rehearsals happened in various places – school halls, back rooms of pubs, anywhere that gave us a space for a reasonable price. The band improved after a couple of rehearsals. I sang through a makeshift PA that offered no voice enhancement tricks except volume, but picked up every passing taxi radio signal. It's not very helpful having your vocal interrupted every minute with: 'Roger, 22, where are you? Over.'

But even this minor inconvenience couldn't dampen my spirits. I was in a reggae band. That was all that mattered. I had some black friends. My dream had come true.

Desmond's Hammond organ and Leslie amplifier were stored in Lawton's house. They looked like huge wooden pieces of furniture. We had found a good rehearsal space in the Wheatsheaf pub, up the road from Lawton's house. The easiest way to get the Hammond and Leslie there was to push them along the pavement. It took more time to get the equipment there than it did to rehearse, but nobody could afford the cost of hiring a van.

One evening at rehearsal in early 1979, a slick, bespectacled, young black guy sporting a natty pork-pie hat turned up. Immediately he indulged in the obligatory hand clasping and high fiving with everybody. He shook my hand and introduced himself as Lynval Golding. He looked different from the others. It wasn't just his fastidious dress sense either. He had an aura about him, an indefinable shininess that personal success delivers to some people. For a local musician, success in those days meant playing a gig outside Coventry, but this guy started telling stories about touring all over the country with the No. 1 punk band of the moment, the Clash. Even the immaculate creases in his Levi Sta-Prest trousers weren't as sharp as those credentials.

Eventually Lynval ran out of stories, so we began playing a song. Within a few verses Desmond motioned for us to stop. Immediately, Lynval and Desmond pounced on Lawton's reggae rhythm guitar technique. Together they hopped about in a macabre impromptu dance, shaking their right arms so that their fingers made a snapping sound, their voices loudly deriding what they had just heard.

'No maan, no maan. Blood claat!' Desmond repeated over and over again, the word 'claat' exactly a perfect fifth in pitch above 'blood'. They made several attempts to communicate to Lawton what they wanted to hear, but apparently he did not have the necessary musical chops to evince the particular sound that they were looking for. I felt sorry for Lawton. Ridicule from one's peers is a bitter pill to swallow. These guys were merciless with one another. Somewhere the politeness gene had got lost and the diplomacy gene had never been inherited. This was a completely different scenario to the whimsical folk scene that tolerated all kinds of amateur performance. This was a dog-eat-dog world that I'd entered, where everybody behaved like a pit-bull.

They mostly talked as if I wasn't there. I didn't much mind, because I didn't understand Jamaican patois anyway. When Desmond discovered that I didn't know what he was saying much of the time, he made it his business to talk patois all the time. He couldn't understand how you could be black and not understand the language. I couldn't be bothered to explain. He wouldn't have listened anyway. I should have

119

tried conversing with him in French, perhaps then he might have seen the error in his logic.

Eventually the rehearsal finished. Lawton packed away his guitar and, looking visibly shaken, bade everyone goodnight. Aitch asked the landlord if it was okay to leave the equipment there overnight, because nobody fancied wheeling it back up the road. He reluctantly agreed.

I offered Desmond a lift in my car back to where he lived in Radford. Lynval asked if he could come too. On the way, Lynval suggested that I meet up with some of his friends the following evening. Apparently they were looking for a singer for a new band. I dropped them off outside a nondescript house somewhere just off Beake Avenue in Radford. Before he left the car, Lynval pressed something into my hand. 'That's the address. Be there about 7.30 tomorrow evening. Desmond will be there too.'

The words 33, Adderley Street, Hillfields were scrawled in pencil on the inside flap of an empty giant Rizla packet. Indeed these were exciting times. It was the end of May 1979.

When I explained to Terry what had happened at rehearsal, he looked perturbed.

'Who is this bloke, Lynval?' he asked.

I explained as best I could, but I wasn't exactly sure and therefore sounded like it.

'I hope you know what you're getting yourself into,' was all he said in reply.

I should explain that Terry was one in a million when it came to putting up with my crazy ideas and mercurial decision-making processes. He did what all men should do with their partners, gave them the space to make their mistakes or triumphs, without fear of recrimination. When I look back on this time, I realise he probably felt particularly threatened by my sudden penchant for hanging out with cool black dudes from the Coventry music scene, but if he did, then he was secure enough in our relationship not to show it.

The following evening at the appointed time, I knocked on the door of a one-up, one-down terraced house in Hillfields, an area infamously populated with varying ethnic groups, some more recently arrived than others, who lived cheek by jowl with students, druggies, dealers, pimps, prostitutes and dole scratchers. The door swung open to reveal a resplendent Charley Anderson dressed in a light tan, neatly pressed safari suit, flashing his trademark toothsome smile.

'Come in, come in, everybody is here already,' he said, motioning me into the house. This was difficult, because the front room was small, but full of people. A long '60s-style sofa that had seen better days took up almost the entire length of wall by the door. It was just about possible to squeeze through without bumping into the end of the sofa. Ensconced on this sofa was a tall, blond, angular-featured man rolling a conical spliff on the back of a record sleeve. Next to him sat a beautiful dark-haired young woman with piercing violet-blue eyes. Her face reminded me of a young Elizabeth Taylor. They were obviously an item. I couldn't help noticing their studied stylishness. She was dressed in a black polo-necked jumper and black ski pants, artfully accessorised with cheap jewellery, which magically looked expensive on her. He was dressed in a cream-coloured Ben Sherman shirt and light tan Sta-Prest trousers that finished about an inch above his black loafers, exposing an expanse of white sock.

Charley introduced them to me as Neol and Jane Davies. They were the only white people in the room. We smiled at each other. Nervously I scanned the room for Desmond and Aitch. Both of them were sitting on the floor rolling spliffs.

A young, mixed-race, almond-eyed boy was strumming an unplugged electric guitar in a corner of the room. 'Hi, Pauline, I'm Compton, Commie for short,' he said between strums. He was trying to follow the rhythmic pattern of the record playing in the background. I could just about hear that it was 'Kaya' from Bob Marley's album of the same name. Even at first glance, his reggae skank guitar action looked so much better than Lawton's heavy-handed attempt. I self-consciously perched on the sofa next to Jane, secretly wishing that I wasn't wearing flares. Spliffs were passed until another tap on the door heralded the entry of a tall, slim, smooth-faced and strikingly handsome young black guy, who introduced himself as 'Gappa' – but everyone called him 'Gaps'.

As I looked around at everybody through the thick ganja smoke, I noticed the door to the kitchen swing open. A homely looking young black woman poked her head into the room and whispered something to Charley. I could just see a little girl, no more than three or four, hanging on to her skirt, staring wide-eyed at the assembled company.

Immediately, Gaps called out: 'Hi, Sonia, got any tea?' She smiled at him and disappeared back into the kitchen, re-emerging after a few minutes with a large pot of tea, a pile of cups and a bottle of milk on a tray. She handed it to Charley and went back inside. That was the last I saw of her on that particular evening.

When the album had finished, the spliffs had been smoked and the tea drunk, Charley suggested that Neol play his record. Neol's long slender fingers reached into Jane's handbag and extracted a 45 rpm vinyl single in a plain white cover. I could just about see the words *The Special A.K.A. Gangsters vs. The Selecter* crudely stamped onto one side of the sleeve.

I didn't know it at the time, but 5,000 of these singles

had been pressed up and released via Rough Trade. The Special A.K.A. was slowly building a huge countrywide following, due in part to the success of their dynamite live performances, but more importantly due to their song 'Gangsters', which described the vicissitudes of the music business using a new musical hybrid punky/ska. The Selecter track, an instrumental written by Neol, had been gathering dust on a shelf for the past two years, but had been hastily tarted up with the addition of a ska rhythm guitar track and invited along for the ride by Specials kingpin Jerry Dammers because he didn't have enough money left for the Specials to record a 'B' side. Overnight the Selecter had gained its own distinctive momentum. It had even been played on DJ John Peel's BBC Radio One show, on which he had erroneously said that it was a Specials song. Neol Davies had immediately phoned him between songs and put him right.

Neol delicately slid the record out of the sleeve and, holding its edges by his palms, gingerly stepped over the floor paraphernalia and elegantly knelt down beside the red Dansette record player in the far corner of the room. He dropped it onto the spindle and waited while the player's internal mechanisms whirred and clunked before spinning the precious record into life.

By this time, I was very stoned. The spliffs were even stronger than those that Lawton rolled. As the record began I was mainly aware of the curious jumpy beat, which was not as smooth and relaxed as the Jamaican reggae we had just been listening to. Then a haunting trombone melody kicked in which was good enough to withstand many repetitions. Charley was listening to the record with his head bobbing in time to the metronomic tchk, tchk of the rhythm guitar. At intervals he murmured: 'Yes, maan. Rocksteady, Rasta,' whenever he heard something he really liked.

Then an unearthly-sounding guitar took up the trombone melody, but this time the musician's dexterity pulled and pushed the melody within the confines of the beat. The music was reshaped, until it took on a deeper poignancy that was somehow missing in the trombone's efforts.

Instinctively I knew it was an accomplished piece of work. Everything about the music and the sound was so much better than our mediocre rehearsal efforts. When the record finished everybody congratulated Neol. He smiled beatifically, then loped back over to the Dansette and played the record again. Nobody complained.

While it played, various people made comments about the mix and sound balance of the instruments. Compton was eager to know how Neol got his weird guitar sound. Neol told him that he used a chorus and delay pedal. Much of this techno-speak went over my head.

Then Neol addressed the whole room. 'I need a band,' he said, 'to build on the success of my single. That's why we are all here tonight.' Then he broke out in a broad smile and started singing Gary Glitter's 1973 hit, 'Do you wanna be in my gang, my gang, my gang.'

The incongruity of the moment made us all laugh and we shouted back in unison: 'Oh yeah.'

Jane looked lovingly at Neol and Neol looked lovingly back at her, content to see his brilliance reflected in her eyes. I could see that they would be a force to be reckoned with in the future.

And thus the 2-Tone band that became known as The Selecter was born. For once I was in the right place at the right time.

PART TWO

BLACK & WHITE

SIX

WHITE HEAT

Between 1979 and 1981 everything changed, my identity, my music, my style, in some ways my very being, as I became a fully paid-up member of the 2-Tone movement. Reinvention seemed part of me these days. Perhaps it is easier for an adopted child to adapt to new situations? That risk-taking capability had been finely tuned over the years. I'd never harboured any deep-seated dream to be a pop singer, but when the opportunity presented itself, I grabbed it with both hands. I was reminded of the title of Black Power leader Bobby Seale's book *Seize the Time*, written while he was incarcerated; it summed up my attitude to this exciting new career path that had opened up. This is the most rational explanation that I can offer for why I threw up a well-paid job with promotion possibilities to follow a bunch of argumentative guys into the decadent world of pop music.

Although we got together in Charley's front room, the deal between us wasn't completely done and dusted. I was the last piece of the puzzle that was to become the Selecter and as such, I had to prove my mettle to Neol, who I have always thought was none too keen to have a female member gumming up the male workings of the band.

In retrospect, I have no idea why any of them thought that it would be a good idea to have a girl in the band. There was enough evidence already that women in bands who were not of the wallflower, backing-singer variety were a liability, because the press and media tended to focus on them to the detriment of the band. Somebody, I guess, must have thought that this was likely to happen, so I was paired with Gaps Hendrickson, who could sing, look handsome and dance divinely, but essentially was a very shy man on stage; not a leader. In Neol's defence he is quoted as saying: 'As soon as she sang, it was obvious.'

Early photo of Selecter in Charley's kitchen. Photo by John Coles

I think I shall take that as a compliment.

But more to the point, I think he was astute enough to realize that just another seven blokes in a ska band was not a favourable comparison to the Specials. So a woman in the band was a talking point for the press and made the band visually different. As if we needed that when six of the band were black?

Charley and Neol had been in bands together in the past and both had taken on the duties of lead singer, but I think that neither wanted to be the vocal linchpin in a band that was destined to gig outside Coventry. Our main aim was to capitalize on the success of the instrumental track 'The

Selecter', which was easy, because vocally it was like starting with a clean slate.

Even the name, The Selecter, was in doubt at one point during this period. Charley wanted to call the band Stryder. Under normal circumstances, that name might have suited a late-'70s rock band destined to play working men's clubs, but these were not normal times. The Selecter was being manufactured to do a job – to give flesh and bones and musical acumen to a 'B' side of an increasingly successful record (it was released as a double 'A'-sided record, but only Neol Davies seems to remember that particular fact!). Every month saw the record inching its way up the charts. It seemed pure madness (no pun intended) to throw away that particular piece of immediate identification. So the name The Selecter stayed.

I was duly summoned to a rehearsal at the end of May 1979. All I can remember is where it took place. The Binley Oak is a large, unprepossessing pub in Paynes Lane, Hillfields. Historically the building dates from about 1850. It was rebuilt in 1885 on the larger scale that is seen today. In 1896 it was the headquarters of Singers Football Club, later to become Coventry City FC. In fact, the old Coventry City football ground was just up the road. These were the directions that I was given to find it. Not as good as a sat nav, but good enough.

I was asked to present myself for vocal inspection in the very cold and draughty back room of the pub. Everybody was already there when I arrived and a solitary microphone in the middle of the room awaited me. Since I had never auditioned for anybody before, I didn't understand the significance of what I was about to undergo. I told them I had a song, 'They Make Me Mad', and would it be okay if they jammed around those chords while I sang it to them. The band picked up the simple minor chord sequence very quickly, especially Desmond, whose distinctive 'creamy' Hammond organ sound could lift any run-of-the-mill song into orbit. His bouncy intro set up the awkward entry of the vocal in half time.

I had performed this song in rehearsal with my former, now-aborted band, but these guys ripped up the blueprint and refashioned it anew. Lawton had taken my defection badly. There was no way of sugar-coating the bitter pill of rejection that he had to swallow. I doubt whether he has ever forgiven me for such duplicity. But the truth was that the song had never sounded as good before. The Selecter laid the rhythmic and musical basis for it to come alive. Suddenly I was singing in an uninhibited manner, almost shouting the chorus 'They Make Me Mad'. My voice gushed out of my mouth with the force of an oil-strike. Pure anger moulded every syllable. It was a totally cathartic experience and set the vocal tone for the band. It surprised me, but I knew it was right for the kind of band that we hoped to become. It was a raw, strident tone, not at all like the ladylike folksy vocals that I had been delivering hitherto. There was a 'new kid on the block' and I liked her. Apparently, so did everybody else.

We spent the whole of the month of June rehearsing there or anywhere else around town that would have us if the back room at the Binley Oak was unavailable. Not every day, but probably three times a week. I was still working at the time and had to fit around my night work rotas, which involved working all day, all night and half the next day. Sometimes there would be very few patients that needed X-raying during the night, other times it would be busy all night and the next half-day would feel interminable. It was exhausting, but a good way to make extra money for clothes and records.

There was another bloke who worked in the radiography department, Philip, a very camp young man who had a penchant for Freddie Mercury. He sang in a band too. Its name was Silmarillion (not to be confused with the band that became Marillion). Presumably he was also into Tolkien. Terry and I had been invited to see them gig. I was not particularly impressed, Terry even less so, but Philip could hold a tune rather better than his white boiler suit managed to hold in his portly Pickwickian frame. As regards his black nail-varnished fingernails? Well – let's not even go there!

Nonetheless he was determined to make it, with all the ferocity of an X-Factor contender. He had the self-assurance of a pantomime dame and regaled me at every opportunity during our working day with how many gigs he had done, what songs he was writing and how best to present himself. Philip's constant self-obsessed banter could make the time fly by during long stints administering barium enemas to unenthusiastic patients with faulty bowels. Philip and I would do what we had to do while discussing the latest Kate Bush release. An appreciation for the divine Ms Bush was really the only thing we had in common.

I wanted to confide in Philip about the new band that I had joined, but unfortunately he never seemed interested when I explained that the music we were doing was 'sort of reggae'. He thought reggae was boring and unsophisticated, whereas Kate Bush's 'Wuthering Heights' was pure genius. So I shut up, content to know that it looked as if The Selecter's first show would be far away from Coventry. Philip hadn't managed to negotiate such a feat yet.

Strangely enough, a few months later The Selecter's first hit record 'On My Radio' was reviewed on BBC Radio 1's teatime record review show, *Roundtable*, by none other than Ms Bush herself, who gave the song a resounding thumbs up, while remarking that my falsetto vocal on the chorus reminded her of 'Wuthering Heights'. I hope Philip was listening.

By the end of May we had a set list of about ten songs. There was an instrumental opener, a version of the Upsetters' 'Soulful I', which featured Desmond's considerable abilities on Hammond organ. The sound of his playing, coupled with the energy of his antics behind the keyboard, were guaranteed to get people's attention. We didn't know it at the time, but we were on a steep learning curve. Each of us rose to the occasion because subconsciously we knew that this was a way out of the rat race. This was a way to express how we felt about the society we lived in, but above all, it was a new way.

Slowly, we were familiarising ourselves with each other. I began to realize that I was the only person in the band with a bona fide job, although Neol had recently worked at Lucas Aerospace in Coventry. In fact, he had penned the lyrics to 'Too Much Pressure' while there, after experiencing 'the day from hell'. Everybody else was either on the dole or ducked and dived in and around Coventry.

Charley's place became an 'open house'. Many Selecterites hung out there of an evening, listening to his old ska, bluebeat and rocksteady records. It was an easy time between us all. I was in my element, eagerly assimilating a new music, genuinely interested in all aspects of ska and reggae culture. I quickly realized that there was a general absence of women involved in the early days of ska music. Much later I discovered that there were quite a lot of women who sang back then, but given the heavily patriarchal Jamaican society, male singers were favoured. Women singers were considered less important and ended up forgotten or as backing singers.

An exception to this rule was Millie Small. Of course I'd

heard her sing 'My Boy Lollipop', along with most of Britain, back in 1964. This jaunty slice of pop had sold 600,000 copies. Charley was at great pains to point out to me that it was a bluebeat song, not a pop song, and the first Jamaican record to rock the British nation.

Our first show was in Worcester. I can't remember the name of the venue. Thank goodness things like mobile phones, Twitter and Facebook had not been invented yet, otherwise I am quite sure that our careers would have been stillborn before we had got to the end of the first song.

By this time, we had the music in embryonic form, but unfortunately not the style. I fetched up with an Afro, which was trendy all through the late '60s and mid-'70s, but in 1979 it was beginning to look rather tired. The immense candy floss creation that graced my head in 1968 for the physics class denouement now looked as though it had shrunk in the wash. It was a more manageable Michael Jackson *circa* 'Off the Wall'-sized ball, more associated with the disco crowd than any conscious reggae band. To add to the illusion that I was a backing singer for Chic, I was wearing pink spandex trousers and a tight white T-shirt scattered with pink sequins! Embarrassing to admit but true. My style choice had been made more out of ignorance than any real sense this was the ensemble I desired. The truth was that I didn't know how I was supposed to dress for this kind of music, so I just copied what I'd seen black women wearing on *Top of the Pops*.

Charley's locks were long by this time, so he was cool in that department, but his fawn safari suits were well out of order. Desmond, Aitch, Gaps and Commie still didn't know in which camp their hair belonged, much less their clothes, an assembly of denim flares, badly patterned sleeveless jumpers, and an assortment of hats, none of which were pork pies or trilbies. Money was the main issue of course. Any extra money was spent on marijuana; there never seemed to be a moment when there was not a spliff on the go or being rolled or stubbed out.

Dope smoking in this extraordinary quantity was new to me. I smoked occasionally, but not every hour of the day in which my eyes remained open. In this world of weed, clothes were a low priority. So was punctuality. I learned patience is indeed a virtue when the clock runs according to a Jamaican man's understanding of 'soon come' time. Charley was never late, because he was clever enough to make us all meet at his house, but Desmond and Aitch could be up to two hours late, which made people very fractious before we'd even fetched up at the gig.

The Worcester gig was in a draughty, rundown, wooden-floored hall with a proscenium arch stage at one end better suited to sermons than live gigs. There was no in-house PA. Our sound was made audible through a mish-mash of different-sized speakers borrowed from a Coventry sound-system and mostly inaudible microphones, operated by an inadequate mixing desk set. A surly-looking hanger-on, the imaginatively named Chris Christie, was enlisted to operate this audio mess. No matter really, because we played to three people, not even a dog in attendance.

Welcome to the world of the haphazard happenings, because that was how our gigs came together. Everybody was late all the time and when they did arrive, they had invariably left something behind at home, so somebody had to drive them back to get it. There was a never-ending list of obstacles to be overcome before the band could even start out on the road, let alone do the show. But with the brass-neck bravery of youth, all the problems got solved and somehow we would end up on stage. That's when the magic happened. All seven of us together was a magical, alchemical thing to behold, as anybody who was conscious back in 1979 and saw the 2-Tone tour would agree.

Gaps and I had the words taped across the front of the stage, just in case we forgot them. This led to a lot of movement on our respective parts as we followed the words along the front of the stage. Thus developed our style of running and skanking anywhere and everywhere. In those days the hour we spent on stage was probably akin to a three-hour gym workout. Even in Worcester.

The Worcester gig happened on 2 July 1979. The band that turned up to the next gig at the F Club in Leeds on 10 July 1979, a scant week later, was almost unrecognisable.

In the intervening week, Neol and Jane had taken it upon their collective selves to sit us down and give us a good talking-to about image, how we presented ourselves to the public. They said that it was not enough to have personal style, we had to fashion a coherent band identity. They suggested that we look at the kind of stuff that the Specials were wearing and adapt it to our own tastes. We were also informed that we needed to do a photo shoot as soon as possible. These guys meant business, I thought.

Jane took me on a shopping expedition. She favoured second-hand shops. This caused a problem with some of the guys in the band because Caribbean people don't like wearing other people's cast-offs. They want to buy new clothes with their money, not clothes that other people don't want any more, or worse, 'dead man's threads'. That's why hip-hop artists dress themselves in designer stuff and bling. Black people don't want to look poor, as though they haven't got the money for store-bought clothes. Plus, Charley, Commie,

Aitch, Gaps and Desmond favoured the African heritage-type stuff that Bob Marley and the conscious reggae artists wore, which to my mind looked equally cool.

It didn't bother me very much. I didn't shop at second-hand places, but I knew plenty of white girls who did and they always looked sharp and distinctive, mainly because they weren't wearing the latest deliveries to Top Shop or Miss Selfridge. It wasn't something I was much interested in, but I did like to look fashionable. Hence the pink spandex trousers, which were mightily in vogue at that time in the ladies shops I've just mentioned.

Under Jane's tutelage I started to frequent the second-hand shops that used to be opposite the Arts faculty at Lanchester Poly. Jane had a good eye for stuff and I was happy to follow her direction. We took the 'rude boy' look that Peter Tosh had pioneered in his early ska days and feminized it. It was just a question of changing the proportions of the garments. She picked out some beige Sta-Prest for me, which were probably from the previous ska era, circa late '60s. They stopped an inch shy of my shoes, which I was told was 'cool'. An orange, slim-fit, boy's Ben Sherman shirt was poked through the changing room's curtains to cover the upper half of my body. Next she handed me a double-breasted jacket made of shiny grey material. It fitted perfectly. Job done. We sourced a pair of black penny loafers at a downmarket shoe shop, Ravel. White socks took up the spatial slack between the trouser bottoms and my shoes. We decided that my Afro hair did not suit this new ensemble, so I pulled it up into a small topknot. I felt curiously empowered when I tried the clothes on at home and surveyed the result in the bedroom mirror. The addition of a pair of fake Raybans, strictly for posing purposes, finished everything off very nicely.

'Is that what you're going to wear on stage?' Terry asked as he passed our bedroom door and caught the first glimpse of the new image.

'Think so,' I said. 'What do you think?'

'Different.'

Not exactly a thumbs up, I thought, but I instinctively felt that I was on to something and I wasn't going to let anybody's lack of enthusiasm get in the way.

The photo shoot came next. The photographer was a local young man, John Coles, who hauled us off down under the flyover which crosses the Pool Meadow roundabout. It was a spooky twilight shoot and all the more effective for it. When it got too dark we ended up at Charley's house yet again, posing for photos in the kitchen. I think I like these photos the best out of all the other more obviously expensive shoots we did later. The photos capture the joy of a band at the beginning of its life, assured that success is its for the taking, all it has to do is keep playing and following the yellow-brick road.

By this time Charley and Neol had made contact with John Mostyn, a band manager in Birmingham, who ran the Oak Agency. Hitherto his main claim to fame was as Brent Ford of the imaginatively named band, Brent Ford and the Nylons. I'm told that he used to go on stage with the leg of a pair of tights on his head. Whatever turns you on I suppose.

John Mostyn was already booking shows for the Specials, picking up on the buzz surrounding the 'Gangsters v. the Selecter' single, so when John realized Neol's instrumental had metamorphosed into an actual band, he was more than happy to book us too. This is why many of our early gigs were as support to the Specials. The first of these shows was at the F Club in Leeds.

When the band gathered outside Charley's house, ready

for the gig in Leeds on 10 July, all of us looked much more polished. People had suit bags holding modish get-ups. We also had a couple of roadies, Grant Smaldon and Rob Forrest, two young Coventry lads who spent much of their time signing on and hot-knifing dope at Gaps's flat in Pioneer House, Hillfields. Rob, who dearly loved the band, had acquired an old, badly re-sprayed, battered and rusty green Bedford van, which he offered us as transport. We were now a fully functioning band. Next stop Leeds.

The F Club (the F stood for Fan and it was sometimes known as the F Club at Brannigans) was a moveable feast in those days. It was smallish, with a capacity of about 250 to 300. We were supporting the Specials – our 'big break' as Horace refers to it in his autobiography, *Ska'd for Life*. Gee, thanks Horace. Much obliged to you, sir, for pointing that out (touching one's forelock is optional)! 'Gangsters' was riding high in the charts and the Specials were capitalising on its success and also on their notoriety from the tour that they had done with the Clash the year before.

On arrival we were informed that there would be no soundcheck for us, because the Specials' soundcheck had gone on too long and now everybody had gone to the pub next door. So, while the band set up their gear in front of the Specials' noticeably more expensive equipment, I familiarised myself with the layout of the dressing room. There were no separate facilities for the lady of the band except the toilet – a fact that you get used to fairly early on if you are the only female in a band. Plus anybody can come striding into the dressing room any time they want, which is not so good when you are only half dressed. Failing to knock on this particular day was the unholy duo, Rex and Trevor, the renowned original Specials 'rude boy' roadies. They politely introduced themselves: 'Wh'appen, sis.'

By now, I had learnt that this greeting was a friendly and usually benign exchange between black males and females, even if you weren't bona fide siblings. So I said: 'Hello.'

The subtext of the glance exchanged between them was definitely: 'Shit, we've got a right one here.'

'You singer, right?' enquired Rex.

Without waiting for an answer, I noticed them check out my new ensemble of Sta-Prest, shiny grey jacket and loafers. I must have passed muster because Trevor immediately suggested, with a particularly cheeky, yet endearing grin, that the thing I most needed at that moment was (no not that!)… a hat.

He escorted me to the Specials' dressing room with Rex chortling along behind. We were alone in the room, because the Specials were preparing for the show in the pub. I noticed that their dressing room was a proper room containing comfy armchairs, a three-seater sofa, heavily stained, but a sofa nonetheless, and a fridge with assorted beers and soft drinks, and a plate of sandwiches and bowl of fruit on the rickety table. Our dressing room was part of the cloakroom: rows of hard, bench-like seating with hooks to hang clothing. It reminded me of the changing rooms in my school's gym. Knowing where you were in the pecking order of the bands did not confine itself to the position on the bill. The worth of a band is in the detail.

A dense cloud of acrid ganja smoke hung in the stale-smelling room.

'You want something from the rider?' Trevor asked as he saw me eyeing up all the goodies. He handed me a bottle of lager.

So this is a 'rider'. I'd heard Neol and Charley use the word when talking about gig fees and whether they should ask for a rider. Obviously they hadn't asked for one from this promoter.

'Yeah, thanks,' I stammered out. Trevor handed the bottle to Rex, who removed the cap with his teeth. Quite a party trick, I thought. I took the proffered bottle. Then I was shown an array of hats. I tried on a few, but they all looked a bit too butch for my purposes, until I alighted on a dove-grey fedora with a dark grey ribbon hatband. As soon as I tried it on, I felt perfectly attired.

Finding the right hat for oneself is a fraught business. Hats can make some people look totally ridiculous, either because their facial physiognomy doesn't fit the hat or because their ears stick out or something. Some men look like Freddy 'Parrot-Face' Davies in a hat, others look like Humphrey Bogart. I wanted that Humphrey look; that cool, 'if I snap my brim at you then you'll do anything for me' look. That's what the grey fedora gave me. It was perfect. I looked at Trevor with that look of 'Please let me have it, I'll pay you', but to no avail. He said that I could borrow it for the gig. Thus the image was born, it just hadn't been named yet.

It was at this point that we collectively found out what it meant to be the 'support act'. The sound and lighting crew returned from the pub about half an hour before we went on. Lengthy negotiations ensued. It would cost us £10 if we wanted the sound guy to operate the mixing desk and PA. Basically this meant that he made sure the instruments and vocals were audible to the audience, but without any 'fairy dust' additives, such as reverb on the vocal mics or echo effects on some of the instruments. These 'extras' were reserved for the main band, so that they sounded better than the support. Unbeknown to me in those days, the sound guy would also turn the PA to half volume for the support band, so that when the main band came on they would sound louder, which obviously sent a surge of adrenalin and anticipation through the audience. So many tricks of the trade had to be learned. The lighting guy also wanted a tenner to switch on the lights while we performed a half-hour set. They both knew we would pay up, because there's no point performing if the sound is inaudible and the band can't be seen. We were only being paid £50 in total, so there wasn't much left after the agency took their cut, to pay for petrol and the roadies. But we didn't mind. We had an audience to impress.

The gig is still vivid in my mind. We began playing to quite a few seemingly disinterested folk propping up the bar or sitting at the tables and chairs at the edge of the dance floor. Despite the money that had been exchanged with the sound and lighting crews, the sound mix, the onstage foldback and the constant, single state red stage lighting were woefully inadequate. But we must have been making the right kind of noise, because after the first song the people at the bar suddenly came down the front clutching their pints, followed by others who had been waiting in the stairwell or round the sides of the room for the main act. Soon they tried dancing, but suddenly realised that it was impossible while holding a pint of beer. So they downed tools and started skanking. Not a bad result to be better than a pint of beer at your first proper gig.

Gaps and I stole looks at each other as we skanked up and down the front of the stage, our vocals fearlessly intertwining over the urgency of the Selecter music, until a look passed between us during a song in the middle of the set that telegraphed the message: 'Hang on in there. We are doing all right, just keep it up to the end.'

I loved it when Gaps danced. He really was the most elegant

141

dancer out of the whole 2-Tone assortment of wannabe Fred Astaires. He seemed to come into his element when he moved his legs and body, flailing his arms or holding them in stylish positions to the beat of the music. He made the instrumental 'James Bond' come alive with his toasting, a technique of chatting on the microphone, and he looked exceptionally menacing even though, as I said before, he was a shy, quietly spoken man in everyday life.

In Leeds everything came together, the harmonies, the Selecter sound, the songs, Gaps's dance routines, my stage persona and cockney patter. The crowd was baying for more by the end of the show, but there wasn't time for an encore. The band was told in no-nonsense terms that we had to have all our gear off the stage in ten minutes, because the stage had to be properly set for the headline act, the Specials. As the rest of the band stripped the stage down and packed it away in our van, I went back to the empty dressing room, sporting a grin as wide as that of the Cheshire Cat. Taking the opportunity to remove my sweaty clothes while there was still some privacy, I was less than pleased when Trevor reappeared demanding his hat back. I reluctantly returned it, while trying to cover what little dignity is left to a woman who has been caught wearing not much more than her bra and knickers. He stared at me for a few moments with a renewed respect, before remarking: 'You looked good onstage, sis.'

To demonstrate this newfound respect, he promptly dropped his drawers as he exited, up-ended his backside, reached back with his hands and spread the under-side of his testicles. I was later informed that I had been 'turkey necked'. I realised that I was now officially 'one of the boys'!

We were all elated after the gig. Something was happening in the world of music and we had somehow thrust our fingers

Gaps Hendrickson and me leading from the front

into the life-giving force of the Zeitgeist. The resultant shock of the new was 'le ska'!

The very next day I went into town to a men's outfitters, Dunn & Company, which had a double-fronted store opposite Sainsbury's on Trinity Street. There was a strange hush in the shop, probably more due to the fact that there was a soft carpet underfoot than a rogue woman standing in their midst. The shop was run along the lines of the comedy sitcom

143

Are You being Served? As soon as I stepped into the shop, a man approached me with a tape measure around his neck.

'Can I help you?' He choked back the 'sir' part of his standard, reflex-action patter and stood staring at me, as if he had just noticed a slug on the floor.

I explained why I was there in my best patrician tones and after a barely imperceptible rise of his left eyebrow, he asked my hat size, which completely stumped me. It hadn't occurred to me that hats had sizes. Helpfully, he went to the back of the shop and reappeared with a selection of dove-grey hats.

I loved their hats. They were beautifully made, with just the right proportions and lined with white silk stamped in the middle of the crown with the 'Dunn & Co' logo in curlicue script. I tried on a couple rather self-consciously until I found one that fitted. I now had my own hat and always shopped there whenever I needed a replacement, which fortunately was not too often.

Eleven days later, on 21 July 1979, we supported Madness and the Specials at the Electric Ballroom in London. How many bands can say that they played a prestige London show within seven weeks of getting together? Not many, but we did. We were on a steep learning curve. Not only that, we also garnered our first review from *Sounds* journo Giovanni Dadomo, who begins his article being totally surprised that the venue is rammed at only 8.30 p.m. and asks the reader to forgive his vagueness because 'it is hard to be a saint in a sauna'. He freely admits that he has no idea whether the band on view is related to the 'B' side of the Specials' 'Gangsters' single or not, but he seems impressed by the 'two all-action vocalists'. Unfortunately I find it hard to forgive him for saying that I introduced the songs in 'a squeaky oop north accent somewhat reminiscent of the late "Clitheroe Kid"', only to realize on closer scrutiny that 'the squeaker is quite definitely a girl'. Fortunately he later mitigates this unflattering portrayal by saying 'a much better singer than talker'. More importantly though, he loves the band, likening us to the Specials, and signs the article off with '[The Selecter] conspire to make dancing the only way to walk.'

He was not wrong when he described the venue as a sauna. Water dripped from every inch of space on the auditorium's walls. When I first read the review, I hated him for likening me to Jimmy Clitheroe. A chubby, middle-aged pipsqueak in a schoolboy outfit was not the 'image' I was going for! But the rest of it – whoah! What a review for only your fifth gig ever!

Fortunately no more reviewers ever alluded to the 'Clitheroe Kid' again. And it will be Giovanni Dadomo who will be talking in a squeaky voice if I ever meet him in the future!

The review now posed a huge problem. I was still working, albeit sporadically – lately I had been phoning in sick on rather too many occasions. I often joked with Philip, my fellow radiographer, that I had had a heavy night after a gig and I wasn't in a fit state to work the following day. Thankfully and to his credit, he didn't say anything to anybody, but he was beginning to wonder what kinds of venues my new band was playing in. To make matters worse, he read all the music papers hoping that one day his sorry-arse band, Silmarillion, would be reviewed. I had told him the name of my band, but I'm not sure that it registered with him. He never referred to us by name, just 'your band'. I hoped he had forgotten it. Otherwise if he read the gig reviews in the papers he would begin to put two and two together. Fortunately, the reviewer had not named any of us individually, because in those early days, we had no PR company giving out press releases to would-be reviewers.

I expressed my worries to Charley one day while listening to some records round at his house. Apparently Neol had told him that Paul Rambali, an *NME* journo, wanted to do the first in-depth interview with the now rapidly emerging Selecter. Our names would appear in public once the article was printed. Suddenly I was scared. Everything was moving so fast. What was I going to do about my job? After all, I was up for promotion soon to senior radiographer. Was I prepared to destroy my career and throw away three years of hard training just to follow what could possibly turn out to be a damp squib? There were hardly any guarantees in life, but none in the music business. All these questions messed with my head, until Charley said: 'Why not change your name, P?' (He always called me 'P'.)

The simplest ideas are always the hardest to think through, but a name change cut to the chase immediately. But to what?

By this time, Gaps, Desmond and Rob had arrived. They busied themselves rolling large spliffs, while listening to Charley's old bluebeat record collection. People love a game when they are stoned. Inhibitions roll away and people blurt out the first thought that comes into their head. Everybody started pitching in ideas about a name change. Most of the ideas were unworkable, particularly when Desmond, while eyeing me lasciviously, shouted out: 'Pauline Pum-pum'. For those readers not acquainted with Jamaican patois, pum-pum is a woman's vagina!

The wonderful thing about 'free-forming' with words is that happy accidents occur. So when Charley lay on his back puffing out smoke rings after pulling on a large chillum, and said: 'What have we got...Pauline...she's black...Pauline's black...black Pauline...'

'That's it,' I shouted excitedly, 'Pauline Black.'

As soon as I said it, the name felt right. It fitted me like a glove. It was a statement of truth and intent all at the same time. Yes, I was black and I wanted to sing about what it meant to be black. But more than anything I wanted my family to finally say my name. Pauline Black. They could never bring themselves to say the B word. After years of being called half-caste or coloured, I could say it loud and proud, Pauline Black.

At that moment I felt as good as Muhammad Ali probably did when he kept taunting his opponent Ernie Terrell in 1967 with the words: 'What's my name, fool? Say my name?' Ali said it in retaliation against Ernie Terrell, who had insisted on calling Ali by his former name, Cassius Clay, which Ali considered his 'slave name'. I wanted to assert my new identity, fashioned in my own image, not somebody else's idea of who I should be. As far as I was concerned back then, my adopted name was as good as a 'slave name'. My rebirth was complete. The 'rude girl' I had invented had a new name, Pauline Black. Black by design!

I used the name in public for the first time in Rambali's article, ingeniously titled 'They Still Bear the Skas'.

This staved off the danger of being found out at work, but only for a short while. We were getting more and more gigs further afield and requests for interviews, so it was only a matter of time before my secret life was discovered. In an attempt to stave off the inevitable, I went to my doctor with a cock-and-bull story about a bad knee and very obligingly he signed me off for six weeks.

During July and August, The Selecter travelled up and down the English motorways, gigging and building a reputation on the circuit. On 11 August 1979, our trusty Bedford van broke down just a few hundred yards from the gig in Middlesbrough at the notorious Rock Garden. We had been warned in advance that you entered here at your peril, particularly if you were a predominantly black band. The local skinheads were tough and heavy and as someone usefully described it: 'It was a cross between a Viking pillage and a far-right rally.'

The venue occupied a corner plot and we could see in the distance a small crowd of skinhead fans waiting for us. Rob and Grant, our trusted roadies, advanced towards the venue on foot with a degree of trepidation, but as soon as the reception committee heard that it was The Selecter in the van, they ran pell-mell towards us. This was a most unnerving sight when you were actually in the van and had no idea of the conversation that had just taken place between them and the road crew. Neol and Charley got out of the van trying to look mean and moody, because they were both over six foot, but it was completely unnecessary; the advancing horde were clutching bits of paper or torn-off wall posters advertising the gig and all they wanted was to have them signed and talk to us, which everybody dutifully did. They then pushed our van to the venue, where they helped our roadies unload the gear. That was it, this band of tearaways were now our 'official' protection for the day and chaperoned us to the local pub and chippy, where nobody bothered us at all. The gig was rammed. These kids understood what we were trying to say. The moral of the tale is, take people as you find them. It was us who had preconceptions that day and it taught us a lesson.

After this, we got ourselves a manager. Her name was Juliet De Vie and she was twenty-one years old, a bottle-blonde puppy of a girl, but beneath the puff-candy exterior lurked a will of iron and a mind like the Enigma machine at Bletchley

Park. When we first engaged her, she was working at Trigger, a PR company that by then had become the 2-Tone HQ, in Camden, adjacent to the tube station.

Rick Rogers, the Specials manager, owned Trigger's cluttered, makeshift office. It was up some rickety stairs at the back of a tiny arcade, which also conveniently contained a loafer and Dr Marten's shoe shop on the ground floor. Meetings normally took place in a greasy spoon café around the corner. It was all marvellously informal in the early days and, come to think of it, in the latter days too.

Our choice of manager was largely down to Neol Davies, who has always been an incurable flirt, and was smitten by the physical charms of Ms De Vie on sight. Besides it was a good idea to have another woman on board, not that anybody had sought my opinion before engaging her, but her managerial presence chimed with the anti-sexist ethos of the 2-Tone label.

As soon as we had management, our ad hoc schedule became structured, thanks to Juliet. No longer were we running hither and thither like headless chickens looking for a gig.

Suddenly we were added to the bill of a benefit concert in aid of One Parent Families in London on 21 August. It was headlined by the Specials. Initially John Cooper Clarke was on the bill above us and we were bottom, just behind Linton Kwesi Johnson, but at the last moment JCC went to the States and we and LKJ were bumped up the bill, while all-girl band the Modettes were brought in to take up the slack.

I loved Hammersmith Palais, the famous venue immortalised in song by punk band The Clash, whose taped records were now on permanent rotation in the bus thanks to Rob the roadie. It was an old-school dance hall, smaller than the nearby premier venue, Hammersmith Odeon, but it was big on history. The building dated back to the 1920s. It was a place where the 'unwashed' masses congregated to hear music, from jazz, big bands and tea dances to the currently in-vogue punk and reggae.

The stage was at such a height and width that the rapport with the audience was perfect. The auditorium was wider than it was long. There is nothing better than seeing a wide stretch of upturned faces all pointed at the stage and smiling and enjoying the music. Somehow the alchemy that happened between audience and performers at the Palais made you enjoy the music whether you wanted to or not.

However, on this particular night the stage was a small round bandstand, not able to support the burgeoning needs of two seven-piece bands who bounded around the stage as if their very lives depended on it. Therefore a lorry was hurriedly dispatched to get a new one and a motley load of bits of staging and risers arrived that had to be quickly assembled before the doors opened. Everybody pitched in amid much grumbling from the bands and tears from the lady promoter who didn't realise that a large venue like the Palais required a powerful PA rig and a proper stage. Nonetheless, a good night was had in the end. As they say, all's well that ends well.

We came to realize that 'benefit' gigs were often badly organised and benefited nobody much after all the 'expenses' were taken into account. Indeed, I often wonder who is the real beneficiary? In my experience it is usually the egos of the many flaky do-gooders that attach themselves to these charity gigs like ticks to a mangy dog.

Word went round backstage that John Lydon was in the audience. Him I had to see. I rushed out front with Gaps for company and as we pushed our way through the scrum at the bar we saw a huge crowd jostling for a better look at a pimply, skinny white boy, who was doing his best to ignore them. Oh, the price of fame!

Other luminaries present and correct on that particular evening were a brace of Pretenders, Elvis Costello and an exuberant Iggy Pop, who may or may not have been in the company of Mr Rotten. My eyes were popping out of my head as I clutched my pint of bitter shandy and shuffled in and out of the assembled mob.

The Modettes came on to the stage amid a bit of heckling from some of the more uncouth sexist elements in the audience. This was my first live experience of an all-girl band, who competently played their instruments and wrote their own material. Vocalist Ramona fronted the band. She looked just like Jean Seberg in Jean-Luc Godard's 1960 movie *A Bout de Souffle*. She sang in English, but with a heavy French accent, mangling the words of the song, but nonetheless possessing that *je ne sais quoi* that many French girls use to maximum effect. I'd been told that their guitarist Kate Korris had formerly been a member of the Slits, an all-girl band that I admired, but the revelation for me on that night was the powerful drummer, June Miles-Kingston, who sat gorgeously stony-faced behind her equipment, holding the whole, wobbly, jelly-like sound together. They won the audience over by the end of the set. After all, London was their stomping ground and this was a London audience, notoriously fickle and expectant. What could The Selecter offer?

Respected *NME* music journo Charles Shaar Murray reviewed the gig eleven days later, on 1 September 1979. He provides a vivid, if somewhat fanciful, rundown of Selecter personnel. Neol Davies is described as 'fearsomely be-shaded and looking like he's never dropped any pills' and again, I am initially mistaken for a boy, 'a ska-oriented Michael Jackson', until on closer inspection he refers to me as 'a real live Rude Girl'. Impressed with our 'tightly constructed Proper Songs', he suggests that we may give 'the Specials a taste of serious competition in time to come'.

Peter Coyne of *Record Mirror* saw the gig in much the same way: 'they play harder than the Specials and their demonic, danceable sound is pleasurably akin to being whip-cracked across the skull with white-hot barbed wire'.

Praise indeed! But the man of the evening as far as The Selecter was concerned was LKJ. His albums *Dread, Beat & Blood* and *Forces of Victory* were also on heavy rotation in the van. He eloquently articulated the very things that we felt so strongly about. Single-handedly he had invented a new lexicon to describe the often violent events in Britain that impacted on its black Caribbean citizens. When he strode to the microphone that night his mighty presence just ate up the stage. Unfortunately, his backing tapes had gone missing in transit, so it was a very short set. The highlight was a version of 'Sonny's Lettah' declaimed in his usual incendiary verse to a spontaneous rhythm supplied by massed handclaps and a smattering of drums provided by June, the Modettes' drummer. Definitely a night to remember.

Back in Coventry it was time to record. Jerry Dammers, in the wake of the enormous success of 'Gangsters', which peaked in the pop charts at No. 6 in July 1979, had signed the Specials to the Chrysalis record company. Ever a stickler for detail, he negotiated one of the best recording deals imaginable at the time. He'd asked for and been given his own label, 2-Tone, and the monetary facility to sign and record up to ten bands of his choice. Madness had been the first recipient of this deal. They had already recorded 'The Prince', a musical eulogy to the famed Prince Buster, one of the original luminaries of the Jamaican ska movement, and if Charley was to be believed, one of his long-lost cousins. Now it was our turn to record our debut single as a seven-piece band with the aid of a £1,000 recording budget from the 2-Tone label.

Neol decided to use Roger Lomas, the same record producer who had helped him record his instrumental song 'The Selecter' in 1977 in a tiny four-track studio in Roger's back garden shed on Broad Street, in Foleshill. Roger Lomas was now producing bands at Horizon studios, a converted stables adjacent to Coventry station, owned by local businessman/entrepreneur Barry Thomas.

Horizon was a bitch of a studio for access. I lost count of how many times we risked serious back injury lugging our equipment up the vertiginous wooden staircase to get to the studio, poor Desmond with his enormous Hammond and a Leslie. That normally sorted out the men from the boys.

Horizon housed a 16-track recording machine and mixing desk, not exactly state of the art, but a big improvement on Neol's first recording excursion for The Selecter. Roger Lomas proved to be an easy-going, gnome-like man, with an interesting party trick of touching the end of his nose with his tongue. His long hair and penchant for form-fitting, flared jeans made him look as if he would be more at home producing a heavy metal album. But he was an excellent bloke who knew his onions when it came to the recording process. He really liked what we did, the foremost prerequisite of any producer. Otherwise you just get an off-the-peg production sound from a jobbing hack who doesn't give a damn about your music and is just using your money to get himself into a good studio and get his mates in to play overdubs.

He used an in-house studio engineer, Kim Holmes, and

tape-op, Moose. All of them were used to working late, late hours in the studio. We recorded three songs, 'Street Feeling', 'Too Much Pressure' and 'On My Radio' over a three-day period. Most days we were in the studio until the sun came up.

It was my first time in a studio. I thought that music was recorded with everybody in the room just as you performed it live, but straight on to tape. I did not know about the wonderful process called 'overdubbing', which allowed a musician to put his part on separately. Each instrument was independently miked up so that if a mistake was made during the process of the recording, then it could be repaired at a later date. Therefore a song could be orchestrated and a proper arrangement decided upon.

This was a phenomenally quick learning curve. Initially the band records their individual instruments onto a backing track. In order for the musicians to know where they are in a song, the vocalist is expected to provide a 'guide vocal'. Often, the band takes an inordinate amount of time to get the backing track down, so that the poor vocalist is hoarse by the time they come to put down their lead vocal overdub. And usually things have to be done in a hurry, especially if you are a novice band on a tight budget. As soon as you enter a studio, the clock is ticking and time means money. We had only three days to record, arrange and mix three songs. Crazy times.

Roger was incredibly patient and helpful. He realised that I didn't know about studios and helped me double-track my vocal to give the sound depth. He also came up with the idea of doing the chorus response 'On My Radio' in a falsetto voice. Magic: this and the odd-time signature of the bridge section was enough to lift an ordinary song into a classic one.

His only problem was that he had a 'catchphrase'. Just like Bruce Forsyth has 'Nice to see you, to see you nice', Roger's was to give you a thumbs-up on greeting while innocently saying: 'All right Boy'.

To those of a nervous disposition, which meant any black person in a white person's company in those days, this was tantamount to a red rag to a bull. The word 'Boy' is a hangover expression from slave times when applied to a black man. Back then and even in the civil rights years, it didn't matter how old the 'Boy' in question was, it could be a young man or an old man, they were both addressed in the same derogatory way. It wasn't nearly as bad as being called 'nigger', but not that far off.

At first I didn't notice it. I just accepted that it was one of Roger's conversational tics; annoying but certainly not meant in any kind of racial manner. Roger liked the band and was putting his heart and soul into the recording process, so how could he be construed as a racist? However, there were more sensitive souls in the band than Neol and me. The former Hardtop 22 faction had taken real offence at this greeting. They didn't realise or certainly could not be convinced that there wasn't some kind of distinct racist overtone to this catchphrase. Gaps often sang 'Simmer Down' under his breath whenever the phrase was heard.

Therefore a deep resentment was forged towards Roger, which rumbled under the surface for many months. Later this catchphrase would lead us to make the worst decision of our short-lived career. But that was still a way off.

On 26 August, the day after liberation from the confines of Horizon studios, I was standing on the Lanchester Poly stage giving it big time to the packed house of students that had assembled for the Specials' triumphant homecoming gig.

Even a large posse of 'townies' had wisely been allowed in, otherwise they would probably have caused a riot outside – 2-Tone, they seemed to be saying, belonged to the whole of Coventry, not just to a bunch of work-shy students. We were in support, but I was on cloud nine. Here I was seven years later in the Main Hall again, not sweating over exam papers or watching a famous band passing through on tour, no – I was in a band on the verge of breaking through into the big-time. As Batman would have said, if he could have seen into the future: 'Poor, deluded girl!'

I didn't care, this was the best delusion that I'd ever had, particularly when it was topped off the following day by our first gig at the Lyceum, in London, supporting mod-revivalist band Secret Affair and fellow Coventry girl-made-good, Hazel O'Connor.

With the gig coverage in the local newspaper, all pretence of illness was over. I took the only step left open to me, I paid one last visit to the radiography department at Walsgrave Hospital to tender my resignation to the Superintendent Radiographer and to clear out my locker and say goodbye to some close colleagues. Far from being an embarrassing admission, my seemingly successful career change was met with interest and delight and much well-wishing for the future, even from some of the old stalwart doctors that worked in the department. I almost felt guilty that my subterfuge had gone on for so long. As I jauntily walked out of the hospital, my footsteps faltered as I suddenly realized that my future was now unpredictable. I'd left behind the surety of steady, plodding promotion in a good, worthwhile job, for the mercurial dizziness of supposed fame and perhaps fortune. I resolved then and there that I would have to make my new life work come what may, because there was no way that I wanted to re-enter those hospital doors and have to ignominiously beg for my old job back.

But I'm getting ahead of myself. We had a pivotal gig to do – a return to the F Club in Leeds, but this time as a fully fledged recording band with an identifiable image, an aggressive 'take no prisoners' attitude and a hastily forged pedigree in the dance halls of England. And what's more, headlining. The rider was fabulous.

The gig sounded and looked almost professional. Our set was now paced properly and worked to a crescendo for the last song, 'Too Much Pressure', in which we had initiated a splendid piece of theatricality. Mid-song we all had a mock fight in the centre of the stage. Strobe lighting added to its visual impact. Recently, there had been an escalation of trouble at some of our gigs. The Specials also suffered a similar plight at their shows. We had begun to be targeted by some members of the extreme right NF Party, who hid among the skinhead fraternity. Regularly, these fascist elements came to gigs to cause trouble. They would deliberately start fights with other members of the audience, or orchestrate repeated shouts of 'Sieg Heil' at the stage when we were performing, accompanied by raised right arms in the all-too-familiar Nazi salute. At first this behaviour happened sporadically, but gradually it increased in frequency and ferocity. We hoped our 'mock fight' would demonstrate to the audience that the business of fighting looked horrible and was ultimately futile in settling problems. It worked for a while. Audiences were shocked. The fighting was kept under control.

We played a gig in Bristol on 29 September in Trinity Hall, an old church hall youth club, just before embarking on the 2-Tone tour. 'On My Radio' had just been released and the reviews for the single were brilliant. Everybody in the band was feeling good.

The evening started out well, despite Trinity Hall being a cavernous, depressing meeting place overlooked by a new redbrick fortress, the local cop shop. The soundcheck was late, because the PA equipment arrived late and took ages to set up by the owner. A reggae/ska disco tried to take up the slack when the punters were let in early, despite the soundcheck not having finished. We all stomped unceremoniously off the stage. We were already acting like prima donnas and we had only been gigging for three months. Gaps and I had an interview to do, so we accompanied the journalist to a pub around the corner from the police station. As soon as we walked in, the landlady looked at us and pronounced audibly within the pub: 'No, not in here.'

A swift glance around the place showed me what she meant. No blacks in here. We could have argued it out with her, but who would have wanted to drink in the damn place after a reception like that. The landlady's reaction had soured the evening and the mood swiftly went downhill. Gaps and I were simmering with anger and we probably off-loaded quite a lot of this on to the interviewer. We decided to return to the venue and carry on the interview in a backstage corridor, but just as we settled into chairs to chat about how well things were going with the band, five young blokes making a sharp exit saw us and begged sanctuary in the relative safety of our dressing room. They told us that a gang of Mods had tried to set on them for no reason at all. We let them hang out for a while, then they filtered back into the crowd, honour still intact.

We resumed the interview, only to be angrily interrupted by a harassed promoter, who had obviously bitten off more than he could chew when he decided to book a 2-Tone band. 'If you don't get out there now, there ain't gonna be no gig. It's getting charged out there,' he shouted, a look of abject terror on his face.

He was right. We began the gig and the infectious sound of the music soothed the growing tensions between the different factions for a while, but halfway through the set the dark mood crept back in. In a bid to acknowledge that there were different factions present, I greeted each of them, Mods, skinheads, punks.

Immediately the Mods chanted in time-honoured fashion: 'We are the Mods, we are the Mods, we are, we are, we are the Mods.'

The 'Army and Navy' parka brigade made a lot of noise. The sound of 500 pairs of Doc Martens pounding the floor is deafening in a confined space. We played the music again, but a group of skinheads to the left of the stage lowered their braces to their waists and raised high a large Union Jack right in front of the audience. Gaps and I tried to ignore the triumphal flapping of the 'Butcher's Apron', but the flag offered a focal point for the aggro that had simmered all evening. 'Too Much Pressure' stoked the fiery tension in the room with another ton of coal. We fervently hoped that the mock stage fight would act as a release valve, a catharsis, forcing the disruptive elements in the audience to confront their hostility. Unfortunately it didn't have the desired effect; after the all-too-familiar stage invasion a small skirmish broke out and escalated like a forest fire finding dry tinder. The battle that everybody came for happened even though the music they had just danced to had the message of unity attached to it in capital letters.

That was when I realized this wasn't just about us spreading a 'unity' message, it was about us being caught up in the maelstrom of competing teenage tribal factions. Until recently such *Lord of the Flies* disputes had been bloodily settled on the football terraces, but 2-Tone had the misfortune to coincide with a police crackdown on the beautiful game's crowd violence. Robbed of causing trouble in their usual territory, disruptive elements had found a natural home at our gigs. All we had to do was figure out a way to deal with such divisive monsters without being eaten alive. Since we were mostly black in our band, the resonances that played out in the larger society were reflected in our tiny microcosm. Some of it was very ugly. As usual, I was caught in the middle and forced to take sides.

The Selecter's main problem at this stage – although we didn't see it as a problem – was that we were all so earnest about society's ills. We wanted to write political songs about socially charged stuff. We were talking about the life on the street from a largely black perspective. The predominantly white audience that followed the Specials found it difficult to identify with us. The identifying markers were not there; there were too many blacks and, horror of horrors, a woman fronting the band.

Acceptance and identification are two separate things. For a band to be really successful, a large section of the population has not only accept the message conveyed in their songs, but also identify with them. The listener has to want to be in their gang because basically we are all tribal in our youth. We never gave people, black or white, the chance to identify with us, or perhaps the 'times' were just not conducive to such a thing happening.

The 'sus' law (the power to stop and search by the police, if they had 'reasonable suspicion') was enforced on the streets. This archaic, draconian law, based on the Vagrancy Act of 1824, meant that any young black person just walking on the street or standing on a street corner with others could be picked up and taken down to the police station, searched, questioned and generally harassed, until maybe one of them lost their rag and became abusive, whereupon the police would then arrest them for public disturbance or obstructing a police officer. This caused deep resentment and divisiveness in the black communities of Britain. It was a calculated operation. The police knew exactly what they were doing. The 'divide and rule' tactic is a favourite of the thugs of the Establishment.

Insulated as I had been from the black population in Coventry before joining the band, I had nevertheless been picked up by two policewomen on my way to work at the radiography department in Coventry, and driven round to the employees' entrance of a big local department store, where two people intently peered through the window at me and to my relief shook their heads and went back inside. Even though I was not the person sought, the policewomen hauled me down to the cop shop and interrogated me for two hours, asking me at great length where I had been on a particular day three weeks before, and for more personal information than I was prepared to divulge. When I procrastinated about this I was met with the usual police rejoinder: 'If you're not guilty of anything, then what do you have to worry about by telling us what we want to know?'

Eventually they could see it was leading nowhere. They drove me back to work and had the audacity to explain everything to the superintendent of the X-Ray department, who was told that they were looking for a shoplifter and I fitted the description. Their definition of a description was any young black female. I was mad as hell on that day. This was my introduction to the 'sus' law.

The idea of multiculturalism hadn't yet been invented, so a general racism pervaded society. Coventry was a violent city. At that time, nothing united the tribal configurations of the youth more than the general unspoken policy of hating the blacks or newly arrived Indians and Pakistanis. All of us, including Neol, understood this implicitly. Our music tried to convey it explicitly. At first we were clumsy with our message. In those early days, all the bands, us, the Specials and Madness were fiercely committed to an anti-racist stance. We had been pushed up out of the masses, not imposed by some corporate music bigwig who wanted to have a bash at this new 'multi-ethnic' look. We were the real deal.

As much as racism mired the streets of Britain in 1979, sexism was rife in society too. The boiler-suited and monkey-booted feminist movement was making itself heard in Britain for the first time, much to the chagrin of Britain's as yet unreconstructed men. Some of these ladies also beat a path to the door of the 2-Tone movement. Sometimes it felt as though we were speaking for all the disaffected youth in Britain. That was a heavy, heavy burden, particularly in Coventry, where jobs were scarce. Once the Motor City of England, by 1979 Coventry city centre was just a rundown, concrete urban sprawl, with a ring road that only seemed to help you find the M1 going south, something that many city dwellers suggested was the only good thing about Coventry. The 2-Tone movement gave many young Coventrians hope, where before there had been none. Perhaps naively, The Selecter and the Specials wanted to spend their musical careers highlighting these problems. Unfortunately, we were dragged into the 'entertainment business', which was seriously at odds with 2-Tone thinking.

The next crucial item on The Selecter's agenda was sorting out which record company we should sign to. 'On My Radio', which hadn't been released yet, was recorded for the 2-Tone label, but it had turned out so well and our popularity was rising so swiftly that album deals with major labels were now a possibility. Arista and Chrysalis wanted us. One day the band turned up at Charley's house for a meeting, only to find a Rolls-Royce outside. The MD of Arista, accompanied by his right-hand man, the preposterously named Tarquin Gotch, had travelled all the way from London clutching a recording contract. The incongruity of a Rolls-Royce parked in a deprived area was lost on these London chancers. We reasoned that if they didn't understand this irony, then there was no way that they could ever understand the music we played. They went away empty-handed. Chrysalis took a more 'softly, softly' approach and offered us a good deal. We signed. If it was good enough for the Specials, then it was deemed good enough for us. After all, Jerry Dammers was no slouch in the business. He had single-handedly negotiated the 2-Tone label and monies to fund it from Chrysalis already. We were invited to become joint directors with the Specials in furthering the aims of the 2-Tone label.

We signed to Chrysalis/2-Tone on 10 October 1979. The day before we recorded our first John Peel session at BBC Maida Vale. On the day of the signing we recorded 'On My Radio' for appearances on *Top of the Pops* and for *Multi-Coloured Swap Shop*. The day after there was a photo session with top rock photographer Brian Aris, who had the unholy job of trying to make us look like a big-time band. He even managed to subdue Desmond's antics. Then we taped videos for *TOTP* and *Swap Shop* appearances. Chrissie Hynde's band, the Pretenders, were also at the *Swap Shop* TV studio, promoting their newly released single 'Brass in Pocket'. Chrissie and Jimmy Honeyman-Scott absconded with Neol and me to a pub for a lunchtime session and filled us in on what was expected of the newly famous. A lot of drinking, hell-raising and drug-taking apparently. Both of them had had a lot more practice at the rock-and-roll lifestyle than we had. But look where that got poor old Jimmy. He was a really sweet guy.

From the outside it looked as if things were going brilliantly, but inside The Selecter musical dissatisfaction had already begun to rear its ugly head. Desmond began smoking and drinking much more and his personality markedly changed. This huge man would often lumber across from stage right to left and start berating Charley for his bass playing, in much the same manner as he had dissed Lawton's guitar playing. An audience just saw two people haranguing each other.

Charley's bass playing certainly wasn't on a par with that of Horace from the Specials, but it was adequate for Selecter purposes. He was also a good focal point. The sight of a slim, elegantly tall, red-locked Rastaman in a three-piece tonic suit flailing his Marleyesque locks around while playing bass with his big spider fingers was a definite winner for both a hungry press and rapt audiences. There had never been anything like it before. It was as original as my 'rude girl' get-up. Charley was sick of being made to look bad by Desmond, who would play air bass, in full view of the audience, to demonstrate to Charley how his bass lines should sound. Desmond was no diplomat, and would often take his grievances into the dressing room.

Other grievances harboured by members of the band began surfacing too. The tunes were beginning to take on a rockier flavour, spearheaded mostly by Neol's playing style, whereas there was a faction headed by Charley that wanted to promote a more reggae flavour. Commie and myself thought that the hybrid we had going was the right way. Charley, Gaps, Aitch and Desmond favoured the 'old school' ska sound. Funnily enough, not one of them ever suggested that a horn section might be a good addition, because that is what makes for that kind of authenticity. We remained a guitar-orientated band, with both lead and rhythm present. Many reviewers thought we had a more authentic sound than the Specials (even Jerry Dammers has been quoted as saying this too), but how could we have done without horns?

Amid these machinations, the Selecter bandwagon rolled along, gathering ardent fans and garnering rave reviews. Finally came the day, despite our ongoing wrangling, when we made our joyous mark in front of the youth of Britain. The Selecter performed our newly released chart hit 'On My Radio' for the first time on the only music TV show that mattered in the UK in 1979, *Top of the Pops*. The show itself was recorded at the London BBC studios in White City on 17 October, two days before the legendary 2-Tone Tour began.

It was an arduous but exciting day. Like most bands, some of us didn't know how to behave once inside the hallowed halls of the Establishment TV. The worst part of it was hanging around interminably in a windowless dressing room with only a few utilitarian chairs. Nervous bands left to their own devices tend to roam and get up to things that they shouldn't. Trying to round up seven people to do the endless rehearsal run-throughs of the band's hit song so that faceless people in front of banks of TV monitors could get camera angles for the evening's 'live' performance was hard work. Our manager, Juliet, was running hither and thither like a sheepdog snapping at the heels of various members who had gone AWOL, while laughing and chatting with the powers-that-were in order to achieve maximum damage limitation.

Desmond was the most unruly, because he had a well-

Gig ticket October 1979, Selecter spelt wrong, as usual

developed method of confusing white folks with his riddle-me-ree backchat and could wind up the most laid-back of people within minutes. If any white authority figure approached him he would just let his lower jaw hang down, move his face forward until it was a few inches away from theirs and adopt a quizzical expression before saying: 'Wh'appen maan?'

When they returned an inevitably blank expression, he would exclaim 'Cha bloodclaat' while delivering a menacing stare, usually accompanied with a snap of the fingers of his massive right hand. Rest assured, it was probably very intimidating for the recipient, but most of the tight-arses at the Beeb in those days deserved such treatment. Unfortunately, it also reinforced all their stereotypes about us black folk. They had decided that we were trouble even before talking to us, which meant that we played up our given roles to the hilt. Well, who wouldn't, given half the chance?

Charley was banned from entering the staff bar both

before and after the recording because he refused to take off the hat that covered his locks. Charley told the jobsworth commissionaire on the bar entrance that he wore the hat for religious reasons, patiently explaining the rules of Rastafarianism to him, the finer points of which fell on deaf ears. A great deal of fuss ensued, with much 'pussyclaating and bloodclaating' and I could see that the producer and director of the show were thinking: 'Hmmm…future note… watch out for The Selecter.'

I stayed out of the argument because it seemed contradictory to me that Charley, most other times, particularly when performing on stage, had absolutely no problem about whipping his loose locks around for artistic effect. I couldn't understand why he didn't just do that in the bar, but I had come from the other side of the fence. I didn't know very much about the strict codes of the righteous black man's religion from Jamaica, Rastafarianism.

Fuel was then added to the fire when I was coerced into entering the bar with my hat on which, of course, because I was a woman, didn't seem to matter. A huge row erupted from Charley as to why it was okay for me to wear a hat, but not him. Fair point. This ugly scenario was only quelled by the intervention of Juliet who hauled us all down to the studio for the recording.

We were the penultimate act, just before 'Buggles' performed 'Video Killed the Radio Star'. Since we were on so near the end we got the chance to watch the fabulous Suzi Quatro strut her stuff, Lena Martell bore the pants off everyone and XTC, my favourite, easily stealing the show with the imaginative 'Making Plans for Nigel'.

The performers mimed to the backing tracks, which had been pre-recorded some days before, because in those days

Charley, Gaps and me larking about, 1979

the Musicians Union were able to enforce a rule that the original recordings couldn't be used, they had to be done again so that engineers and all extra or uncredited musicians would be gainfully employed. All hail the Union. It was an excellent idea, but very time-consuming in an already full band schedule. Since these tracks were hastily recorded and mixed in a few hours, they were sometimes not as exciting as the original record. Probably the average viewer at home wouldn't notice, but the artists did. So the visual aspect of the performance has to be spot on, because the audio part is probably not as good as the record. We more than made up for any audio deficiency with our onstage antics. We looked sharp, original in both dress and song. Who else could have got a song decrying the BBC-owned Radio 1 past the censors and made a hit of it, seemingly without anybody really listening to the song's sentiment? The Selecter definitely had the last laugh on that particular day. Mind you, Buggles played their trump card the following week, when they went to No. 1 and killed the radio star stone dead. Our highest position in the official singles chart was No. 6. I wasn't complaining. Our first single had gone Top Ten.

I was overwhelmed with excitement when I watched the broadcast a few days later on TV. It was an unnerving experience watching what seemed like a facsimile of myself running, dancing and singing on stage, fronting a band of people who I hardly really knew, but looking like I belonged in that milieu, looking like I meant business.

Suddenly, a maddening thought popped into my head. I wondered whether the mother who had given me up at birth for adoption might be watching. She was only seventeen years older than me, perhaps she was still young at heart and into music just like myself. Would she recognise me? Would she feel proud of me? Would she come looking for me in the light of my success? Was I worth something at last?

For a split second I felt like Jimmy Cagney's character, Cody Jarrett, in the movie *White Heat*, who utters these immortal

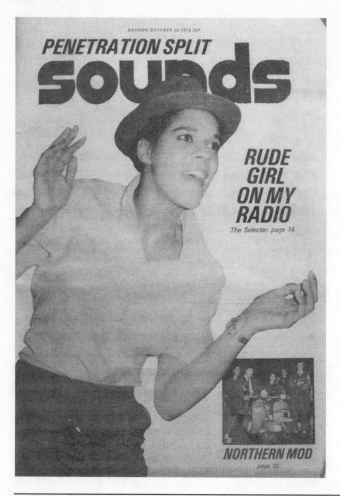

words while firing his gun into the giant gas tank: 'Made it, Ma. Top of the world.'

The 2-Tone explosion had begun.

SEVEN

'A BIRD'S EYE VIEW'

On 22 September 1979, *Melody Maker* music journo Frank Worrall wrote: 'The Selector [sic!] are going to be real contenders.'

Could things get any better? Yes they could; we were invited onto the bill of the legendary 2-Tone tour.

I had never been on tour before, so staying each night in a hotel, rather than driving interminable distances home after each gig was a completely new experience for me. Until now, we had done disparate dates, rarely consecutively, so the 2-Tone tour was the stuff of dreams. We rode on a proper bus, albeit not the sort with bunk beds, lounges and a kitchen that would be introduced to us later, but the kind of bus that takes you to the swimming baths when you are at school. Indeed, the whole tour smacked of a school outing. It reminded me of a school field trip with no holds barred. As far as The Selecter were concerned, any mode of transport was an improvement on our old, beat-up, green Bedford van, which could now be found propped up on bricks, tyres long gone, in the car park of the infamous Hillfields high-rise, Pioneer House.

The idea behind the 2-Tone tour was to make it like a package review show. Immediately I had in mind the Motown show that had sailed through England in my teens. It made sense: keep the ticket price low and maximise the entertainment. Even though the Specials, Madness and The Selecter were lumped under the same ska banner, we were very different bands. The 2-Tone logo and identity attached to each of our respective singles was like a corporate kinship, a unique vision that people could buy into, not only with the product, but with a dress code and most importantly an ethos, that of unity and harmony between races and between men and women. Jerry Dammers's genius created the Walt Jabsco logo alongside the inspired use of black and white chequers to establish an undeniably cool visual that gave our audience, increasingly made up of young kids from many varied races

The 'Rude Girl' image perfected 1980. Photo © brianaris.com

and backgrounds, a chance to subliminally absorb a radical political statement, while getting on with the serious business of dancing.

Even the tickets were purposely kept low in price. You could see three bands, each of them with a top chart single, for the princely sum of £2 or £3. What a bargain. Dance venues were our main stamping ground, which meant no seats and punters packed in like sardines. Looking back at old printed itineraries for the tour, we had to bed, water and feed 44 people every night for 40 nights. Sometimes those figures swelled to probably more like 54 people when managers, friends and family turned up. It was organised chaos most of the time.

The tour manager who had to coordinate this mess was Frank Murray, a likeable Irishman who previously managed Thin Lizzy, so he was used to the antics of wayward rock and rollers. He was firm but fair, sometimes manipulative but most often relaxed. If you were in the trenches and thinking of going over the top, then you would definitely follow this man.

The pecking order for stage was always The Selecter on first, then Madness, lastly the Specials. It was expected that the opening band would get the worst deal, normally a half-empty hall with lots of punters propping up the bar, but the word of mouth and general media mayhem about the new 2-Tone phenomenon meant that venues were full about twenty minutes after the doors opened. Many also might think that seeing three bands all doing ska music would be too much, but we had very different takes on the ska beat. The Specials mixed their ska with rock, Madness mixed theirs with music hall, and we mixed ours with reggae and a soupçon of rock and soul.

Vocally the differences between the bands were even

starker. The Selecter had the surly coolness of Gaps and gender-bending me, sometimes harmonising, sometimes singing lead individually with a whirlwind on-stage energy. In contrast, Suggs gave Madness a definite Ian Duryesque flavour while Chas Smash did his nutty dance and rallied their fanatical following. Terry Hall brought the Specials an unmistakeable post-punk whine flanked by a charismatic toasting rude boy, Neville. What was not to like? We had all bases covered.

The Selecter's manager Juliet De Vie and I were the only women on the 2-Tone bus who were gainfully employed and not giving gratis blow-jobs. The fragrant Juliet was a welcome respite from the sweaty-boy smell that infiltrated the bus after very hot gigs.

In his book, *Ska'd for Life*, Horace Panter says that mostly he sat up the front of the bus. I don't remember it like that. I remember him and the terrifyingly cool Terry Hall holding queenly court on the back seat. Horace probably sat up the back so he didn't have to see the dubious shenanigans that were going on in the middle of the bus, but I always figured that Mr Hall sat there because to get there he had to traverse the entire length of the 56-seater tour bus which gave all us mere minions so much more time to admire him on the journey. I have to say I had never met such a bunch of prima donnas as some of the Specials. I don't accuse Neville Staple of this behaviour, but the remaining sextet should have been sent down by 'Judge 400 Years' for a long spell of personality rehabilitation.

Jerry Dammers, the Specials keyboard player, main songwriter and mastermind, was a bizarre figure, with his gappy mouth, Thunderbirds puppet walk and Rupert Bear trousers. His precarious sense of style and dress were simultaneously studiedly comic and cool. He affected the demeanour of the fool, much as Robert Graves's Claudius did. Jerry used this character trait to hide his astute and somewhat manipulative business brain. He very cleverly fooled people into doing his bidding most of the time. Some people didn't mind, some railed against him. He's never been able to utter more than a few words to me any time I've ever had the misfortune to be in a place where we had to make conversation. He was one of those people who has a conversation while looking over your shoulder, hoping for somebody who would be far more interesting to talk to than you.

The Specials guitarist, Roddy Radiation, in those days, was young, mostly drunk and full of spunk. He had the face of an angel, but the punk credentials of a stroppy schoolboy. The one good thing you can say about Roddy is that he has never changed. As a musician he gave the Specials their edge, something that often rubbed Jerry Dammers up the wrong way.

Strangely enough, Jerry and Roddy used to share a room on the 2-Tone tour. I still have the rooming roster. On a rare night off in Manchester, I knocked on their Piccadilly Hotel room door because I had run out of Rizlas. I was entertaining in my room on that particular evening and it was too late to go out and buy skins at one in the morning. I was very stoned at the time but, according to my recollection, young Roddy opened up the door clad only in a Specials T-shirt and holey socks. Trying hard not to look while he unselfconsciously manipulated himself, I blurted out: 'Got any skins, Roddy?'

He was so totally drunk that he was barely focusing on anything. He smiled one of his lop-sided, loopy grins and nodded in the general direction of a table messily covered with half-eaten take-aways, beer bottles, torn fag packets and dead spliffs. As I walked over to the indicated Rizla packet, I noticed his rooming mate lying prostrate on the bed, with a fully clothed, dishevelled young woman rocking back and forth. They didn't sound as though they were having much fun. Indeed the only sound that could be heard was the slow, rhythmic, rock-steady creaking of the bed. Meanwhile, Roddy climbed up onto a chest of drawers, voyeuristically absorbed in some serious post-gig business. I collected the skins and made a sharp exit. All in a day's work for 2-Tone boys.

Much is made of Neville Staples's sexual antics and those of his procurers, the rude-boy roadie duo, Rex and Trevor. Yes, all of that is true, I saw many a silly young girl backstage being groomed by the duo for future sacrifice on the altar of Nev's cock. Unfortunately for those who supposed that an invite for coffee back at the hotel meant exactly that, it was probably a 'rude' awakening. But for the more willing participants, it was probably a mouthful too much, if the mythology surrounding Neville's alleged sexual exploits is to be believed. Often, I would scoop up some sobbing, penniless young waif who had failed to deliver her 'pum-pum' for that particular night's use from a lonely hotel corridor somewhere in Britain and allow her to use the other bed in my room. Of course, when the rest of the boys saw her downstairs in the morning and she told them what had happened, I think they all thought that I was sleeping with girls. I'm afraid not, besides, you never knew where their girls had been!

Our manager Juliet was not present all the time. She and Rick Rogers, the Specials manager, had Trigger, their PR company, to run in London. When she did join the tour I was glad of her company. I rather enjoyed a woman being in charge of us unruly Selecter lot and she knew her onions when it came to PR. She was getting us a lot of reviews and interest, which all helped to build our profile.

The gigs were universally packed. So much so that sweat dripped off the walls and the ceiling at many venues. One particularly avid fan leapt from a balcony during our set at the Top Rank, Cardiff gig. I assume he lived after his spectacular vault.

My twenty-sixth birthday was celebrated at a now-defunct venue, the Plymouth Fiesta. I was lucky enough to be presented onstage with a huge birthday card signed by all three bands after the last encore. Lynval then led the whole audience in singing Happy Birthday. This was a magical, life-enhancing moment, but it just as quickly turned into the first of many nightmarish moments. Post-show, most band members were well fortified with beer and assorted drugs. Desmond, whose unpredictable behaviour was beginning to cause concern, began acting up, due to something that had been said to him by one of the bouncers. The burly security guys were eager to clear the dressing rooms as quickly as possible and close up for the night. Unfortunately they were being less than polite. Suffice to say that as we were getting changed out of our sweaty stage clothes in a less than convivial communal dressing room, Desmond suddenly shouted: 'Bloodclaat white man.'

Within moments I saw three bouncers and several of The Selecter holding Desmond's struggling body almost at right angles (remember he was a big man) while he sunk his teeth into Chrissy Boy from Madness's left cheek. His manhandlers dragged him off, leaving a scared and stunned Chrissy Boy clutching his face. Desmond was too heavy to carry for long, so his feet were re-deposited on the ground, but he hadn't finished with his 'Hannibal Lecter' routine. He lunged at one of the bouncers and tried to bite him too. The bouncers then decided to go and find reinforcements. That was when things turned ugly. Somebody, maybe Frank Murray, ran into the dressing room and told us to get Desmond out of the building as quickly as possible, because the bouncers were coming for him armed with baseball bats. That's the last I saw of Desmond that night.

The atmosphere in the bus took on a distinct chill the following day. The Selecter began to get a reputation for being rude, argumentative and at times violent with each other. The Specials had the same problem with two of their members, namely Roddy and Jerry, who were always having differences of opinion, but they hadn't resorted to biting each other yet! Unfortunately, we didn't know then that Desmond was ill, let alone that soon his mind would degenerate even further until his stage persona was compromised too.

The Specials' Neville Staple still has my undying respect for the attitude he exuded on stage. This was a young, black British male, adored by men as well as women for his cocky, devil-may-care persona, but not afraid to subvert stereotypes. Terry Hall may have been full of the studied sarcastic stage chat, but to see Neville astride a PA stack singing 'Monkey Man' and gesticulating at the skinheads in a mock chimp way was to see real rebellion. That moment in the set always spoke to me, far more than seeing some sleepy-eyed boy-wonder laconically singing his lyrics as if he couldn't really be bothered. If that's cool, then you can keep it. Give me a man who nails his colours to the mast!

I can't tell you how sick I used to get of the *Sieg Heil*ing bonehead skins. I'm sick of saying stuff in interviews about how 'lovely' it was on the 2-Tone tour. Some of these shirtless, bleached-jeaned, braces-dragging-round-their-arses bastards made it total misery. If you scratch their surface they have 'racist' written all the way down their centre like a sickly sweet stick of BNP rock. At gigs I always pointedly directed the chorus of 'They Make Me Mad' at them.

Madness jumped ship halfway through the tour to go to America. I think they wanted to distance themselves from the media flak that was unfairly directed at the tour. Some of the more unscrupulous newspapers erroneously dubbed the 2-Tone movement as 'racist', because of the violent skins who were targeting the gigs, ostensibly to make trouble. The Specials and The Selecter did our best to answer such accusations, but Madness didn't seem to have the stomach for controversy like the rest of us. Their jaunty, boyish image was in danger of being sullied with political fall-out, so they de-camped. Cowards!

I think they also wanted to steal a march on the Specials and get to the other side of the pond first. Ultimately, the Specials nailed America much better than Madness, the latter's quintessential Englishness being somewhat lost on the brash American sensibility.

Madness was replaced on the tour by Dexy's Midnight Runners, a soul band, just a few months from breaking through with a stupendous single release, 'Geno'. They had their own resident mad man, Kevin Rowland. I always noticed that Desmond and Kevin gave each other a wide berth whenever their paths crossed.

Just before Madness left us, there was a night on the television when there was almost a wholesale takeover of *Top of the Pops* by 2-Tone records. All three bands appeared on the show. Since we were on stage first every night, *TOTP* used a pre-recording of ours, but the Specials and Madness were able to do a fresh recording, thus pushing their singles further up the charts. Never in my wildest dreams did I imagine that we would find ourselves with a hit single and be a major movement in the pop market within the space of a few short months.

Suddenly we were catapulted into a world where people did things in order to 'make the show go real nice!' This could mean anything from helping you get your dry cleaning to providing you with the drug *de jour*. This was a whole new world and not necessarily a brave one. Weakling that I was, I soon found myself out of my depth.

The best you can hope for as a woman designated as 'one of the boys' is to be tolerated. Most men are on automatic pilot when it comes to women. For them, women have a dual role. They are either shaggable or not. If the woman in question is the lead singer of a popular band, then this often renders her definitely un-shaggable. Therein lies the rub, as they say.

For almost two months, I was doomed to watching grown men act like prepubescent schoolboys at an Ann Summers party. Therefore I spent an awful lot of time on my own while everybody else, with the noted exceptions of the monk-like Horace and the studiedly aloof Terry Hall, were pursuing the Bacchanalian triple tour delights of sex, drugs and alcohol. Don't know when they found time to do their laundry!

The flipside of the gold coin that I had just been tossed was loneliness – hours of it in impersonal hotel rooms up and down the country. Unfortunately loneliness can lead to poor decision-making, especially when fuelled with gratis lines of cocaine. I had never taken cocaine before. In fact, I had never given cocaine any thought at all before the 2-Tone tour. I smoked marijuana without a second thought, and had done so recreationally at weekends for years, but cocaine was out of my price range and out of my social sphere. I discovered that cocaine makes an essentially shy person rather gregarious

and on some days, the life and soul of the party. Regrets? I had a few!

The Selecter's rollercoaster ride hurtled down the track towards Europe, taking in Holland, Belgium, Norway, Sweden, Germany and Italy on the way. I had never been outside Britain until then, and I found it hard to comprehend that so many foreign fans turned up at our gigs, fully kitted out in black and white clothes, and sang along to the songs at our performances. Their English was practically non-existent, but they had memorized our songs' words. They were tuned into that youthful musical sixth sense that can detect meaningful new sub-cultures inside their radar range. Slowly but surely we stealth-bombed Europe with the 2-Tone message. During this initial raid I also caught the eye of a Swede, Stockholm-based photographer Hatte Stiwenius.

Life seemed to be zooming along at breakneck speed,

while all sorts of career-enhancing or sometimes threatening decisions had to be made. Mike Read and John Peel commissioned us for much-coveted radio sessions. During these lengthy Maida Vale recordings, coffee breaks were spent deciphering the impenetrable gobbledy-gook-speak of our chosen lawyer and accountant, who were negotiating with our prospective record company, Money. Record deals, just like time and tide, waited for no man or woman. Out of natural loyalty to the Specials and perhaps a misplaced sense of trust in Chrysalis, we stuck with 2-Tone. In retrospect, not the best business decision, but that's where our hearts were at the end of 1979.

We were a band that had been catapulted into the big time within six short months, unlike the Specials who had had two years to build up their touring chops. It is a testament to the strength of us as both musicians and people that we managed to make it in the way that we did, given the short preparation time.

Now we faced our biggest hurdle. Who would produce our first album? The bar had already been set very high by the Specials when Elvis Costello had consented to produce them. Neol wanted Roger Lomas to carry on in the producer's role. On the face of it this was reasonable enough. Roger had managed to produce two hits from Neol's songs, the instrumental 'The Selecter' which had kicked off the whole seven-piece band idea and the quirky single 'On My Radio' that had established the band as more than just a faceless semi-hit wonder.

In my opinion, we had already made one stupid mistake. Our first band single should not have been a double 'A' side. 'On My Radio' should have been the first single and its flipside 'Too Much Pressure' should have been the second single. But

Neol and the rest of us at that time agreed that the fans came first and they should have value for money. This is true, but we had plenty of cover tracks in the live set which would have been adequate for 'B' sides. Also, these cover tracks would have generated much-needed royalties for the original Jamaican artists. More importantly, it would have established Gaps Hendrickson as a lead singer too.

There was much heated discussion as to whether we should have a change of producer. Charley argued that we needed a 'name' producer from the Jamaican reggae world, not a home-grown, almost unknown from Coventry. Mikey Dread was suggested, and Dennis Bovell, who had not only produced 'Silly Games' for reggae artist Janet Kay, but also earned his punk credentials by providing the sounds for the very successful all-girl band, the Slits. Charley stood his ground. He felt unhappy that although the band was predominantly black, two white men, Neol and Roger, were calling the shots and trying to push the band further away from its roots. It was bound to happen, particularly when Roger's catchphrase of 'All right, boy' resurfaced as an argument for not employing him further for the first album.

I was stuck in the middle, that miserable 'between a rock and a hard place' void, where most mixed-race people find themselves from time to time. I'd always wanted to promote my black credentials, but these seemed very different from Jamaican credentials. In the same way that Roddy Radiation was in love with the illusion that was James Dean, I was in love with the illusion of Angela Davis and the Black Panthers. I was dancing to a black American aesthetic, not a Jamaican one, even if I was the lead singer of a band that did Jamaican music. I was confused. I had to make a choice and in 20/20 hindsight I made the wrong one. I should have supported

Neol, but I didn't. I supported Charley in his quest to bring in somebody who would authenticate our sound. The trouble was it didn't need authenticating, or if it did, then we chose the wrong producer.

For whatever reasons, the big guns Mikey Dread and Dennis Bovell did not take up the offer. A real pity, because I think they would have taken our raw material and really made something of us, not necessarily because they were Jamaican but because they were fine producers. Instead we got Errol Ross. I didn't like him after five minutes in his company. His unctuous demeanour coupled with his hustler mentality did not impress me. He had 'slick willy' written all over him. Charley, who had known Errol for some years, was obviously very impressed with Errol's business acumen. Errol loftily explained that he had a production company called Positive Productions.

'Positive productions produce positive outcomes' was his favourite mantra.

As I recall, he immediately complained about the hotel we had been booked into in Brussels. I'm not sure what his complaint was, but the upshot of his displeasure made some members of Charley's faction start questioning whether we were being treated as befitted our status. Fuel was added to this fire when somebody suggested that perhaps the Specials had stayed in more upmarket hotels and had bigger riders at gigs than us during their European tour. I couldn't see anything wrong with our accommodation or our well-stocked riders. Compared with our respective homes, the hotels were downright palatial. It seemed to me that the bottom line was that The Selecter had not had the degree of chart success that the Specials currently enjoyed and therefore there were not so many 'goodies' available to us yet, but if we were patient and worked hard, then soon those things would materialise. At first, their querulous objections were only low rumblings, muttered in the back of the tour bus or in shared hotel rooms, but Errol amplified these whenever possible and their sound would get louder as we progressed around Europe. The split had started.

We arrived back in London just in time for the Christmas festivities and a three-night run at the Michael Sobell centre in London supporting the wonderful Ian Dury and the Blockheads. These gigs were a fitting end to a fabulous year and were a barometer of how far we had progressed as a band. There was only one problem. We were driving each other mad.

EIGHT

TOO MUCH PRESSURE

Fans and me outside Sheffield Limit Club, 1980

The Selecter reported for recording duty on 1 January 1980. It was a new year and a new decade, anything seemed possible. We were well rested, refreshed and raring to get on with recording our first album. Three leisurely weeks stretched ahead of us to get the honed perfection of our live set down on to tape. We were secure in the knowledge that each of us was now on a regular wage of £100 per week, due to a Chrysalis advance. No more signing on or working while we were not on the road. Even the roadies were on a retainer. The Selecter was generating money. A publishing contract was still to be resolved, but that particular bugbear could wait for a while. We were a happy band again. All that remained was to deliver a killer album. We awaited the arrival of our new producer, Errol Ross.

A first album should be the easiest to realize in the studio. The band has usually been polishing the songs for years and the constant repetition in professional surroundings tightens and finesses any wayward song structures. However, as soon as Mr Ross arrived it was as though we were all novices again. In some ways we were, but we had done radio sessions in the BBC Maida Vale studios by this time. We knew the runnings, even if we weren't totally seasoned professionals. Most of us knew what was expected in a recording studio. A producer should put the musicians at their ease and subliminally create a working environment where they feel that they can create good music; endless hoary old lectures about how to create positive vibes are not the way to achieve such a result. Charley seemed enthralled by Errol's smooth, silver-tongued homilies and platitudes, almost treating him like a mentor, but oblivious to his corrosive production style. Prior to his engagement, he had apparently been a mediocre bass player, who decided to retrain as a sound engineer. To my knowledge, the Selecter album was his only successful recording. Certainly in his current résumé he lists no others. In my opinion, he single-handedly ruined the sound of our first album, *Too Much Pressure*, although fortunately, not the songs. They were too good and couldn't be harmed, but his production skills were minor at best and majorly ruinous at worst.

We chose Horizon studios again, which was a big mistake. The studio engineer Kim Holmes and the tape op Moose naturally bore their allegiance to Roger Lomas. They were often less than receptive to Errol's 'positive productions' lectures too. Errol made the mistake of bullshitting so much about his technical studio prowess that when he did need advice, Kim and Moose were not very helpful. It was a mess from beginning to end. It took over a week to record the basic instruments. Gaps and I were expected to provide guide vocals for every song. Every session went on into the wee hours of the night, so by the end of the week our voices were very hoarse. Then Errol expected us to record our vocals with voices that were well below par. I politely asked him to do the instrumental overdubs instead while we gave our voices a few days' rest, whereupon I received a pompous lecture about my 'less than positive' attitude. Needless to say, my attitude became 'less than positive' by the second and for anybody who has stood downwind of me when I'm raging, they will know what I mean. I think our exchange went something like this: 'You must think positively, Pauline. What do I mean by this? Banish all negative thoughts, see only the good in every situation. Therefore instead of being negative about the vocal sound, why not think positively and ask yourself how best to use this sound to your advantage.'

To which I positively answered: 'How about sticking it up your arse.' Unfortunately, probably not the most considered response, but once a rude girl, always a rude girl I guess!

I've worked with many producers over the years and I think most would say that I am a very reasonable person in a studio. I've never had a bad session with Roger Lomas at the helm. He always likes the recorded vocals to sound as good as possible. After all, the vocals carry not only the words and message of the song, but the lyrical melody that the punter in the street likes to whistle, so why would anybody go out of their way to make them sound worse than necessary?

I think that Charley secretly wanted Mr Ross to oversee all future Selecter projects, because Errol began dispensing advice to us about how to behave, how to be professional, how to make it big in the music industry. Anybody would have thought that he was Berry Gordy. All this would have been helpful if he had led by example, but somebody who bills the record company (and indirectly the band!) for the use of his shoe leather because he had to walk a few hundred yards from Bond Street tube station to Chrysalis Records in Stratford Place for a few A&R meetings, is, in my humble opinion, a first-class wanker.

I recently googled Errol Ross. I was surprised to discover that there are two producers named Errol Ross. The first produced one of my favourite albums, *Blackheart Man* by Bunny Wailer, the second (our Errol Ross) tells people that his 'superpower' is being: 'A people's person with good communication and teaching skills'! He currently runs a karaoke bar in Spain.

If only we had engaged the services of the former.

Nonetheless, even Errol Ross couldn't completely ruin the *Too Much Pressure* album. The excellence of the original songs could not be marred by badly recorded sounds or a lack of creative ideas. Fortunately for us, Neol and Desmond had plenty of creative ideas. I even penned a song while in the studio, 'Black & Blue', which summed up my state of mind at the time.

> *Feeling so angry, minutes tick by*
> *Stuck in one room, living a lie…*
> *So Black & Blue, Life knocks you about,*
> *Black & Blue.*

I was honoured when Rico Rodriguez, one of the original Skatalites, provided a beautiful bluesy trombone solo in my song that captured the melancholic quality of this personal lament.

Charley adapted the Millie Small hit 'My Boy Lollipop' into a paean for ganja weed. It was renamed 'My Sweet Collie (Not a Dog)'. I was surprised that Charley hadn't written any original songs. Desmond had written 'Danger', which dealt with the violence on the streets in the late '70s.

To be fair to Errol, Elvis Costello didn't do a particularly good job on the Specials' first album either. It was as if neither producer, the white or the black one, knew how to handle this curious hybrid, the 2-Tone sound. Perhaps each band would have been better off employing a mixed-race producer!

There was still another hurdle – an even higher one – for the band to get over: how to split the publishing monies between us, before signing a publishing contract? Nothing divides people more than money, or a perceived lack of it if it looks as though somebody else is getting more. None of us had any real money; nobody had savings or the like. But suddenly we had to think about signing a contract which would be binding for the next three years. Such an undertaking was bound to cause friction between us. Resentments built up about how the money would be apportioned, which did not help the creative process. Things began to fall apart.

Neol's songs had been years in production and were fully formed beasts when they were brought to the rehearsal room. Obviously we all added our stuff and the songs were significantly improved, especially 'On My Radio' and 'Missing Words', but when it became apparent that Charley thought the publishing money for all the original songs should be split seven ways, our interpersonal relationships began to unravel. Neol thought he deserved the lion's share for his songs, particularly as so far he had written all the hits; others thought differently.

Being a songwriter myself on the first album, with two of my tracks reaching the final cut, I wanted to be in agreement with Neol. Also, I thought it provided an incentive to develop us all as songwriters if the songs were individually rewarded. Naively I thought that a bit of competition in songwriting could only produce better material. But I put these considerations on a back burner. I felt obliged to back the black fraternity. Neol magnanimously acquiesced to our demands. Charley got his way. Did we make the correct decision? I don't know. I was told that bands who split monies equally between themselves generally stay together longer.

That should have been the end of the discord, but unfortunately the pot of resentments had been heated to boiling point. Even though it had cooled somewhat, it still simmered. Collectively, we may well have been a 'melting pot', but the black/white divide had asserted itself. It was as if Neol was perceived as 'the greedy white man', while the rest of us played 'needy black folks'. And some were more needy than others.

Our first professional photo-shoot nailed our style. The pictures captured us at our best. They made us look threatening and surly, but with that all-important cool factor. We looked like no other band on the scene. We were the business. On photographic paper we were the embodiment of the 2-Tone ideal: blacks, whites, men and women, working class with a social conscience. None of us had a dad hidden away somewhere in a country parish, or harboured colonialist, upper-middle-class origins. Too many musos masqueraded as men of the people, when nothing could be further from the truth. Unlike some of our contemporaries, we were the real deal.

Despite that, unfortunately, the shallow foundation we had built our unity upon was beginning to crack. The career we had built so quickly, initially held together by the mortar of expedient camaraderie, was being eaten away with the constant acid rain of mistrust, mismanagement, misbehaviour, misogyny, malevolence and the occasional misadventure.

Desmond's personality became increasingly unpredictable. When we supported Rockpile, Ian Dury and the Blockheads and Elvis Costello at the NEC Arena in Birmingham, Desmond was so incensed with Charley's bass playing halfway through our set that he deliberately pushed over his Hammond organ at the sound of the rhythm section. The music was brought to an abrupt halt while our trusted roadies righted the keyboard and the rest of us tried to calm Desmond down in full view of the audience.

None of us knew how to handle Desmond any more. Lynval Golding tried talking some sense into him if he happened to be in town, which was rare in those days, because the Specials were now the next big thing and had little free time. Besides they were struggling with their own internal divisions. I don't think that these tête-à-têtes had any significant effect on Desmond. Once I was told about a ganja-smoking duel that Desmond had with Silverton Hutchinson, the former Specials drummer. It lasted for three days and nights. Eventually Desmond was in such a state that he had to be helped home. It was suggested that Desmond's mind, fragile at the best of times, was never the same after that.

But I had a bigger problem on my mind than Desmond's mental state. The Swedish photographer who had taken a shine to me in Stockholm had made it his business to fetch up at a few other shows during the European tour and then came to London for further photographic opportunities. An attraction to each other had begun a sporadic sexual relationship which, on my part, was used mainly to alleviate the boredom of hotel rooms. There had also been a regrettable one-night stand with one of the musicians on the 2-Tone tour. The upshot of these sexual misadventures was the unfortunate discovery that I was pregnant.

I was not married at this juncture, but I'd been with Terry for seven years. Needless to say he took quite a dim view of my condition after I confessed that, including him, there were three potential fathers. My only explanation was that loneliness often led to poor decisions, but it fell on deaf ears because he had also been lonely while I was away, but hadn't chosen to sleep with others. I could see his point, but I probably didn't realize how deeply my actions had hurt him. Contraceptive pill taking and touring don't mix – at least not in those days. I don't actually remember forgetting to take the pill, but I must have done.

An abortion was the only sensible option. He/she would be thirty years old now, a sobering thought. But I do not regret my decision. I have never been mother material. In fact, I do not have a maternal bone in my body. Besides, with the album recorded, the artwork finalized, the next single chosen, TV appearances, a short European tour and a forthcoming headline UK tour, a baby was out of the question. Any feelings I had about the subject were buried. Terry and I never spoke about it again.

On a lighter note it was time to choose a support band. One might think that, with our first headline UK tour looming, the obvious choice was support from another good band to enhance our sound but not interfere with it. A no-brainer. So what happened? We asked the all-girl ska band Bodysnatchers and the female-led indie band, Holly and the Italians, to join us on tour.

In many ways it made sense to give women the opportunity to showcase their music. The punk movement had pushed many very good female musicians to the fore – the Slits, Poly Styrene of X-Ray Spex, Siouxsie Sioux and Chrissie Hynde, to name but a few. I felt part of this continuing post-feminist movement and Juliet and I agreed that it made sense to highlight this in our choice of tour support.

The Bodysnatchers had first come to my attention when they had supported us at a gig. I loved the sheer chutzpah of their lead singer, the gorgeous, tall and tanned Rhoda Dakar, who sang with a charmingly idiosyncratic, richly nuanced voice, perfectly suited to their somewhat shambolic rocksteady sound. Her style was Mod-inspired but nonetheless highly individual. Her hair was a glorious Mr Whippy, gravity-defying beehive. She was completely at odds with, but a perfect foil for, my rude-boy image. The Selecter suggested that they were signed to the 2-Tone label, which didn't meet with universal approval within the 2-Tone camp. Some voiced concern about the band's relative inexperience. They had only done their first gig in November 1979. By their own admission, they were not competent musicians and they were about to jump under the media spotlight, which by this time was waiting patiently for the label's first failure. Ironically, Roger Lomas was drafted in to produce their first single, the Dandy Livingstone song, 'Let's Do Rocksteady', backed with an original composition, 'Ruder Than You'.

Holly Beth Vincent, the main squeeze of Mark Knopfler in those days, and I had first met when The Selecter and her band, the Italians, were invited on to the bill to play with Blondie at the Hammersmith Odeon on 22 January 1980. It was a big opportunity for both of us. 'Three Minute Hero' was about to be released the following week and Holly was picking up a lot of radio airplay with 'Tell That Girl To Shut Up'. Ms Harry even invited Holly and me to her dressing room for a photo shoot to mark the occasion. She was a very gracious lady while the necessary photos were taken and on stage a superlative performer. This was one of the best nights I can remember on stage with The Selecter.

Debbie Harry, me and Holly Beth Vincent, 1980

Holly and the Italians proved to be a great opening band on that night too. After seeing their performance, The Selecter decided to invite them on the *Too Much Pressure* tour because we hoped that they would provide a different sound palette, a welcome respite from the relentless ska off-beat, for the audience. Holly was a pertly pretty Chicago-born singer-songwriter who wielded a deft guitar lick and played music with a punk/pop edge. She looked as though she could more

195

than hold her own on any stage.

On paper the three bands looked like a perfect combination: all fronted by strong women, all with individual styles. It was a done deal. The Selecter busied itself with a first appearance on BBC's *Old Grey Whistle Test*, a showcase gig at Le Palace in Paris and *Top of the Pops* in the interim, then joining up with our two chosen supports for an all-day rehearsal at the Roxy in Harlesden. Before we knew it we were playing in front of 1,500 people every night on a 30-date UK tour.

Immediately we realized that we had made a mistake in electing to have Holly and the Italians as second on the bill after the Bodysnatchers. The fact that their music had absolutely nothing to do with ska or reggae – something we saw as a plus – was not enough to stop the diehard, unreconstructed male 2-Tone fan from spitting, bottling and heckling them off the stage every night. Understandably Holly got upset and although they struggled on for a while, their reception got so bad that they were forced to leave the tour.

Too Much Pressure was released on the 2-Tone label on 15 February 1979. We were playing much the same venues as on the 2-Tone tour and packing them out just as successfully with us as headliners. The buzz surrounding the tour sent the album to No. 4 in the charts the following week. Even though it was well reviewed, many of us in the band knew that production-wise it could have been so much better. Unfortunately, our second single release, 'Three Minute Hero', despite the success of the album, didn't do as well as expected, rising only to No. 16 in the charts. We did *Top of the Pops* again, but our energetic performance wasn't enough to push the single any further up the charts. In my opinion, it was not as good a song as 'On My Radio' and was badly recorded. The title was catchy enough, but the melody and production could have been better and the saxophone solo sounds like a kazoo! Only Errol Ross knows how he managed to do that! By then, many of us were sick to death of Mr Ross. He was *persona non grata* at the 2-Tone label's parent company, Chrysalis.

Even the Bodysnatchers' first single, produced by Roger Lomas, had made the Top 20 and they had only been playing for three months. Some of the male members of the band consoled themselves with playing 'musical beds' with a few of the Bodysnatchers while on tour, but even that delightful pastime couldn't reduce the malaise that had set in among us. The record company A&R wanted answers and decided to bring Roger back into the fray. Needless to say, Charley took this badly, although Neol and I were very pleased. He was given the task of re-mixing 'Missing Words' for the third single while we continued touring.

Out on the road, Juliet proved relatively useless at controlling our increasingly bizarre behaviour. She was out of her depth when our arguments really kicked off in the dressing rooms after gigs. To make matters worse, she committed the cardinal sin of forming a romantic relationship with our tour manager. That was a definite 'no-no' and undermined her authority.

After Holly and the Italians left the tour, we drafted in another 2-Tone-inspired act, Coventry band the Swinging Cats, to take up the slack. They had formed at the end of 1979, so they had something in common with the Bodysnatchers. It was also an opportunity to give Coventry musicians a leg-up onto a bigger stage. On the strength of this tour, they later signed to 2-Tone and released a single, 'Mantovani/ Away' (CHS TT14), which sank without trace despite the first 20,000 copies being sold at the giveaway price of 50 pence. To be fair, it was an imaginative piece of music, but by then the backlash had begun. Perhaps we should have been more business-minded with our choice of support and not quite so charitable but, in our defence, it seemed the right thing to do. The Specials had helped us so it was only right that we did the same thing.

Prior to the tour, Juliet had pointed out that the Bodysnatchers didn't have any flight cases for their backline. So The Selecter decided to pay, no expense spared. What major band would do that for their support act these days? None, but we did. So when some people accuse The Selecter of leaving the 2-Tone label to sign with Chrysalis, implying that money was all that motivated us, then I see red, because nothing could be further from the truth. We spent our hard-earned money on giving both these bands the opportunities that we enjoyed. Misguided maybe, but we thought we were living up to the ideals of 2-Tone.

The quirkiness of the Swinging Cats proved a hit with audiences, so the relentless hail of bottles and gob that had greeted Holly and the Italians most nights ceased. The Bodysnatchers were content to be shoved up the bill to second place, and everybody was happy for a while.

Then one morning in March, the strain of touring became too much for Desmond. We were late as usual – par for the course, I know, but bloody infuriating. Why is it when people join bands, they consider that they can act like children who don't want to go to school? It's a job. Get used to it. Gigs and records don't get done unless you put a bit of bloody effort into it!

I was sitting on the front seat of the bus. The two support bands were already on board. We had been waiting for stragglers for the past three-quarters of an hour. At last, Desmond, Charley and Aitch lurched out of the hotel, oblivious to how long they had kept us waiting. Apparently, Desmond took exception to the 'look' on my face as he came up the stairwell of the bus. All I remember is that he stared at me aggressively for some moments before shouting: 'Wha'ppen? You t'ink you're the Queen?'

Then he flung himself at me, pushed me down on the seat, put his hands around my neck and began throttling me. Six people had to drag him off. The Bodysnatchers and the Swinging Cats were so traumatised by this and the frosty fall-out that later on they refused to ride on the bus with us. I wish I had left the band then and there. I didn't dare tell Terry what had happened. When I look back on the incident, it was obvious even then that there was something decidedly wrong with Desmond but, because of the unpredictability of his moods and violence and his propensity to drink a bottle of whisky a day before the show, nobody ever wanted to displease him.

There was a double standard in the band. Certain members paid lip service to the 2-Tone ethos that espoused non-sexism, but couldn't live up to that ideal in the real world. For example, The Selecter played a homecoming show at Coventry Tiffany's. Naturally, the wives and girlfriends of the band members wanted to come along. We had been on tour for months and this, at last, was their chance to see their conquering heroes on stage in front of their friends and neighbours. However, some members had got used to the nightly attentions of female fans. They didn't want their partners to cramp their style, so these unfortunate ladies had been told not to attend.

However, what the guys hadn't reckoned on was the ingenuity of cuckolded wives and girlfriends. Collectively these ladies came round to my house on the evening of the gig and asked me to put them on the guest list. What was I supposed to do, say no? Terry, realizing my dilemma, kindly offered to escort them to the show. Suffice to say, they had a wonderful time, even though I was a pariah in my own band for quite a while after that particular stunt. But secretly I harboured a feeling of triumph against such rampant misogyny. What's good for the goose is also good for the gander. Oh, bondage, up yours!

The tour was over and we needed a hit, quickly, if we were to maintain the momentum of a successful band. Roger Lomas's hastily re-mixed album version of 'Missing Words' backed with a cover of Justin Hines and the Dominoes' 'Carry Go Bring Come' would hopefully fit the bill. Chrysalis even gave us a small video budget for this release. Some of the video had been shot in a telephone box outside Brighton Top Rank, just before we performed there (in those days a video was predominantly used on *TOTP* if the band were on tour and couldn't make it to London for the show).

The video didn't get much airplay. It was not particularly original in concept and the melancholic mood of the song was lost in too much over-exuberant posturing from the rest of the band. Perhaps the director should have wielded a firmer hand, but he was probably intimidated by our general stroppiness. The power of band videos as a marketing tool hadn't yet been realized. MTV wouldn't appear on the scene until August 1981. The Selecter would be gone by then.

Our 6:1 black:white ratio fronted by a woman singer was unique and had been our main weapon when first trying to get the band noticed. But in the commercial world of Chrysalis it was also a major obstacle. How did they market such an image to an overwhelmingly white audience? Particularly when you'd already got a band that had a more forgiving racial mix (only two blacks to five whites) and, even more importantly, a young, white, good-looking front-man. Once we were 'in-house' we were at their mercy. The Specials always commanded bigger video and marketing budgets for their product. Chrysalis seemed content to let us coast along in the Specials' slipstream, which had been fine in the beginning when we were learning the ropes, but we were now in danger

The Selecter, 1980 – the 'don't fuck with us' look. Photo © brianaris.com

of coming severely adrift, unless we united ourselves behind a strong band manifesto.

Maybe it would have been easier if we had been a reggae band, instead of a new musical hybrid. We were just one headache too many for the record company. We never learned to play the social games. It was almost impossible for us to hide our feelings when confronted with hostile journalists or Keith Chegwin-type TV presenters. We never appeared on *TOTP*, *Tiswas* or *Multi-Coloured Swap Shop* dressed in comedy gear like Bad Manners and Madness, in order to ingratiate ourselves with our audience. Bad Manners gleefully donned grass skirts for one of their singles. If anybody had suggested that to any of us, they would have had their head ripped off, figuratively speaking of course. Gaps's favourite rhyme, which he would mutter under his breath if some white record company executive pissed him off, was: 'Gobble gobble gobble, munch munch munch/Six thousand savages sitting down to lunch.'

That was as funny as fuck. But really it was just all too much pressure.

NINE

WAKE UP, NIGGERS!

In April 1980, following the release of the *Too Much Pressure* album in the rest of the world, The Selecter tried their luck in America. We were sensibly following in the wake of Madness and the Specials, so we hoped that American ears had been already primed for yet another take on the 2-Tone sound. Stories and rumours abounded that the Specials had not exactly taken America to their hearts – or vice versa. A photo of Terry Hall sticking two fingers up to nothing much in particular other than the iconic Statue of Liberty in the background hadn't helped when it appeared in the media. Neither did it help our preconceptions of what to expect.

I'm not altogether sure why none of the 2-Tone bands really made it in the States. After all, the Clash were currently tearing up the place with their punky reggae-meets-rock-and-roll recipe, so our poppier take on that basic sound should have been a successful clincher. Perhaps one of the reasons why none of us reached the upper echelons of the Billboard 100 chart was that the cognoscenti on the east and west coasts, who had possibly explored a broader horizon than the World Series (the only world event happening in one country that I know of!), may have been open to new fashions in music, but the vast expanse of 'good ole boy and girl' ten-gallon hat wearers and wet T-shirt bosom jigglers inhabiting the midwest and beyond thought we were a bunch of aliens that had just landed in their backyards. In America's defence, a small number of black people regularly attended each gig and either left bemused or, if they were sympathetic reggae enthusiasts, congratulated us on a job well done, but seemed somewhat baffled as to why we played everything at such breakneck speed.

When it had first been mooted that a tour of the Land of the Free was on the cards, my excitement knew no bounds. In my mind, America was like a Mecca, an alma mater, the well-spring of my earliest political thoughts. The opportunity to finally see it at first hand felt indescribably lucky. Despite Terry Hall's two-fingered gesture, I was prepared to give America the benefit of the doubt, particularly since we were going there armed with a new music and style that couldn't fail to knock some sense into the meanest of ornery hombres.

We flew into Vancouver in April 1980 and worked our way down the western seaboard. This Canadian city proved to be an exciting and vibrant place to kick off a tour. Everybody had a day off to acclimatize, because it was our first experience of jet lag. If only the tour agent had told us that we were expected to play two shows the following night, then perhaps we would have taken it easy and not rushed around the city savouring the many delights. Two performances a night was a new phenomenon for us. We used up huge amounts of energy in our stage shows, so to do that twice in a night was initially very difficult. After Vancouver we realized that we would have to learn to pace ourselves. Next stop American soil – Seattle, then Portland, Oregon.

The motel we booked into on the outskirts of Portland after a lengthy overnight drive fulfilled our romantic vision of being on the road in America. My room even had a waterbed.

Selecter members left to right: Neol Davies, Commie Amanor, Desmond Brown, Charles 'Aitch' Bembridge, Jane Davies and Gaps Hendrickson at a truckstop somewhere in the USA.

Unfortunately the front desk omitted to tell me that it needed to be plugged in and warmed up for some hours before you sleep on it. Oblivious to this, I treated the bed as trampoline and joyously bounced around on it for the next half an hour while I phoned several friends in England just to tell them: 'Hey, guess what? I've got a waterbed in my room!' This information was generally met with squeals of delight.

An hour later we left to do the show, returning in the early hours of the morning, completely exhausted after another couple of tiring shows. I remember collapsing into my bouncy bed and falling asleep almost immediately. A couple of hours later, I awoke with a serious case of hypothermia. God alone knows what would have happened if I hadn't woken up. I might have died, because my core body temperature was seriously low. I was shivering uncontrollably. I knew that my condition had something to do with the waterbed. But what was wrong?

Then I saw the typewritten notice pinned by the side of the bed. It was headed: PLEASE HEAT BED BEFORE USE with copious instructions about the dos and don'ts of waterbed use. Too late now. My teeth wouldn't stop chattering as I dragged all the bedding off the bed and made myself a nest on the floor. I crawled under the blankets, hoping that they would be enough to alleviate my obvious hypothermia. It took me almost two hours to stop shivering.

Everybody laughed at my nocturnal misfortune the following morning as I related my story at the breakfast table. By this time, I guess I could see the funny side of it too, but the upshot was that I developed a bad cold and laryngitis. Almost immediately I lost my voice, which pretty much remained AWOL until I got back to England. It did nothing to improve my mood. I felt totally miserable. A singer with a hoarse, croaky voice is rarely a happy bunny, particularly when two shows a night, plus endless interviews are expected at every venue. Nonetheless, America loved the band.

Nina Myskow interviewed me poolside at the Tropicana Hotel after our first gig in Los Angeles for the British tabloid, the *Sun*. By this time I could hardly speak due to laryngitis, exacerbated by the after-effects of a particularly energetic gig the night before. She vividly describes the band's performance style as 'stolen from a frog on pep pills'. Towards the end of her article, she says: 'The voice may be hoarse but the accent is distinctly middle-class. Pauline is the adopted daughter of white English parents, so hers is a truly two-tone tale.'

It's interesting that she picks up on my middle-class accent. People often remark on it, as if I ought to talk like a cockney given where I grew up. I suppose they are correct in their assertion; the way I talk is odd, given my upbringing. To put it into context, let me advance this hypothesis: Mick Jagger talks like a cockney, but really he's a nice middle-class boy from Surrey. It suits his purpose to 'culturally slum'. Nobody has a problem with that. Nobody pretends that they can't understand what he says.

I grew up in a place where I would be asked to repeat everything twice in a shop or even if I was just passing the time of day with strangers. It wasn't because they didn't understand me the first time, it was because they didn't expect to understand me. As far as they were concerned, black people had come from somewhere else, somewhere foreign. Rather than take the time to listen, they stared, so they missed what was initially said to them. It is probably a natural way for people to be when confronted with something or somebody out of their ordinary social sphere, but I used to get incensed at this behaviour when I was younger. It's like the way many of us talk loudly and somewhat childishly to elderly people, who are actually perfectly *compos mentis* with non-impaired hearing. The only reason why we do that is because they are old.

From an early age I picked up on this annoying trait of strangers asking me to repeat everything I said, so I decided to speak in a manner that nobody could misunderstand, crystal-clear English, with no discernible regional accent. Unfortunately, give or take a few vowel distortions, this is similar to how many middle-class people talk. But for me it is not a pretence, or a way of shuffling up the class ladder from my working-class beginnings, it is just a way of being emphatically understood in the country where I was born. I also enjoy the double take that some people make whom I have never met before, but with whom I have enjoyed a prior telephone conversation. Their reaction often says much about their personal prejudices. My motto when I was younger was, if they're going to stare, give them a bloody good reason to.

But issues about accent aside, this article is quite disturbing to read. In retrospect I think I was just covering up my real feelings and blurting out anything that would keep people from probing too deeply. It is obvious that I didn't want to upset my mother, who collected many of these often incorrectly reported newspaper articles. I hated this new chore of being interviewed. Nobody ever wanted to talk about the music, just personal stuff.

We stayed at the Tropicana Hotel at 8585 Santa Monica Boulevard (the famous Route 66) in Los Angeles; in the greater scheme of things, it was possibly a dump of a place, but its fame preceded it. It had been the former residence of Jim Morrison of the Doors and Tom Waits. Frequent guests had included such luminaries as Janis Joplin, Van Morrison, Bruce Springsteen, Eddie Cochrane, the Beach Boys, Led Zeppelin, Martha & the Vandellas and Frank Zappa. It was a first stop on the way up the rock-and-roll ladder, as well as a place to stay once you'd made it. Sadly, it is no longer there. It was demolished in 1988 and replaced by the Ramada Hotel, another landmark gone from old Hollywood. Apart from the black tiled swimming pool and the rock mythology that surrounded it, the next best thing about the Tropicana was the fact that it housed Dukes Coffee Shop, which was also regularly used by the dead and not-so-dead denizens of

Poolside at the Tropicana waiting for Ms Hunt. Photo ©
brianaris.com

the pop and rock world. The Selecter soaked up the stories of long-gone heroes like a sponge.

I adored the American breakfast – the many ways to have your eggs was a constant fascination for me. Plus the culinary delight of having blueberry pie and ice cream delivered to your motel door at any time of the day or night. These were innocent pleasures compared with what some members of the band were experiencing. The main thing I remember about the Tropicana stay was that Charley managed to damage his back while in the shower with some ladies, which warranted a visit from Jack Nicholson's doctor, at great expense I would guess, and having to blow out a couple of LA shows, at even more expense!

The Tropicana was the embodiment of late '70s/early '80s LA excess. Dealers, groupies, drug casualties, strippers, musos, porn stars and maniacs floated in and out of rooms which usually weren't their own. There were banana trees growing outside my first-floor room balcony and below a huge swimming pool which only seemed to see any action when someone fell in. Our first press conference was held beside this pool. It was also my first introduction to my teenage crush, the mighty Marsha Hunt.

There is a time in the lives of most women when they can be considered to be at their best, much like a sun-burnished, juicy, ripe peach that has been picked at just the right moment to preserve its freshness. For Ms Hunt, I suspect that time was in May 1980. She fetched up by the poolside of the Tropicana with a tape recorder and microphone, eager to interview us for her weekly report on British bands performing in Los Angeles. Armed with her taped insights, she hopped on a plane to London once a week to deliver her work. The whole band was smitten when they first saw her, it was like a *Tom*

& *Jerry* cartoon, where the cartoon characters' eyes come out on stalks, their tongues flop out onto the floor and their hearts beat like jackhammers. To add to her sexual allure, Ms Hunt was rumoured to be Mick Jagger's 'Babymother'. Gone was her signature Afro. Her liquorice-coloured hair now hung long down her back, forming a cloud of natural beauty that gently bobbed with her every elegant movement. The perfection of her brown skin and the languid sound of her mellifluous voice completed a picture of overwhelming femininity. Desmond's opening line to her was 'I've always wanted to fuck you.'

To her credit, she just smiled at him as though he were a court jester, before getting down to the serious business of collecting usable soundbites for her show. I could hardly believe that this woman, to whom I had been in thrall since the age of fifteen, was interviewing us. I croaked my way through her kind questions, totally mesmerised by her cool and self-assured demeanour. Unfortunately she was in a queue of several other journalists and her allotted time was up. The record company press officer was eager to get as much journalistic throughput as possible, so the interview was wrapped up quickly. Before she left, she asked if it was possible to do a more in-depth interview for a magazine that she wrote for. She specifically wanted to interview Neol and me, presumably because she thought that in our capacities as songwriter and lead singer of the band, we would have the most to say.

She offered to collect us in her car and drive to her house later that day. Naturally we accepted her offer – anything to get out of the hotel's stir-crazy environment.

At her surprisingly compact home in a quiet suburban LA street, we were almost immediately herded into a bedroom

Marsha Hunt graciously hoisting my unpublished novel,
The Goldfinches, into the air at a book fair in the mid-'90s

to have a look at her sleeping daughter, Karis. The child was
probably about ten and at first glance there was no mistaking
that she carried the genes of her famous father. I felt that this
was a ritual that had to be acted out every time a stranger
came to call. It was as if Karis validated her mother's '60s lifestyle choice as the concubine of rock royalty.

Despite having encountered the goddess of my teenage dreams

in Los Angeles, I found the actual city, at least the small part to which the band had been exposed, curiously underwhelming. The endless roads lined with anonymous-looking single-storey buildings, some of which were shops, often gave the appearance of a shanty town more than a seething metropolis. Of course, there were skyscrapers to be seen in the far-off downtown area, but nobody from the record company seemed eager to show us these delights. So for a bit of exercise, or just to relieve the boredom, some of us rambled around the streets near the hotel or ventured further along Sunset Boulevard to the touristy Sunset Strip to buy cheap tacky souvenirs.

On one such exploration of the hotel's immediate hinterland, a police car slowly cruised past me, then turned around and stopped close by. Two burly cops got out of the vehicle and approached me. I was asked what I was doing. Since I was alone, I felt extremely apprehensive about their enquiries, particularly because both of them were armed with handguns in hip holsters. I answered their questions as politely as possible under the intimidating circumstances. As soon as they heard I was English, they visibly relaxed. They explained that one of the local residents had spotted me walking in the area and dialled 911. I was warned that it was unusual to see people walking in suburban streets. Los Angeles residents drove everywhere, so automatically suspicion was aroused when strangers were seen on foot in the neighbourhood. The upshot of this was that I promised never to do anything as stupid again as use my own legs as a means of exercise in Los Angeles, unless it was in a park. The same thing also happened to Desmond. I would have paid good money to listen to his LAPD encounter. I doubt whether he greeted them with the same opening gambit that he used on Ms Hunt.

Such vigilance on the part of the police seemed misplaced, when I considered that they might have been more gainfully employed apprehending the constant bevy of young, tall, tanned, blonde girls with large bags of coke who frequented our gigs and the Tropicana. The Land of the Free certainly lived up to its name when it came to sexual favours and gratis lines of cocaine being doled out. Our colourful minder, Steve English, picked up one of these young honeys almost as soon as we checked into the Tropicana. Her name was Duffy, she was cute as a button, and along with all the other would-be 'starlets' who waited tables and served beer, she was just waiting for her opportunity to step on to the silver screen. Unfortunately, in reality she was just another 'boy toy' who would get old and used up as quickly as the grams of coke she racked out by the pool.

We hit the road again in our comfy, well-equipped tour bus, driven by our bona fide redneck driver Romain, whose constant refrain was that he usually only drove for Dolly Parton. Quite what he had done to deserve us remained a mystery, but we seemed to get on okay as we chatted our way through the deserts and wastelands on the interminable night drives in America. Anybody would have thought that aeroplanes hadn't been invented. We reached El Paso after driving almost 800 miles across the Arizona desert from Los Angeles. En route, I saw a staggeringly beautiful sunrise in the desert at 4.30 a.m. It was one of those moments when I just felt blessed to be alive and doing something I loved. It made me think about how far we had come in the space of less than a year. Everybody else was asleep. It was bliss not to talk. I felt more alone when everybody else was awake.

I was eager to cross the border into Mexico from El Paso. It was similar to the nondescript border that Orson Welles filmed in one of his movies. The hills surrounding the city were flame-red and shimmering in the heat. Once in Ciudad Juarez on the Mexican side, I was surprised to find its dusty streets awash with beggars, mostly blind or deformed women and children. I vividly recall being passed by a young boy whose severely twisted body only allowed him to walk on all fours like a dog. He had a rope tied around his neck which an older woman, presumably his mother, used to lead him along the streets. She intermittently tugged at it to make sure he kept up with her. The poverty and cruelty on display were mind-boggling, and made all the more shocking as 1980s El Paso was known as the blue jeans capital of the world, producing over two million pairs every week. Yet a few hundred yards across the border people lived literally like dogs. The Americas were proving full of contradiction. Overwhelmed by the abject squalor and deprivation, I shamefully put some dollars in a few begging bowls and fled back across the border to the comfort of my air-conditioned hotel. Dog-boy haunted my dreams for weeks afterwards.

Despite such acute reality checks, the excitement of conquering a new territory for 2-Tone hadn't jaded The Selecter yet. We knew that on the whole Americans didn't 'get us', but for us it was a challenge rather than a demoralizing experience. Americans have a surprising lack of what British people pride themselves on – irony. Without it, American audiences rarely understood what the hell we were on about. There was a lot of irony in songs like 'On My Radio' and 'Three Minute Hero', but I think most of it went over the heads of the average American audience. Plus there was the problem that if you are mixing up black and white people in the band, well, that is okay, but stick to rock music or reggae music, don't try and fuse the two. That way lies serious confusion! American audiences are not big on hybrids, unless they tend to be of the 'mule' variety! Beyond the major cities, our anger-fuelled music was stubbornly misunderstood. Perhaps we were asking too much from our audiences to immediately embrace an anti-racist stance. After all, it had only been twelve years since Martin Luther King and Bobby Kennedy had been mercilessly gunned down. Wounds like that took a long time to heal.

The chief problem was that radio stations in 1980 were still segregated. As far as American radio was concerned, there was black music and there was white music and although crossover hits regularly happened, these categories still prevailed. 2-Tone music didn't lend itself to either side of this accepted racial barrier, being essentially black in origin but, apart from The Selecter, white in personnel and sensibility. It owed too much to punk music for mainstream tastes, but was not similar enough to the great reggae entrepreneurs like Bob Marley for it to be embraced by important black stations.

Faced with such a dilemma, the main radio stations on either side of the ethnic divide chose not to play it. This rendered us dependent on college radio stations and thus a primarily white audience. There were exceptions to this rule, such as maverick radio DJs like Rodney Bingenheimer, who played his own eclectic mix of new releases on KROQ, a rock station in Los Angeles that championed the 2-Tone music and style in much the same way that John Peel had furthered its appeal in Britain. But unfortunately there weren't enough of these defenders of the faith countrywide and the music fell into the yawning crack between black and white America, then largely disappeared once the bands returned home. Some bands overcame this musical apartheid but ours was not one of them.

As we journeyed through Texas, it became apparent that

non-musical racism was alive and well too, despite all the civil rights victories. I lost count of the times that I went into shops and was treated like dog dirt until they heard my accent and discovered that I was British and then everything changed and it was 'please' and 'thank you' and 'hope you have a good day, y'all'. That was how it was in the cities, but it was just plain hostile if you strayed off the interstate roads.

I remember a truck stop somewhere in the 'Deep South'. The restaurant was full of noisy lunchtime diners, all of them white. The sight of six black people and three white people laughing, joking and chatting with each other as they stood in line waiting to be seated rendered the entire place dumb. Eventually we were seated. We were then ignored for fifteen minutes by the two waitresses on duty. America is a place that normally prides itself on its service industries. Nowhere up north had we encountered such blatant unwelcoming behaviour. The tension in the air was palpable. Hungry as we were, we just got up and left. Just before the door shut behind us, the loud hubbub of conversation immediately started again, as though the past fifteen minutes had been a figment of their collective imaginations and, at last, they had woken up from their joint nightmare.

The worst racist incident we encountered was when music journalist Garry Bushell and a photographer were sent to the states to do an interview with us for *Sounds*. Music journos would move heaven and earth for an American assignment. These junkets made up for the hard slog of reviewing crap bands in crap venues in the back of beyond in Britain.

Garry's idea was to spend a few days with us on the tour bus while we trucked through the Texas leg of the tour. He came up with the bright idea of photographing us down by Southfork Ranch, where the popular, glossy soap *Dallas* was filmed. *Dallas* was huge in Britain at the time. The British TV audience had taken the main character, the scheming, but charming JR, to its collective heart. We thought it would be fun to do the photoshoot in such gloriously ironic surroundings.

Romain was not too happy when he heard about our plan, but he was in no position to disagree with it. He dutifully drove us out to the ranch and parked on the side of the country road. A white picket fence surrounded acres of land belonging to the imposing house that was just visible in the distance. A huge sign displaying the name 'Southfork Ranch' hung above the gated entrance. The band piled out of the bus and began to pose for photos in the entrance. Apart from the sound of our general excitement, it seemed as silent as the grave.

Ten minutes later, as we were sitting on the picket fence, smiling and mugging for the camera, a flat-bed truck turned up with several burly men on the back all ominously sporting baseball bats. It pulled over to the side of the road behind the tour bus. Immediately Romain approached them and I can only assume that he explained who we were and what we were trying to do. The ensuing conversation with the strangers became heated. It was at that point that I noticed that we began to group along racial lines. All us black folk knew instinctively that the problem was us. The white members of our party were free to come and go between us and enter into conversation, but the six of us became dumb, which I hasten to add was not our usual modus operandi. It was scary. Suffice to say that we were hustled back on to the bus and Romain told us all to shut up if we wanted to get out of there safely. I was later told that the menacing strangers had said to Romain that 'If those niggers don't get off that fence and back on that bus right away, then there is gonna be trouble.'

The Selecter on a dirt road outside Dallas, 1980

Well you can't say fairer than that, can you?

I'm not sure that the American tour ever recovered from that piece of 'good ole boy' advice. But it did make us all feel like counter-insurgents in their big old country. We were pleased to get back to civilisation as Austin beckoned. The city that spawned Janis Joplin welcomed us with open arms and made up for such appalling treatment.

Garry Bushell still relates the Southfork diplomatic incident, except he has embellished it over the years. No, Garry, nobody actually shot at us. Believe me, I would have remembered that!

219

The Selecter travelled a zigzag path across the States and Canada until we reached New York on 20 May. Our music garnered a lot of good reviews and love along the way. People began to sit up and take notice of us: one member of rock royalty in particular, Mick Jagger, who attended our New York City gig at Hurrahs.

Record Mirror journalist Mike Nicholls describes the place as 'a swanky, uptown club full of failed fashion plates' in an article about us, entitled 'How The West Was Won' from 14 June 1980. While trying to get a bird's eye view of the stage from the raised DJ podium, he was surprised to find himself in the company of Mick Jagger and Jerry Hall. He notes that 'not only was he [Mick Jagger] there, he was actually dancing and to all intents and purposes enjoying himself.'

The wear and tear of the tour is highlighted in the same interview with Mike Nicholls. At a Greenwich Village in-store album signing in New York, this is what Neol had to say about whether he liked America and its people: 'They're just a bunch of idiots. Posers. They're not interested in our music, they just think they ought to be here.'

Mike Nicholls answers: 'That's how the scene operates here,' and suggests that we 'should make the best of it', particularly while we 'keep selling tickets and albums'. He tells Neol that we 'might as well accept it'.

'We don't have to accept anything,' Neol retorts.

Nicholls muses that for someone in a band whose self-avowed purpose is to get people dancing, perhaps Neol is taking everything, including himself, too seriously. Bored with Neol, he tests out Desmond, who eagerly tells him about his visit to a local hospital's ER department that morning with a rash on his arm where he was made to wait in line for ages while white patients were seen ahead of him. Nicholls marvels at Desmond's – presumably unexpected – Midlands accent. He continues: 'Pausing only to raise his [Desmond's] spirits with a few shots of duty free, we went for a stroll around the East Village. Desmond related a typically daft anecdote. "I tell you, when we got into town I asked this guy where there was a park to go and walk around. So he directed me to a car park, the foolish bastard."'

It had been a long, hard slog to the East Coast, but on arrival our management reported that the notoriously hip club, 'Whiskey A Go Go' in Los Angeles, had invited us back for a further week of sold-out shows. What that meant was four nights with two shows a night. We were already exhausted, but what band in their right minds would turn down such an offer? We valiantly tried to invigorate our jaded spirits for the big push back across the continent. My voice had at last improved and the band's spirits were lifted with the clement weather, constant attention and laidback atmosphere of the West Coast. My main memory from one of those shows is when Hollywood star Bette Midler came backstage for a meet-and-greet session after one of our shows. At first I didn't recognise her, because until then I had only seen her elaborately dressed for her stage shows. The woman who presented herself in front of me that night was dressed like a bag lady: heavy tweed coat, hat pulled down over her eyes. It was only when I peered closer and saw her face that I realized who she was. She clutched her prodigious boobs with both hands and said in a broad 'Nu Yoick' accent: 'Don't it hurt your boobies jumping around so much on stage?'

We both collapsed on each other in fits of laughter. It takes a well-endowed girl to know the concerns of another! The divine Ms M was indeed divine as we discussed the relative merits of Playtex bras.

Band interview in Horizon studios, 1980 – tough decisions ahead

The Selecter returned from America a leaner, harder band and went straight into Horizon studios to record our next single, 'The Whisper/Train To Skaville', but we were now so lean and hard that it would take only the slightest knock to fragment us completely.

TEN

SELLING OUT YOUR FUTURE

We left America on 1 June 1980. As soon as I arrived back in Coventry, I experienced an acute dose of culture shock. For the previous week we had been enjoying the largesse that Los Angeles nightlife had to offer. We had been driving up and down the Sunset Strip in an assortment of hired Thunderbird or Cadillac cars. Now I was journeying into Coventry city centre on the number 31 bus – what a leveller! I still lived in a two-up, two-down terraced house in Earlsdon and the car was a beat-up, old, blue Vauxhall Viva.

It was as if nothing had changed, but everything had. I needed some stability in my increasingly fluid life. It was not just the band that was in danger of fragmention, I was too. Not only that, but my relationship with my partner Terry suddenly felt very distant. It's difficult to be in a relationship where one of the partners is perceived to be living it up in far-flung corners of the world while the other stays at home and goes to work every day. These were not the days of mobile phones and e-mails; communication was sporadic when in a foreign country. The cost of international phone calls was prohibitive on a wage of £100 per week.

To make matters worse, every time I arrived back home I was full of what had happened on tour, without recognising that Terry had been on his own for weeks and probably didn't

My favourite magazine cover, 1980

want to listen to my litany of band intrigues. Somehow, I knew that we had to strengthen our commitment towards each other or run the danger of splitting up, which would have been such a waste after eight years. So I discussed with Terry the possibility of us getting married. I wanted to make us a permanent item. Fortunately he felt the same way.

Terry booked the wedding in Coventry registry office for

224

8 July 1980. He picked a time to coincide with his lunch hour. That morning he left for work at 8 a.m. dressed in his usual casual manner, blue Levis, shirt, jacket, coat and umbrella, just in case it rained. I think he wore a tie that day as a grudging nod towards the solemnity of the occasion.

I left for Horizon studios at 10.00 a.m. The Selecter were embroiled in recording a selection of tracks for our fourth single. We had chosen 'The Whisper', 'Cool Blue Lady', 'Rock and Rockers' and 'Train To Skaville' as likely candidates. This was our second day in the studio. I had dressed in my usual rude girl boyish manner, because a photographer wanted to do some informal shots of the band hard at work in the recording studio that morning.

Terry had been told that we would need two witnesses at the wedding. Since we had invited no relatives to celebrate our union, we decided to ask the bands' two roadies to attend. Rob Forrest, having been with the band from the beginning, was our trusted compatriot in our musical adventures. He had recently been joined by Hartford, a strong, mean-looking, personable young black guy, who hailed from Gloucester and spoke with a broad countrified accent. Hartford didn't look for trouble, but it unerringly found him. They were the perfect pair, one white, one black; one crazy, the other sometimes even crazier! But both supremely loyal to the band. I'd sworn them both to secrecy about my impending nuptials. Terry and I wanted a no-fuss, no-frills wedding. It would have complicated our lives far too much to have had it any other way. So at 11.50 precisely, I donned my trusty trilby and all three of us sneaked out of the studio and walked the short distance to the registry office.

My future husband was there already, pacing up and down outside the medieval building housing Coventry Registry Office. We nervously smiled at each other in acknowledgement of the incongruity of the situation. We could not have looked less like a bride and bridegroom if we'd tried.

The four of us climbed the winding wooden staircase to the reception desk. We were ushered into an impressive oak-beamed room with a splendid vaulted ceiling, 'the Black Prince Room'. The four of us looked rather woebegone in this large room which probably accommodated 50 guests when full. After a short while two elderly, conservatively dressed ladies entered. One of them introduced herself as the person who would conduct the ceremony.

'Are you still waiting for guests to arrive?' she enquired.

She directed her question at Terry, whom she had deemed as the most sensible-looking of our quartet.

'No, this is it,' he said.

'Oh,' was her only reply. She bustled over to her friend and after a brief, whispered exchange between them, asked us if we had brought along a tape recording of some music for the ceremony.

'No,' said Terry. 'Perhaps we should get on with it, because I'm due back at work soon.'

The two ladies looked most concerned at this turn of events. Then I piped up: 'I don't want to say the "obey" part of my marriage vows either. I don't mind saying, "to love and honour", but not the "obey" part.'

I had read somewhere, probably in *Cosmopolitan*, that it was only women who had to say this, it was not part of men's vows. The magazine article had said that the word 'obey' was optional. That was good enough for me.

The officiating lady peered over her reading glasses, gave me a withering look, but grudgingly agreed to remove the offending word. Rob and Hartford did their best to stifle their giggles. I pointedly stared at them and they shut up. She then asked the sixty-four thousand dollar question: 'You do realise that marriage is a very serious matter?'

The phrase hung in the air as heavy as mercury. I knew that if I looked at Terry and he looked at me, then we would probably both burst into laughter. For years we had said that we would never get married, seemingly content just to live together, but here we were doing exactly the opposite. How did that happen?

She repeated the words.

'Yes,' we both said, somewhat irritatedly.

Seemingly satisfied, if not convinced, she opened her book and began to read from the marriage service. Terry and I dutifully turned into parrots. There was only one more hiccup.

'Do you have the ring?'

'No,' Terry answered.

'We don't need one,' I offered by way of explanation.

I noticed that her partner pursed her lips and looked very worried by this turn of events. A wedding without a ring, whatever next? The lady reading the service was now completely flustered. Yet more lines had to be cut from the service. In an effort to get us out of there as quickly as possible, she took a deep, steadying breath and cut to the chase. Before we knew it we were pronounced husband and wife, documents were signed, Terry was on his way back to work and I was on my way back to the studio to record the vocal on 'The Whisper'. Job done. We are still married. No photos exist of our nuptials.

■ ■ ■

As Terry and I drew together, the members of The Selecter moved further apart. This period in the studio should have been a joyful and creative time. Nobody had to do anything other than write songs and perfect their musical chops, but unfortunately the bickering between us never ceased.

In the wider musical world, the level of intolerable tension at ska gigs was reaching boiling point too. Far-right groups, National Front and British Movement members and sympathisers, made it their business to target 2-Tone bands. This gig review of Desmond Dekker and Madness at the Lewisham Odeon in *Record Mirror*'s 14 June 1980 edition by Mike Nicholls, a respected music journo, painted a worrying trend: 'The lemming-like pseudo-skanking was bad enough but the constant "*Sieg Heil!*" was pathetic.' He notes the confusion of this section of the audience, who were '(correctly) applauding Desmond Dekker while he was singing the immaculate "Israelites", hardly a race the BM/NF (does it really matter?) are known to have endeared themselves to.' He later observes that 'Madness did little to discourage the chanting.'

This review marks the beginning of a distinct sea-change in the accepted thinking of the music press about all things 2-Tone. The 2-Tone movement was no longer the next big thing; indeed, would soon be last year's old thing. The media was becoming disenchanted with us. Perhaps we were not the promised antidote to the fascist thugs after all? We may not have been the remedy to society's racist ills, but collectively we did much to hold a mirror up to society and show the racism at its very heart.

I think the 2-Tone movement positively changed many young people's views about discrimination and social politics, unlike the new Turks who were now snapping at our heels intent on embracing more Thatcherite ideals. Margaret's jackboot was readying itself to give left-wingers a bloody good kicking. The era of style over substance was knocking at the back doors of record companies. We had been in America for only six weeks, but that was long enough for a new movement to gain a foothold on the entertainment ladder. Synthesizers that offered a large, colourful array of sounds were the new playthings of young, upcoming musicians.

This new musical generation was growing tired of the monochrome palette of 2-Tone. Their flamboyant, multi-coloured clothing began to make us strictly black-and-white adherents look drab. The peacocks stalked the clubs while us magpies chattered among ourselves, seemingly oblivious to the fact that a new era had dawned on the musical horizon.

Then it happened. The band fell apart. On Thursday 21 August 1980 Desmond left. Just like that. Why? I don't really know. There was never much explanation. It happened on our first day back in Horizon studios after a fun weekend at an outdoor festival in Helsinki, Finland, where we played on the same bill as the Jam and the Tourists. There must have been something in the Finnish water, because the Tourists split up soon after that gig and the Jam split up not long after The Selecter.

Hartford and Rob had just spent the morning getting Desmond's Hammond organ and Leslie amplifier up the Alpine slope staircase at Horizon and setting it up along with the rest of the band's equipment in the main studio. We were engaged in the tricky business of laying down possible new tracks for the second album, guaranteed to bring on a fresh bout of arguments. It didn't take long before a big row erupted about something very trivial. By that time, so much disagreement was going on behind closed doors that for a lot of the time I was left out of the loop. I think the main protagonists were Charley and Desmond. The upshot was that Desmond stormed out of the building, shouting that he was 'done with the band', and he never returned.

Special envoys like Lynval Golding were sent to his house to have behind-the-scene discussions with him, but he could not be persuaded back into the fold. Desmond was having none of it; when he 'left the building' he had done so permanently.

At which point, Charley flexed his muscles. Within a day and a half, the band's ongoing debate was resolved. This polarisation of attitudes had been consolidated in America. The tour bus had been split into two living areas, the kitchen/dining area at the front of the bus and the secluded lounge with two long couches and a big central table at the back of the bus. The bunk-bed area in the middle kept the two sides apart. Charley, Aitch, Gaps, Desmond and, most of the time, Commie occupied the back. Here they listened to reggae music and smoked copious quantities of weed – so much that when you opened the door it was impossible to see the occupants through the foggy clouds of ganja smoke. Neol and Jane, Malcolm and Juliet, the two loving couples on tour, occupied the front half of the bus, mostly listening to Talking Heads, Roxy Music, Dire Straits, the Motels and our tour manager's pet love, Meatloaf! Commie and I straddled the two areas and listened to the Clash's new album *London's Calling* and probably too much Gary Numan. I rarely ventured into the back, mainly because the smoke was bad for my inflamed throat and as a woman you can only listen to 'Pussy Price A Gone Up' so many times in raucously laughing male company before you begin to wonder what the fucking joke is!

These divisions between us had been brought back to Coventry. The band was unable to go forward until they were resolved. We were not the only ones experiencing this kind of hostile separation into opposing camps. The Specials were embroiled in their own band disaster too, brought on by the rigours of their American tour. Our problems were brought about by musical differences, exacerbated by the racial and cultural divisions that had brought us together in the first place.

Charley wanted to push the band into deeper reggae territory. Neol wanted to push the band into a more experimental rock territory. The hybrid of these two musical forms that was the key to our success was in danger of extinction. It was the same insoluble problem we had experienced back in February while recording the *Too Much Pressure* album. Something had to give. Meetings were called. Factions formed. Our management grouped behind Neol. Gradually Charley painted himself into a corner, whereupon the pack hounded him and his ideas. But none of them could bring themselves to actually 'sack' him. That job fell to me by default. It was a hard thing to do, but if we were to proceed to the next level as an established band, then the source of the division had to be excised. If those around you are too cowardly to do it, then somebody has to step up to the plate. I was happy to do so on Saturday 23 August 1980, a scant forty-eight hours after Desmond disappeared over the horizon (no pun intended!). And everybody else was happy to let me. I should have given each of them a white feather!

Now we were five. Three days later we had to record our appearance on *TOTP* with our new hit single, 'The Whisper', which had managed to garner enough Radio 1 airplay to scrape into the Top 30. Gaps and Commie took up the slack on bass and keyboards. I threw out my hat and donned a red jacket. Big mistake. I looked like a Butlin's redcoat. However, it was not all doom and gloom, we were a unit again. The

DOMINANCE & C

Specials' 'Gangsters' had already come out with 'The Selecter' on the B-side.

"So I went round to his place and said, 'Let's get a group together', and we took the nucleus of Hardtop 22 to make up The Selecter, and got Pauline in."

'The Selecter', Charley points out, was written by Neol in conjunction with Brad Special:

"So it's ironic that we end up working with him now."

After a year of existence, and despite considerable UK success, The Selecter by last summer were hugely in debt. "The Selecter were earning *nothing*. Everything was going into paying for the costs of touring — we didn't mind too much, because we thought we'd get really strong

foundations, and in the we'd be a really powerfu Mind you, it seemed a b ridiculous when we got cheque in for the album something like £85,000, still had debts of £9,000

"So it was obvious th only money was to com publishing. But the only who would really benefi that would be Neol, whe

An *NME* interview with Charley Anderson after the split. By this time he and Desmond had formed the short-lived reggae band, The People

---

bickering and back-biting ceased, enabling us to explore new material. We rediscovered what it was to be an original creative band. But, best of all, we discovered an unlikely saviour in the guise of the late and sadly lamented Ian Dury of the Blockheads fame. Fortuitously, he performed on *TOTP* the same day as us. They were promoting their latest hit, 'I Wanna Be Straight'. Ian perceptively noticed we were short of personnel. While both bands shared an elevator back up to our respective dressing rooms after the recording session, Ian said: "Ere, do you wanna borrow Norman to play bass on a couple of tracks until you lot sort yourself some new guys?'

'You bet!'

It's well known that Ian had his own personnel problems within the Blockheads around that time. His arch-nemesis was Chas Janckel. Perhaps he recognised a similar situation with us and felt impelled to sort out our problems, even if he couldn't sort out his own. Who knows? But we were eternally grateful for his interest, and even more for his solution to the

MISSION

of the songs. It seemed
eryone else was just a
n musician, helping him
money. I told him that he
to divide it equally with
st of the group. He didn't
," he laughs.

ugh Neol refused to go
with what the bassist
aying, Charley wouldn't
e matter drop. This
mental disagreement

came to a head when The
Selecter returned to Coventry's
Horizon Studios to begin work
on their second LP.

"The others told me and Neol
to go outside, out of different
doors. Eventually, they asked
me to come back in. But none
of them could tell me. Pauline's
the strongest of them, though:
she was the one who said it. I
felt like going berserk and

---

problem. Norman Watt Roy was the quintessential New Wave bassist.

Ian was as good as his word and within a few weeks of our initial meeting he arrived in Coventry with Norman in tow. The two of them ensconced themselves in a seedy hotel on the Leamington Road for the weekend. Neol had written two songs, the haunting 'Celebrate the Bullet' and the melancholic 'Washed Up and Left for Dead' that laid the blueprint for the second album. They both needed a definitive bass line, the kind of melodic line that was a 'hook' in itself. Immediately Norman started playing on the two tracks, it was obvious that he understood the sparing subtlety required to match the evocative vocal lines and poignant guitar melodies. The precision of his playing, tinged with an indefinable melancholy, remains unsurpassed and makes both of these tracks classics of that Selecter period. The band was moving on, stylistically and musically.

Commie wrote 'Selling Out Your Future' for the album, a sad, lilting, reggae paean to recessionary Britain, pre-dating

'Ghost Town' by many months. A creative wellspring was suddenly at full flood. Carried along on the tide, I wrote 'Deepwater', 'Red Reflections' and 'Bristol and Miami' for the album.

'Deepwater' originated when I noticed a sign for the town on the freeway in Missouri. Population 400. Small-town America. It reminded me of the 'small town' thinking in the band. 'Red Reflections' was about my relationship with Terry and the upheavals that had been caused by my new career. My home life was still a hotbed of discontent, much like the internal strife within the band. Sometimes there seemed no escape from arguments. The only place I found a semblance of peace was writing new songs in the studio.

The next song I wrote, 'Bristol and Miami', was probably my proudest moment in songwriting. As much as I was concerned about the recession and the creeping fascism in Britain, I also thought that what was happening was part of a global phenomenon. The riot in Bristol in April 1980, triggered by a police raid on the Black & White Café in the St Paul's area, was black people's answer to the same kind of racial injustice felt by the black people of Miami who rioted one month later, after a black Marine Corp veteran was viciously beaten to death by the police. Both riots had been triggered by seemingly random events, but in essence were about black people's continued lack of empowerment in society. It had taken an American tour to make me see that these seemingly unconnected events were part of the ongoing black struggle. At that time it was easier to write about the struggles of black people in the world than it was to write about my own within the band.

'Celebrate the Bullet' is still my favourite Selecter song from the album of the same name. It showed that Neol's songwriting abilities had matured, now that a direction had been set for the band. Finally The Selecter floated in calmer waters after the battering that it had taken in its former stormier creation. In my opinion, Neol was way ahead of Jerry Dammers's abilities at that time, because the Specials were still plagiarising old ska songs and serving them up as originals. It would be another year before their demise and before the prophetic 'Ghost Town' would appear on the scene, but we would be gone by then and 'Celebrate the Bullet' would be forgotten.

Curiously Charley and Desmond formed a short-lived band called 'The People', which was rich considering that one of the reasons that Desmond had cited for leaving the band was because he 'couldn't stand Charley's bass playing'! I think that Charley was intent on showing us all how it should be done, but it didn't work out as well as he hoped. After one single release, 'Musical Man' backed with 'Sons & Daughters' on Race Records, they were gone. Some while later I discovered that Desmond had become ill with schizophrenia and his Hammond genius was lost to the world for ever. I sincerely believe that if Desmond hadn't succumbed to mental illness he would have been one of the truly remembered greats of the keyboard fraternity.

As we rehearsed the new material, it became apparent that we would soon have to look for a new bass player and keyboard player. An advert was placed in the music journals. Several hopefuls applied and an audition day was set. Unfortunately I had to go to London on that day for a BBC Radio 1 *Roundtable* show appearance. This show pitted the week's new releases against each other, overseen by a judging panel, which on this occasion was made up of myself, Jake Burns (Stiff Little Fingers) and Pete Townshend (The Who). Meanwhile, back at camp, the band auditioned a bass player,

Adam Williams, and a keyboard player, James Mackie from Lancaster.

When I got back it was a fait accompli, they were both in the band and booked into a hotel near where Neol and Jane lived. I was somewhat hurt that I hadn't been included in the decision-making process. After I was introduced to them and heard them play, I instinctively knew that they were not right for us. They were good players, but stylistically and musically at odds with our chosen aesthetic. I consoled myself with the fact that hopefully I would be proved wrong.

In the absence of Charley to hold back his worst excesses, Neol was now free to indulge his many musical influences, which were growing by the day and included Bryan Ferry, Roxy Music, Talking Heads *circa* their *Once in a Lifetime* album, as well as the more flamboyant Funkadelic, Parliament, Chic and Brian Eno. He even suggested that we get Brian Eno to produce the album. Needless to say, that did not go down well at the record company's A&R. Instead we got Roger Lomas, who ironically went on to have a string of successes with Bad Manners after he finished our album.

The Selecter ship became increasingly rudderless. Nobody knew what they wanted or who they were. Though the songs were good, the music had no coherency from track to track. Band members smoked enough marijuana on a daily basis to remain absurdly paranoid about each other, as well as other bands on the label and gig audiences. These were hard transitionary times in the music business and none of us was strong enough to identify what was required to get us through these choppy waters. This was when our choice of manager began to appear naive, if not downright detrimental. Poor Juliet stood no chance of dealing with us in our present extremism. Things began to deteriorate badly between us, as

The Selecter mark II – the styling for this photo is wrong on many levels. Photograph by Gered Mankowitz © Bowstir Ltd. 2011/Mankowitz.com

a band, and her and Malcolm, our tour manager and now her permanent partner. This ended when they were sacked and the band decided we would manage ourselves. Big mistake. Needless to say, we were not very good at it.

I remember a meeting with Chrysalis Records around this time, when the triumvirate of myself, Neol and Commie tried to conduct a discussion with the MD and Head of A&R about future advances for us. It was obvious quite early on in the proceedings that these advances were not going to be forthcoming until we had a hit. When this had been established, the A&R guy got up and put on a record, pompously announcing to nobody in particular, but meaning it for us: 'This is the future of pop music.'

The record was the future single of arch-New Romantics, Spandau Ballet, '(Work Till You're) Musclebound'.

The three of us looked at each other nonplussed. As soon as the record ended, the meeting was over and The Selecter knew that the party would soon be over. To make matters worse, as we were as usual raiding the Chrysalis press office for freebie new releases we noticed that all the young staff were sporting scarves around their necks and tartan trousers or kilts. The last time we had been there everybody had been wearing black-and-white checked clothes. How times had changed.

Even worse than this, a movie, *Dance Craze*, directed by Joe Massot, had its premiere at the Dominion Theatre that evening. The film had been shot in 1980, and comprised performance footage of The Selecter alongside Madness, the Specials, the Bodysnatchers, the Beat and Bad Manners while on tour throughout the United Kingdom. A soundtrack album of the same name had been released the day before, featuring fifteen of the songs that were played in the film. We had been invited to attend. The timing couldn't have been worse. There in all its glory was the original band banging out the songs with vibrancy and panache, even if some of the members had overdubbed their parts in the studio in post-production. The present band seemed a pale imitation, literally and performance-wise, of that on screen, despite what we ultimately managed to achieve in the studio.

The single 'Celebrate the Bullet' had been released on 6 February 1981. It was unfortunate timing. Just two months before, on 8 December, John Lennon had been shot. Radio 1 DJ Mike Read thought that we were trying to say something clever about this event, which of course couldn't have been further from the truth. The song has a staunch anti-violence, anti-war theme, but irony was never big at BBC Radio. The lily-livered Smashie & Nicey fools at Radio 1 took the song title literally and, as ever, underestimated the intelligence of their audience, while overestimating their own. It was instantly banned.

Chrysalis hurried to put out the album, hoping that when the single was seen in context with the overall sentiments of the album, it would be looked at anew and interest would be stimulated again. This was a sound hypothesis, but even this salvage attempt was blown out of the water when John Hinckley Jr decided to try and waste the President of the United States, Ronald Reagan, on 30 March 1981. No further mention of the album was made on Radio 1. Thus sounded the death knell of The Selecter.

I think 'Celebrate the Bullet' is a forgotten classic of 2-Tone, on a par with 'Ghost Town' in terms of orchestration and arrangement, but with a more oblique message. It was an own goal for Neol Davies. Without a hit single, both the British tour and sales of the album were in jeopardy. Neol had told us all to prepare for success. Now we silently stared into the abyss while arguably making the best album of our careers. I stand by 'Celebrate the Bullet' wholeheartedly. It is a proud album of a proud band. We were rowing against the tide and ultimately were swamped in the mighty swell of the '80s pop market. There was no place for us in the musical world any more. People were becoming bored with music that contained some social message that they only half understood, or couldn't care less about. The only problem was that deep down, none of us had realised it yet.

Also we had embarked on a new way of styling ourselves. Neol's wife Jane had designed the album cover of *Celebrate the Bullet*. Her logo for the band, which looks like a red, white and black 'pie chart' and is affectionately known as the 'piece of cheese' in some circles, is also her design. She was a disaffected art student who had wanted to go to St Martin's but unfortunately, for whatever reason, didn't get in. Neol once said in an interview that this was because she was from a working-class background and thus she was ruled out for entry. This may or may not be true, but suffice to say she had not had the kind of training that allowed Jerry Dammers to create the idea for our *Too Much Pressure* album artwork. She was perhaps not the best person to start styling a band or producing professional artwork at a time when the band's career was in serious jeopardy and could have benefited from a designer with real vision.

Her band styling was absurd. It was decided that I should rid myself of my hat and let my hair show. Essentially, it was considered a good idea to feminise myself so that we would appeal to a wider cross-section of people. In retrospect this was a terrible mistake and I should have had the foresight and sense to resist, but at times I am the kind of person who says 'anything for a quiet life' and, to be perfectly honest, I was by now totally at sea. Neol grew pointed sideburns and looked as though he was Daryl Hall's clone and Gaps looked like a maracas-playing escapee from a soca band. I could go on, but I'll stop there.

I've never been big on diplomacy. The entertainment industry, as I see it, doesn't understand the meaning of the word either. When a band has outstayed its welcome and is deemed to have wasted too much money at a record company, then it is out on its ear and that's that. I could see such a life-threatening storm coming. I'd had enough. I jumped ship and promptly found myself floundering in deep water.

PART THREE

BACK TO BLACK

ELEVEN

DEEPWATER

After leaving The Selecter, I suffered from a recurring dream almost every week for a couple of years. Each night, somewhere in my dream cycle, I lay submerged on the cool tiles at the bottom of a swimming pool. The surrounding water was a deep blue colour. As I looked up there were people sitting along the pool's concrete edge, all crammed up against each other, furiously kicking their legs, their dangling feet looking like frayed bits of grey felt as they thrashed in the water far above. Their shimmering faces were contorted with laughter. They were oblivious to my plight. I had drowned, but I could still see. 'Danger 15ft deep' was ominously written in huge black letters halfway down the wall at the pool's deep end. The words gently swayed in and out of focus with the ripple effect of the water, just like my last few conscious moments. It always said 15ft.

It was easy to attach significance to the dream. The abrupt departure from the band had been overwhelming. Just as I had been unprepared for such quick success, I was similarly unprepared for such rapid public failure. To paraphrase my song 'Deepwater', 'I was in trouble and up to my neck again.'

A new manager, Alan Edwards, a shaggy-haired, charming facsimile of a vertically challenged David Essex, had spirited me away from the claustrophobia of the band's implosion.

At the time, he also managed fellow Coventrian singer Hazel O'Connor who, if I had thought about it for more than a nanosecond, was on a similar downward spiral after her success with 'Will You'; she just didn't know it yet.

Alan suggested that I move to London. He said that it was where the 'movers and shakers' lived. Long conversations ensued at his flat above a row of shops on Highgate's main drag, about the direction of my future career. 'Career' – a new concept for me. Until then I had thought that radiography had been my bona fide career, while the musical success remained somewhere between a dream come true and a nightmarish hobby. I realized that I ought to be thinking more seriously about what I intended to do. Alan opened my eyes to other avenues within the entertainment industry, which was a good thing, but somewhere in our lengthy conversations, I allowed somebody else to make decisions that should have been mine. When budding musos ask for advice about how to get started in the music industry, I always tell them never allow others, particularly managers, to decide what they should do creatively. In my beleaguered experience it is a recipe for disaster.

The hoary concept of 'networking' had begun to find favour in London in the early '80s. Everybody sported a Filofax bursting with names, addresses and phone numbers of people who could 'help' you. Mostly such people were more interested in how you could help them, but since survival in lonely London town was easier with friends, I quickly learned to network just as hard as everybody else. It was tough going. My forthright stage persona was completely contrary to my shy and reserved personality offstage. Slowly I learned to be more outgoing and fearless in everyday life, less guarded and self-deprecatory. This new strategy worked, but often I felt contrived, which made me even more defensive. I was caught in a vicious repetitive cycle, which did my mental state no good at all.

Immediately, Alan negotiated a solo deal with Chrysalis record company. In hindsight, I should have moved on to another company, but although it was not the best deal in the world, it was not the worst. The MD of the company at the time, Doug D'Arcy, was supportive and I think genuinely wanted to see me do well. I was set the task of all new solo careerists – writing a hit. The head of publishing at Chrysalis, Stuart Slater, suggested I try writing with various in-house tunesmiths, a practice that elicited some interesting partnerships. Until then my song melodies were built over guitar chords, but the songwriters I was hooked up with favoured synth keyboards. Suddenly guitars had become a thing of the past in pop music. Synths were the new cost-effective way of running a band. However, I was an old-fashioned girl, I still adored guitar played through a chorus/delay pedal and Hammond organ played through a whirling Leslie speaker.

Under company pressure, I edged further away from the ska sound that had been my public identity and closer to a marketable pop sound. The only problem was that I wasn't writing lyrics that went with that sound. Furthermore, while in The Selecter I had created an alter ego, a feisty, angry, opinionated young woman, who had sprung from the confines of my mind like a bad Jill-in-the-box. I both loved her and loathed her. She was a means to an end; a safety net that I could fall back on when I felt that the things going on around me were getting out of my control. She was now fully fledged, eager for new experiences. Pauline Black existed and she did not want to return to the status of Pauline Vickers anytime soon.

I secretly dreaded the thought of having to go back to

the anonymity of my former day job back in Walsgrave radiography department, tail between my legs, contritely obeying orders from recently promoted contemporaries, especially after the heady lifestyle that I had led for the past two years. Such thoughts did much to spur me on career-wise. My fame monster had been unleashed.

So, eager to please and desperate to escape seeming oblivion, I temporarily moved to London. Terry was not at all happy about the separation, but it was decided between us that if I was going to be successful in the future then I had to be where the music was made and by that time Coventry's 2-Tone heyday was on the wane. When I left home with a couple of suitcases in the summer of 1981 I felt as vulnerable as the young girl that had left Romford to go to the polytechnic in Coventry. I was twenty-eight years old.

Terry on a weekend visit with me in London, 1982

I moved into a large room in an Edwardian terraced house in Heyford Avenue, Vauxhall. Several other people shared the house, ranging in age from late twenties to late fifties. It was an area that had been run-down, but was beginning to be bought up in large swathes by small-time property developers, intent on converting the fine old houses into rabbit-warren-like flats. The particular house I shared was a building site for much of the time that I spent there, lovingly overseen by arch-cockney 'Mick the Brickie', who singlehandedly knocked down walls and installed bathrooms and kitchens where previously old fire ranges and outside toilets had existed.

If I wanted to be a credible solo artist, then I had to write some new songs pronto. Alan suggested that I buy a Tascam Portastudio 144, which was the world's first four-track recorder whose revolutionary design enabled songs to be recorded directly onto a compact audio-cassette tape. Until then recorded sound-on-sound, outside of a studio, could only be achieved with reel-to-reel tape on bulky Revox machines or their ilk. Musicians now had the ability to affordably record several instrumental and vocal parts on different tracks and later blend these parts together while transferring them to another standard two-channel stereo tape deck, which made a stereo recording that could instantly be played on ordinary tape decks. This new creative tool had even been embraced by Bruce Springsteen, no less, to record his album *Nebraska*, so who was I to argue!

A new Yamaha PS 20 keyboard synthesizer was also purchased with my modest recording advance. This handy though expensive piece of merchandise provided one-stop access to many synthesized sounds and drum patterns, most of which, by today's standards, sounded artificial and sometimes downright comical. But it was portable and when headphones were inserted it allowed the player freedom to experiment without annoying other people in the immediate vicinity.

Thus began many lonely days and nights in my London bedsit trying to write new songs. And I did. The first results were considered encouraging enough for me to be hooked up after a couple of months with a writing partner, an up-and-coming young buck, Simon Climie, the future one half of successful late '80s pop duo, Climie Fisher. At the time he had the dubious honour of being the 'toyboy' of former model Dee Dee Harrington, once the main squeeze of Rod Stewart. The first time I visited his flat for a writing session, Ms Harrington was very much in attendance. Probably vetting me for potential rival status.

She needn't have worried. Simon was very talented and a really nice bloke, but with his pallid milk-fed skin, liverish lips and watery blue eyes, he was completely safe from my attentions. I stood uncomfortably in the middle of the living room watching her as she noisily bustled about in front of a mirror, combing and artfully shaking out her long blonde hair and then attaching a belt with holsters on each side containing fake guns to her snake hips, before adding chaps to her long, lean, jean-clad legs. A jauntily angled cowboy hat perched on her leonine mane completed this daring ensemble. Believe me, the effect was dazzling. I felt like a country girl who'd just arrived in the big city.

Writing songs with Simon was easy and despite our stylistic differences our output was relatively prolific. A batch of them were recorded with producer Bob Sergeant at the helm, who'd produced many of the Beat's hits, but they failed to meet with Chrysalis's approval.

In the meantime, Alan had suggested me for a part in a

forthcoming play by a radical new black theatre company, the Black Theatre Co-operative. Inadvertently, I had gone from being at the forefront of a new British musical movement to being in the same position in an emergent black British theatre. During the '70s, there had been an explosion of 'alternative' (anything that wasn't white, straight and middle class) touring theatre companies, aiming to reach audiences outside the mainstream. Gradually the Arts Council was reluctantly forced to recognise and fund them.

Among them was Black Theatre Co-operative. It had been formed in 1979 after London fringe theatres had failed to show interest in Trinidadian playwright Mustapha Matura's now celebrated play *Welcome Home, Jacko*. So he and white director Charlie Hanson had produced the play themselves. Out of this collaboration the company was born. Its remit was to encourage, commission, devise and produce new writing by black British artists and to stage popular theatre that reflected the variety of cultures existing in Britain to as wide an audience as possible. This rallying cry was a tall order given the prevailing white hegemony in British film and theatre, but the fight had to be undertaken if the artistic playing field was ever to be level. I was part of the generation of young black men and women who, driven by the inequities of opportunity, racism and second-generation higher expectations, had begun to flex their muscles in the media and, more importantly, on the street.

The 2-Tone movement and the emergence of British reggae music had heralded this new black awareness. Now the black youth had taken it to the next level. They wanted an answer as to why the police were allowed to exercise the notorious 'sus' laws with impunity. After the watershed riots in Bristol, London and Liverpool between 1980 and 1981, the

Scarman Report was published, which laid bare the depth of indiscriminate hatred and racism within the British police force. There was a rush in the arts and media to embrace this emergent dissenting black voice. Something had to give and for once it was the Arts Council. Money, the lifeblood of all things, was made available for stories to be told about this new multicultural Britain.

The Black Theatre Co-operative benefited from this revised funding policy. A new play, *Trojans*, written by Farrukh Dhondy, opened the Black Theatre Co-operative's seven-week season at the Riverside Studios in Hammersmith. Such mainstream notice was a real coup for what had been a marginalized company. I wrote the lyrics and music for the play with keyboardist Paul Lawrence, who led an excellent five-piece reggae band, featuring the superb future Big Audio Dynamite bassist, Leo Williams. The critics generally gave the thumbs down to the play. Most of them were angrily united against the playwright who, in their opinion, had sacrilegiously turned a Greek story into a black revolutionary one.

Such criticism was to be a common theme in the aftermath of the Arts Council's largesse towards ethnic companies. Every black production was in the spotlight, which made life very difficult for potential black writers and directors and actors. The opportunity to develop a black theatre free from extreme media pressure was denied. Severe scrutiny had a tendency to stifle new ideas and led to a reinforcement of the stereotypical roles that black theatre was set up to destroy.

Fortunately, I came out of this play smelling of roses: 'Certainly Miss Black is the best thing about this otherwise dreadful affair, her voice as expressive and appealing as ever, her backing band impeccable,' wrote Steve Grant in the *Observer*.

The reviews helped me to land another part at the Tricycle Theatre on Kilburn High Road as Betty Mae, the feisty, estranged girlfriend of the near-mythical bluesman Robert Johnson in *Love in Vain*, written by Bob Mason. It was my first speaking part and I found myself on a vertiginous learning curve. I literally taught myself to act during the month-long rehearsals before press night on 15 April 1982. This play also contained live music, brilliantly served up by Julian Littman in the main role.

Liverpudlian actor Paul Barber (Denzil in *Only Fools and Horses* and 'Horse' in *The Full Monty*) played my other love

Black Theatre Co-operative cast for *Trojans*, 1982

interest and regularly 'corpsed' both of us almost every night, much to the chagrin of the director, but to the delight of the audience. I wore a false plait hairpiece and one night he grabbed me at the back of my neck and the plait came away in his hand. Without missing a beat he wrestled with the offending object as if it was a wild animal clawing at his face, eventually getting it under control, whereupon he threw it to the ground and theatrically stamped on it, before uttering in his inimitable Scouse tones: 'I think it's dead now.' It brought the house down. Nobody could stop laughing.

Again I garnered good reviews: 'Pauline Black is particularly good as the girl from the shack next door,' wrote Mick Brown in the *Guardian*. 'Miss Black's performance is brilliant as the frail, helpless Betty,' commented Ital Gama Mutemeri in the *Caribbean Times*.

Acting seemed like such fun. It definitely beat solitary hours trying to write songs for an increasingly uninterested record company. Unfortunately, as far as I could see, but he might disagree, my manager wasn't particularly interested in my theatrical success or my notions of a new career as an actor. For him the big money was in recording or television and film acting, not going from theatre to theatre like a travelling troubadour doing semi-political black plays. He told me that a good career offer had presented itself that I should seriously consider. Hence, by the summer of 1982 I became a presenter on a hideous children's television quiz programme, *Hold Tight,* which was recorded at Alton Towers in front of a live audience. An old press release introduces the show as: 'A new fun and games quiz with top guests for Granada TV.'

The 'top guests' included Toyah, the bin-bag-wearing frights that were Toto Coelo, Depeche Mode, Haysi Fantayzee, Three Courgettes (who?!) and Shakin' Stevens. To add to the corny mayhem, comedian Frank Carson pretended to be 'marooned on a desert island' while teams from two schools competed to be the first to free him.

I hated every minute of it. My co-presenter, thirty-five-year-old Colin Crispen, a former PE teacher, looked like one half of that ridiculous duo who do the '118 118 BT' advert dressed in '70s gear with droopy moustaches. As if that wasn't bad enough, I had to talk to children, something I mostly tried very hard to avoid. Worse still, I was expected to introduce whatever chart band had been booked that week.

A publicity still from 1982. Photo © brianaris.com

This meant that I had to suffer the ignominy of interviewing Buster Bloodvessel of Bad Manners (who I hadn't seen since recording days at Horizon studios, Coventry) on the first show. During the interview, Doug Trendle (aka Buster Bloodvessel) insisted on talking about 'grimble' at every opportunity. As I was not in on the joke, he succeeded in making me look rather stupid. I later learned that it was a code word for their drug *de jour,* 'speed'. They even had the dubious honour of writing and recording the title music for the show.

Kevin Rowland (who I hadn't seen since the 2-Tone tour) and his 'Raggle Taggle Gypsies' turned up to promote their No. 1 hit 'Come On, Eileen'. It was more torture than I could stand. My musical career had stalled and becalmed me on the continually up-ending pirate ship at Alton bloody Towers, while salt was vigorously rubbed into my wounds by super-successful contemporaries. Surely something had to give. But no, the gods were cruel. I must have mightily offended them because they taunted me even further by providing Bob Carolgees and Spit the Dog as interviewees – not an experience that anybody can emerge from with much dignity.

An expensive change of management solved having to do any more presenting jobs of that nature. I ditched the song collaborators, asked Juliet De Vie to be my manager again and with her help got back on track. An album's worth of material had been written at snatched moments during the past year and Chrysalis brought a new producer, Adam Kidron, on board. He had just produced Scritti Politti's album *Songs to Remember* but, more importantly as far as the record company was concerned, he had helped fashion a new sound for the band, which culminated in a hit song, 'The Sweetest Girl'.

True to his word, Adam also helped me establish a new

On the *Hold Tight* set at Alton Towers

personal sound, alternative gospel soul. As I write the words, I wonder how I ever managed to convince anybody that this was a good idea, but fortunately for me, the mouthy Liverpool wag, Pete Wylie, had just recorded 'The Story of the Blues' with his band Wah! Heat. His song was a gospel-tinged rocker too. It was very close to the sound that I had in my head for the songs that I was currently writing. I began to think that I was getting somewhere.

255

Adam was from a very interesting political family; his father Michael Kidron and uncle Tony Cliff were actively involved in left-wing politics, so my songs about IRA hunger striker Bobby Sands, 'Nameless', a young Arab woman's lament for her dead Palestinian lover, 'Cedars of Lebanon', and 'Something's Burning' about the New Cross fire in a

A change of image for 'Shoorah!, Shoorah!' single cover photo, 1983

house where thirteen young blacks burned to death were easy for him to assimilate without lengthy explanations about why I wanted to write about such subjects.

During the summer of 1982 Adam helped me assemble a trusted group of session musicians, which included a fabulous, three-part harmony girl group made up of Lorenza Johnson, Jackie Challenor and Mae McKenna, who had already worked in the studio with Green Gartside. We recorded the Betty Wright classic 'Shoorah! Shoorah!' and a self-penned title 'Call of the Wild' for the 'B' side. We even drafted in Liverpudlian male singing group The Real Thing to back up the girls on vocals. The finished tracks sounded great and radio pluggers were eager to get down to Radio 1 to push the record as a potential hit single. A New Orleans mock-up bordello was built in a south London garage for a day's video shoot in support of the single. Suddenly everything that was happening was fun, in direct contrast to the last laboured efforts of The Selecter. I was happy and ready to start on an album. Unfortunately the song got a lot of radio play, but stubbornly refused to climb the charts.

There was a new practice doing the rounds, whereby musicians went to clubs with remixes of their singles. The DJ would spin it and the artist would do a PA or personal appearance that involved singing live or miming to the backing track. The record company suggested that I do a short PA tour, mainly taking in London clubs, but also ranging as far south as Brighton and as far north as Manchester. It was my first experience of the club circuit. Many of the ones I visited were gay clubs, particularly in Brighton, full of outrageously dressed rejects from Village People. I was unable to deliver the necessary over-the-top exuberance required for such an event. I was being marketed as Millie Jackson, but probably coming across as a frightened rabbit. I tried, but I felt hopelessly out of my depth. The nadir of the tour was a PA at the National Ballroom on Kilburn High Road on a club night when Tony Blackburn happened to be there as MC. Dressed in a ridiculous, luminous-green leprechaun outfit, replete with a bell-tipped pointy cap and upturned pointy-toed shoes, he introduced me to the sizeable crowd. As if that wasn't bad enough, he then proceeded to caper about the stage while I sang to the audience. That was the last time I set foot on a stage in a club. The mere memory of such unbridled ignominy brings me out in a rash.

Another new development expected of artists was to make the rounds of the new commercial radio stations that had sprung up everywhere. The artist turned up to be interviewed by some twerp DJ on air, who, in return for a spot of abject grovelling, played their latest single and said positive things about it. The hope was that the song would be added to the radio station's playlist. For some people this probably came naturally, but for me it was akin to purgatory. I was told that if I was nice then goodwill was built up for future releases, so I tried to be 'nice', never a good fit for me. My rictus grin when answering questions like 'How's your body-popping coming along, Pauline?' must have said it all.

Undeterred after the failure of 'Shoorah! Shoorah!' to make a chart dent, Adam and I carried on recording an album, but this time we augmented the three backing singers with the London Community Gospel Choir. A big rehearsal studio was booked where we could rehearse all the songs with the band, which now included the Blockheads rhythm section, Norman Watt Roy and the late Charlie Charles. The grandiose idea being floated at the time was that the whole album would be recorded live in St John's Church in Smith Square, Westminster, which is often used as a concert venue. This spectacular feat was attempted but abandoned when the mobile recording unit proved totally unsuited to recording

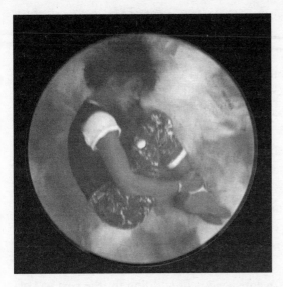

Beaten but unbowed – assuming the foetal position for
picture disc of 'Threw It Away', 1984, © Pennie Smith

amplified instruments in such a venue. I can't even bring
myself to think about the recoupable cost of this venture.

Sticking to my motto of 'forever onwards, undeterred', it
was back to Basing Street studios in November 1983 to record
the album which spawned the single 'Threw It Away' backed
with 'I Can See Clearly Now' in a more conventional setting.
I wrote 'Threw It Away' with Phil Pickett, Culture Club
keyboardist, in a tiny studio under Kew Bridge in mid-1982.
I added lyrics to his eerily beautiful backing track. I loved the
song and my recorded version of it is a favourite from that
time. Again it didn't find favour with Radio 1 DJs. The odious
Peter Powell went so far as to ridicule it on air by dragging it
off his turntable and deliberately throwing it away into the
corner of his studio. To make matters worse, he followed my

song with the Eurythmics new track 'Sweet Dreams' which had been co-produced by Dave Stewart and ex-Selecter bassist Adam Williams. But it didn't end there; after Chrysalis heard the album they feared the political subject matter of some of the songs and shelved it. I was devastated.

I moved back to Coventry to lick my wounds. By that time I'd had enough of the music industry. I seemed to be fighting an uphill battle and my meagre defences had been overwhelmed. Terry was pleased to have me home, particularly after two years of seeing me only at weekends. I enjoyed being back home in familiar surroundings, but I couldn't shake off the feeling that everything I did musically was doomed to failure. Try as I might, I just couldn't get with the bland musical sensibility of the '80s.

My theatre agent suggested I audition for the part of Lola Lola in an adaptation of Josef von Sternberg's *The Blue Angel* at Liverpool Playhouse. It was to be directed by Pip Broughton, a young woman full of left-wing political fervour and eager to make a big splash in the theatre. It was the first time that I had encountered a female director and I liked her fierce energy. I think she liked mine too, because she gave me the part, which was casting against type, a new fashionable experiment in British theatre. I was amazed that she wanted me to play a role that had been made famous by Marlene Dietrich, but if she thought I could do it, then I was happy to oblige. At the time Pip was in a relationship with black actor Joe Charles, so I felt safe in the knowledge that she had some notion about mixed relationships.

The Blue Angel tells a story about a professor and a cabaret singer in 1930s Berlin, who seek each other across barriers of age, class and education, ultimately finding society's hurdles too high to cross. My casting had added race into the mix too.

I moved to Liverpool and boarded in a house just round the corner from Penny Lane of Beatles fame. Released from the stress of having to come up with a hit single, I threw myself into rehearsal, learning to dance and sing in a '30s pre-war cabaret style.

The production was timely for Liverpool. The city was just beginning to claw itself out of the post-riot pit that it had fallen into. Positive images of blacks were suddenly fashionable. Indeed, I discovered that black actor/director Trevor Laird was directing a play with a gritty, realist, anti-racist theme in the Liverpool Playhouse studio at the same time. One evening he and I attended a 'blues' party in Toxteth and I was shocked when he stopped off in the car to pick up some money from a hole-in-the-wall ATM. There in the middle of what looked liked a rubble-strewn, bombed-out site stood a brand new drive-through bank with a money dispenser. It was the last thing that this poverty-stricken area actually needed at that time.

Despite the new multicultural sensibility in Liverpool, I was somewhat taken aback on opening night, 9 September 1983, when I discovered that the programme notes offered copious explanations for the predominantly white theatre-goers about why they would be seeing a black woman instead of the customary cool Aryan woman straddling the iconic gilt chair while crooning the play's much-loved theme tune 'Falling in Love Again'. It suggested that Lola Lola could just as well have been Josephine Baker, the great black American entertainer who had performed in Europe in the '30s. The director figured that such casting added a 'complexity and strength' to the relationship that Lola had with the older professor, who is both attracted and ultimately humiliated by her. I took the stage that night somewhat apprehensively,

Marlene Dietrich would have been proud of me – a
publicity still for *The Blue Angel*, Liverpool Playhouse

wondering whether the audience would accept me in the role,
but I needn't have worried; yet again I found myself battling
white middle-class theatre's conservatism and winning. I
even got a telegram and a bouquet of flowers from Marlene
Dietrich wishing me luck. Unbelievable!

Shortly after I finished *The Blue Angel*, I auditioned for

a fortnightly Channel 4 programme, *Black on Black*. It had already been on the air for a whole series, but the original presenter, the somewhat matronly Beverley Anderson, had left for a BBC news programme. They were looking for a younger presenter to deal with the 'youth' issues alongside the more evergreen Jamaican import 'Miss Lou', Louise Bennett, a much-revered poet, who it was hoped would appeal to the older black generation. I got the job and presented my first show in November 1983.

Having only one programme every fortnight that attempted to cover the needs of the entire black community in post-racial riots Britain was both bravely commendable and incredibly short-sighted of Channel 4, especially as it was transmitted on the graveyard shift at 11 p.m. Needless to say, the programme received a great deal of flak about its subject matter from the very community that it was meant to serve. Rasta youth thought it wasn't representative of them, the older black generation found nothing to satisfy them either and white people dismissed it as ghetto programming and nothing to do with them.

Imagine the furore in Britain if the white community had had a similar fortnightly programme to take on all their issues? But British television was wall-to-wall white-orientated programming, so the Establishment expected blacks to be grateful for this fortnightly sop. As for me, I loved the show despite the inherent limitations. It was a fantastic opportunity to meet all the heroes and heroines of my adolescence and also to discuss political issues that directly impacted on the black community, such as female circumcision, police harassment and racial discrimination, South African apartheid, as well as more frivolous subjects like black hair care, or Caribbean cooking with the extrovert Jamaican Brummie, Rustie Lee.

Every fortnight I would tape a 'live' show in front of an invited audience at London Weekend Television studios on the Southbank. Guests included such diverse stars as Nina Simone, Eartha Kitt, Clive Lloyd, Stokely Carmichael, Viv Richards, John Barnes, Paul Boateng, Darcus Howe, C.L.R. James, Coretta Scott King, Yellowman, Fela Kuti, Gil Scott Heron, Sade, Smiley Culture, Aswad, Afrika Bambatta, Amazulu, Linton Kwesi Johnson, Benjamin Zephaniah, Hugh Masakela and Miriam Makeba.

I enjoyed my job. I even had a marriage proposal from Fela Kuti to become his twelfth wife after he appeared on the show in January 1984. I am glad that I didn't take him up on his offer because shortly after meeting him, his Lagos compound was raided, his mother was thrown to her death from a first-floor window and rumour had it that his wives were raped with broken bottles by the forces of the Nigerian state.

After a few months the executive producer at LWT, Jane Hewland, decided that Louise Bennett's style wasn't working for the show. Trevor Phillips informed me that I would be presenting the shows on my own in the immediate future. If there were any 'heavyweight' interviews to do, Trevor would do them.

Although *Black on Black*'s agenda appeared to be driven by blacks, behind the scenes in the boardrooms it was a completely different story. The higher management echelons that oversaw it and our sister programme *Eastern Eye* were white. The white hegemony still ruled. The *Weekend World* and *The Southbank Show* offices were on the floor above. Lord Peter Mandelson was a researcher on *Weekend World* at the time and every now and again I would bump into him, the Rottweilerish Brian Walden or the urbane Lord Melvyn

On *Black on Black* set with Trevor Phillips, 1985

Bragg in the elevator. Rubbing shoulders with the 'Prince of Darkness' – who could have predicted that!

In an effort to recoup their outlay on my shelved album project, Chrysalis put me together with the newly redundant ex-Specials, and now ex-Fun Boy Three members, Lynval Golding and Neville Staple. Apparently, Terry Hall had informed them by phone that he was leaving the band. Without the eminently marketable white boy fronting the pop trio, the two black guys were out of a job. Under new band name moniker, Sunday Best, we wrote a song together, 'Pirates on the Airwaves', about the newest subversive broadcast method, pirate radio. Suddenly, inner-city urban areas were awash with illegal home-made MW/AM transmitters secreted in biscuit tins. These Heath Robinson devices broadcast pre-recorded programmes on cassette tapes inserted into a portable cassette recorder. The whole mess was powered by a car battery and connected to a long wire antenna (often a coat hanger) slung

265

from a high roof. Tower blocks, those imposing mansions of the poor, offered ideal conditions for illegal transmission of overlooked musical genres on mainstream radio, like reggae, jazz, bhangra and the newly emergent hip-hop.

Chrysalis A&R were very excited when they heard the new song and a video was filmed on the ninth floor of Coventry's most notorious high rise, 9C Pioneer House, in the rundown Hillfields area. The single was released as 7-inch and 12-inch remix versions backed with my track 'Streetheart'. It entered the charts at No. 93 and stalled. It was probably naive of us to assume that mainstream radio would champion a song glorifying their direct enemy, but the failure of this single saw all three of us out on our ears at Chrysalis by midsummer.

I consoled myself with the fact that *Black on Black* was sending me out to America to cover the 1984 Democratic Convention's election of their future leader, who would fight as the Democratic nominee in that year's presidential election. My job was to report on the candidacy of Reverend Jesse Jackson who, if elected, would be the first black presidential candidate.

In 1984 the thought of a future black president seemed a mere pipe-dream, but Reverend Jackson's superb oratory skills and principled fight for his revolutionary idea of a 'Rainbow Coalition' paved the way for the extraordinary events of twenty-four years later.

The director, Trevor Hampton, his PA Julie Villard, and I flew into Atlanta on 5 July 1984. It had been four years since I last set foot on US soil and the wet-blanket humidity of the south had lost none of its ferocity. The producer should have been Trevor Phillips, but he was replaced at the last minute because Trevor's first wife was about to have a baby and wanted him at the birth. Michael Wills,

Trevor's replacement, had flown in a few days before and it was difficult to hide my disappointment when I met him because it was apparent that the whole production team was white. Frankly it worried me to be in a foreign country, covering what was essentially an important 'black' story, without anybody on board who could understand the political nuances of racism that I knew Trevor Phillips instinctively understood as well as I did. The team was competent enough to do the job, but lacked the necessary insights to make the story truly extraordinary.

During a brisk walk before dinner, I noticed that the city-centre population on the streets of Atlanta seemed to be mostly black. The only places I saw white people were in big flashy cars or expensive hotels. When I remarked on this at dinner, my producer explained that all the rich white people that used to live in the city had moved further out into the suburbs after the Civil Rights Act had been passed. This resulted in a three-tier living arrangement: run-down, inner-city black housing, middle-class black suburbs and on the outermost edge white middle- and upper-class suburbs.

As long as nobody forgot their place and tried to move into each other's areas, then the unspoken ancient apartheid of the south remained intact. Such thinking seemed at odds with electing a black mayor, but at least he was a successful first step in a long process.

On my first day there I interviewed America's first democratically elected black mayor, Andrew Jackson. Mayor Jackson appeared personable enough, but I was not used to the slick style of black American politicians. We had nothing of their ilk in Britain. The closest counterpart we had were a few black MPs who were not yet media savvy, such as Paul Boateng and the late Bernie Grant. Mayor Jackson knew how to perform in front of a camera, his unctuous charm oozed from every pore as he deftly fly-swatted my questions about positive discrimination and black voter registration in the rural areas. He had been an important part of the civil rights movement and must have wondered why a British TV channel was allowing me to ask confrontational questions in what probably appeared to him such an unpolished way. Unpolished in terms of what black news presenters were like in America. I had seen several on the local US TV news the night before while channel surfing in my hotel room. Without exception they were a cut above their British counterparts, Trevor McDonald and Moira Stewart.

After the interview, Mayor Jackson politely suggested that he would ask one of his daughters to take me on a shopping trip to Neiman Marcus to look for suitable clothes. He obviously didn't think much of the brand new white suit I was wearing. He also suggested that I get my hair relaxed and styled. My restrained, natural Afro and Top Shop outfit had unfortunately not passed muster. Presumably my hair should have been poker straight in a neat bob and a padded-shouldered *Dallas* power suit should have hugged a gym-bunny body. He probably meant well, but his suggestions made me feel as though I would be better suited to picking cotton!

After the interview, there was a mad dash to Atlanta airport, because a message had been sent by courier that Jesse Jackson would make himself available for a twenty-minute interview while he waited for his next plane. His face lit up with a broad, dazzling smile when he saw me. He was obviously a bit of a ladies' man, but nonetheless he radiated a consummate power and fierce magnetism that seemed neither too slick nor over-contrived, and commanded enormous respect from all who surrounded him. He spent most of the interview admiring my legs between questions, even giving my left knee a bit of a squeeze before he left to catch his plane. I have to confess I was smitten. How I wished that I could have become one of his interns on his campaign trail. He was so much more relaxed than Mayor Jackson. He looked as though he was comfortable in his skin and wasn't worrying all the time about 'what the white folks thought of him'. I'm probably being harsh, but I can only form my opinions on the impressions that each of them gave me.

Until then I had always been conscious of a black/white divide in America, but now I was beginning to see that there were ominous gradations within black American society itself. I did not come from a culture where generations of black people had grown up in well-heeled, middle-class families, who had their own universities, their own strict moral codes, their own prejudices that were every bit as hateful as some white people's.

Next we interviewed a young black family who were not just poor, but dirt-poor. Tony Ghee and his wife had three young children, all of whom had runny noses and running sores on their skinny arms and bandy legs. Their ramshackle wooden house was just a couple of rooms. A rickety couple of worn steps led up to a rubbish-strewn wooden verandah and a wide-open front door. I felt embarrassed to fetch up with a white camera team who were seemingly oblivious to the rank smell of real poverty that emanated from every nook and cranny in the house. Probably they had seen it all before, but I hadn't. I was deeply shocked; this was the Land of the Free, the land of opportunity, Atlanta had a black mayor and these people still occupied humanity's dustbin.

For Tony and his family, and the countless other families sitting on their verandas, who had hostilely peered at us as our car passed along the dusty, rutted road looking for the correct address, nothing had changed. County boundaries were still gerrymandered, which prevented too much inconvenient black voter registration for the upcoming presidential elections and ensured a Republican victory. It seemed to me that Mayor Jackson ought to shift his sorry black arse out to this side of the railway tracks rather than be hanging around City Hall savouring the sweet smell of personal success in his delicately flared nostrils, like so many of the other elected officials.

To make matters worse Tony insisted on addressing me as 'Lady', and treating me as if I was some visiting royalty. I had always found a sense of solidarity in being black among my own kind, so I was disturbed by his deference, it was almost as if he considered himself less than I was. The inequality of the situation forced me to look at what I was doing through his eyes, and I didn't like what I saw. After the interview I would go back to the pleasant, air-conditioned splendour of the Ritz Carlton Hotel on Peachtree Street, whereas the Ghee family would spend their evening and all the evenings that were to follow in this stifling, squalid, cockroach-infested house. For the first time in my life I felt deeply ashamed.

Tony managed to clear a space in the kitchen area so that the cameraman could set up for the interview which, after a couple of false starts due to wailing children, finally got under way. Immediately, the tables were turned. Tony, who had been relatively monosyllabic until then, realized his moment had arrived and, ignoring my first question, just launched into a vigorous, anger-fuelled tirade about the iniquity of the white man and the hypocrisy of the rich blacks who were trying to keep him down. To make matters worse, he delivered this political onslaught in a southern states dialect as thick as the pot of molasses on the kitchen table. I couldn't understand a word that he was saying. If you have ever tried to conduct an interview with somebody who speaks a foreign language in the absence of an interpreter, then you will have a pretty good idea of the dilemma that faced me.

I didn't want to appear patronising by asking him to repeat every sentence; after all, I used to get pretty pissed off with white people who tried that ignominious tactic on me. Somehow we got through the interview, probably without either of us fully understanding the other. I left it largely up to him to say what he wanted and made it the editor's job to decipher what was actually being said. My main contributions were some half-arsed questions and some judiciously placed nods and liberal usage of the words 'really' and 'wow', all said with a sincere note of incredulity in my voice. Throughout the interview local neighbours kept popping in to listen to what Tony said, sometimes nodding sagely or whooping a 'Hallelujah, tell it like it is, brother' at intervals. As the visitors left, they nodded to Tony with a new look of respect on their faces. Our visit had made Tony a 'somebody' in his neighbourhood. I dearly hope that Tony managed to capitalise on his brief moment in the limelight in the ensuing years.

The director, cameraman and PA couldn't wait to leave. I was in a catch-22 situation. I wanted to get out of the stifling house too, but Tony just couldn't stop talking even though the interview had long since finished and the camera equipment had been packed away. Slowly I tuned into his impenetrable accent as he told me about how he stood by the side of the main highways with a cardboard placard with 'Work Wanted' written on it, hoping to be hired as a day labourer by passing motorists, just so he could earn enough money to feed his babies.

How could I tell him that Mayor Andy Jackson was more interested in where his daughters shopped or got their hair straightened than in those black brothers and sisters that still lived in the south's insurmountable poverty trap? That evening the crew and I dined on venison, buffalo and wild boar at Aunt Pittypat's Porch. When the bill arrived and was paid for on our LWT expense account, I couldn't help thinking that the price of the meal would have kept Tony and his family for a good few months of the year. This may sound naive, but it was my first taste of the inevitable dilemma that all journalists probably encounter when sent on assignments to impoverished parts of the world. But I wasn't in Ethiopia or a war-torn, sub-Saharan African country, I was in the land of plenty where the 'American Dream' reigned supreme. It seemed that civil rights had given black folks the vote, but those who had lifted themselves out of poverty were not eager to use their new-found power to lift those who got left behind.

The following day, the crew and I were invited to a 'Men's Day Breakfast' at the imposing pillared colonial West Hunter Baptist Church on the outskirts of Atlanta at the unholy hour of 7 a.m. I had no idea what to expect. On arrival, we found our vocal interviewee Tony on the sizeable, manicured lawn in front of the church, hollering and berating the constant stream of Cadillacs and Buicks purring up the church driveway containing men and their sons in their best silk suits with their wives and daughters in furs and diamonds in the back seats, their hair tonged to shiny, straight perfection. The Academy Awards red carpet has less bling on Oscar night.

A concerned church elder approached Trevor Hampton, our director, and told him that Tony had said he was part of the TV crew. Was this true? The situation was explained to him, whereupon he asked whether we could discreetly do something about removing him, because his foul language and antagonistic demeanour were upsetting the parishioners. Unfortunately Tony was roaring drunk. How he had found out where we would be the following day was a mystery, because he lived nowhere near this affluent black suburb. Tony obviously had profound detective skills. The director had a brainwave. He suggested that I quickly interview Tony again and let him have his say. Then he would give him some money to go away. This strategy worked and within five minutes Tony unsteadily ambled off into the morning, while we got on with the business of interviewing the well-heeled black cognoscenti of Atlanta.

My interviewees were mostly urbane businessmen who were eager to tell me how they had profited from the positive discrimination or affirmative action, as Americans called it, that was now mandatory in Atlanta when it came to doling out the jobs. They told me their stories over liberal helpings of fried catfish, collard greens, biscuits (which were more like bread rolls), hominy grits and lashings of thick gravy. The size of their appetites and large waistlines attested to the fact that they and their families enjoyed the good life. When I asked some breakfast diners what they thought about Tony's plight, most of them looked vaguely embarrassed, some raised a quizzical eyebrow at my interest in such a seeming low-life, but mostly the rejoinder was: 'Some people just don't want God's help.'

I could have understood this rejoinder if Tony had been an anomaly among the Atlanta black poor, but I had seen street after street of people in similar circumstances to him and their lot in life looked just as grim as if the Civil Rights Act had never been signed. A glance from my director told me that I had better calm down and stop antagonizing the assembled company, although I hope my questions gave them a bout of indigestion.

The views held by the parishioners were all the more surprising because the pastor of the church was the internationally famous Reverend Ralph Abernathy, who had stood shoulder to shoulder with Dr Martin Luther King during the civil rights years and even cradled King's dying body after his assassination in Memphis. I briefly interviewed Reverend Abernathy, who proved to be a humble, gentle soul, who fully supported Reverend Jackson's brave run for office. His lined face and expressive eyes gave testament to that old spiritual 'Nobody Knows the Troubles I've Seen'. His spirit shone brighter than the bling of his assembled church brethren. To have had the opportunity to speak to him was a profoundly moving experience.

Next stop was San Francisco, where Jesse Jackson would attempt to be elected as presidential candidate at the Democratic Party Convention held in the Moscone Center. We stayed at the historic Sir Francis Drake Hotel on Powell Street, close to Union Square, where Jesse Jackson was due to hold a 'Rainbow Coalition Rally' the following Saturday evening. The grand, Italian renaissance decor of the foyer was somewhat at odds with the Beefeater-attired doorman. I assumed that, since Americans had a short history, they didn't have to worry when they muddled up the histories of other countries. The breakfast dining room was full of Democratic delegates, mostly from the southern states judging by their accents. They enthusiastically tucked into large stacks of pancakes dripping with molasses and what seemed like a bucket of cream. They were mostly white and wore trousers with elasticated waists to accommodate their ample girths. I didn't give Jesse Jackson much of a fighting chance in the election if these people were representative of the voting delegates.

I will never forget the electric atmosphere in Union Square the night Jesse Jackson spoke to the members of the Rainbow Coalition, who filled every available inch of the famous palm tree-lined square. The effortless cadences of his speech, the rise and fall of the rhetorical questions that he threw out to his enthusiastic audience, were thrilling and captivating. Every disadvantaged social group was present: blacks, Arab Americans, Asian Americans, Native Americans, gays, lesbians, small farmers, disabled veterans, youth, union workers; anybody who was pissed off with or suffering from Reaganomics was there that night.

I grabbed every badge or piece of memorabilia that I could. I did not want to forget the feeling of camaraderie that night. It was as though all my life had been leading up to this singular moment: a black man was raising his head above the parapet and wanted in to the most powerful job on the planet. Not only that, but all the people who surrounded me were sure that he could pull off this superhuman feat. Even the Ku Klux Klan who had marched in a nearby street that afternoon couldn't dampen the spirits of the faithful. On that night, anything seemed possible, even a future black president. No one was more disappointed than me when 2,191 Democrat delegates voted for the colourless, shabby and ineffectual Walter Mondale as their presidential candidate. Jesse Jackson got a very respectable 466 votes. It is worth noting that Joe Biden, a fellow candidate and Vice-President of the USA since 2008, only managed to poll one delegate vote in 1984!

I consider myself very lucky to have interviewed Coretta Scott King, Reverend Ralph Abernathy, Mayor Andrew Jackson, Senator Julian Bond and Mayor Marion Barry in a live televised debate for *Black on Black* from a studio in the landmark Trans-America Pyramid building in San Francisco. These were the movers and shakers of the post-civil rights movement. These people had struggled against murderous odds to achieve voting rights for black people in America. They had been my idols for the past twenty years and here I was sitting among them and being allowed to ask them questions. The word 'humbling' doesn't begin to tell how I felt.

Project forward twenty-four years to the night when Barack Obama made his unforgettable presidential acceptance speech in Chicago. In the small hours of the morning I watched tears stream down the face of Jesse Jackson as he stood in the front row of the audience. I wondered what he was feeling at that moment. A small part of him must have felt defeated after so much personal struggle. I hope not, because his bold stand in 1984 probably showed a young Obama that anything was possible if fought for hard enough.

August Darnell, aka Kid Creole, and me

Soon afterwards, on a more light-hearted note, Granada TV cast me as Kid Creole's (aka August Darnell) love interest, Mimi, in a musical extravaganza, *Something's Wrong in Paradise*, aired on Boxing Night 1984. It was filmed during the summer hiatus between series of *Black on Black*. The whole cast stayed in the Britannia Hotel for the duration of filming, so we all got to know each other by the end of production. Unfortunately, Kid Creole was an inveterate womanizer, who touted his nightly conquests under the very nose of his wife, one of the trio of Coconuts, in the hotel bar. Needless to say, I was not surprised when she divorced him in 1985. The boss-eyed Hollywood actress, Karen Black, star of the movie *The Great Gatsby*, was also in the cast and at every opportunity

277

enjoyed asking me how come we had the same surname. I didn't have the heart to tell her that I had changed mine by deed poll!

A third series of *Black on Black* began in January 1985. The elegant, reserved Beverley Anderson had returned as co-presenter having lost her BBC job when her news programme had been axed. I was relegated to 'youth' and light entertainment issues again, while Beverley dealt with the political stuff. I knew I was treading water as the year progressed. I had lost all heart for making music. The '80s synth sound was all-pervasive and the British reggae scene was now dominated by 'Lover's Rock', a softer kind of reggae prone to excruciatingly sickly love songs. The only alternative was the poppy, reggae soundscape of all-girl bands like Amazulu or The Belle Stars – the latter was essentially a rebranded Bodysnatchers, but without the truly talented Rhoda Dakar.

To make matters worse, I was summarily dropped from my recording contract by Chrysalis and then I discovered that *Black on Black* was to be axed by the new media executive with the grandiose title of 'Channel 4 Commissioning Editor for Multicultural Programming', Farrukh Dhondy, the man who had written the first play I had acted in, the critically mauled *Trojans*. It was no secret that Dhondy considered *Black on Black* and its sister programme *Eastern Eye* ghetto television. He advocated more diverse black programming with more advantageous time slots. These were very laudable aims, but Dhondy's assertions implied that black people could have a choice in programming, which in reality did not exist in 1985.

For any black programme maker to refuse the ethnic programmes would only mean the likelihood of not being offered anything else. The mainstream channels identified skin colour as the only criterion for minority programmes, making it impossible to define black culture in any meaningful way. Instead of building on the success of what *Black on Black* had achieved and fighting to have it moved to an earlier time-slot, Dhondy threw the baby out with the bathwater, and yet still never managed to make black TV programming cross over into the mainstream, although he did write the truly awful, but fortunately forgettable, Channel 4 sitcom *Tandoori Nights*.

My life had reached a crossroads and I had run out of energy and ideas. After a particularly odious interview in the now defunct Widow Applebaum's Café on South Molton Street, with a less than sympathetic music journo, for a feature article, 'Where are They Now', about what members of the bands from the 2-Tone era were doing now, I was so angry and miserable that I stood on Bond Street tube platform seriously considering the prospect of throwing myself in front of a train. It sounds rather dramatic now, but I remember the episode very clearly. It was early afternoon and there were only a few people on the platform, none anywhere near me. It was one of those hot humid days when the underground air takes on a solid physicality and weighs heavy on the body, like water on a drowning man. As a train approached, the welcoming breeze offered by the movement of air from the tunnel cooled my anger. It felt as though it was blowing away the huge burden of disappointment and failure that I had been carrying for so long. A single thought flashed into my head: 'Do it now.'

All I had to do was take a few steps and it would be over. The shocking ease with which I could do the unthinkable must have been enough to jolt me out of my suicidal reverie. I knew it was time to abandon all thoughts of a future pop career. My time had passed. It felt as though there had been a party and I was the last to leave.

TWELVE

DARK MATTER

When I was fifteen, I stayed overnight with my oldest adoptive brother, Trevor and his wife, Barbara. They would have been in their mid-thirties at the time, but largely lived their lives like two fifty-year-olds. That meant that it was lights out at 9 p.m. sharp. To be fair, on this particular night we had to be up at dawn for an early coach ride to Folkestone.

Trevor was a coach driver for a local firm and took his job very seriously. He was every elderly person's friend. Invariably, the little old ladies that planned summer trips to the seaside always asked for him when they approached the coach company he worked for. Indeed there was often a fight between the over-sixties club at the Salvation Army and the over-sixties at the local Rotary club for his services on any given day. Trevor was 'old-school' in style without being an annoying jobsworth. He genuinely had a gene for service, which in these more modern times has been successfully excised from most people's DNA. Often I would accompany him and Barbara on these senior citizen awaydays. The Folkestone trip was with elderly Baptist church ladies, who mainly sang hymns all the way there and all the way back. I sulkily joined in, after much coercion from Barbara, not caring whether Jesus wanted me for a bloody sunbeam or not.

I have never had much of a religious sensibility. Notions of a loving God seem misplaced in the cruel world we live in. However, when I was in my teens, I was quite happy to believe in the existence of the Devil or vampires. People often remark, 'You've got the Devil in you', but never say 'You've got the God in you'. It seems that the definite article is only required for old Beelzebub, but not for the omnipotent one, thus lending Old Nick and his evil cohorts a seductive allure. My fertile imagination was a hotbed for the supernatural to roll in. I guess this is how things are for many young people as they adjust to the onslaught of the hormonal rush that overtakes the body and renders the brain redundant for those difficult adolescent years.

The previous night I had seen a *Dracula* movie for the first time in ITV's 'Mystery and Imagination' series. I mainly watched it because Nina Baden Semper (later of sitcom *Love Thy Neighbour* fame), a British/Caribbean actress, played a vampire in the story and I hardly ever saw a black person on television in those days. Denholm Elliott was Dracula and Susan George was Lucy. It had been so scary that I had to sleep with my bedroom door ajar and my bedside light on that night. Vampires always seem to have a profound effect on the psyches of suggestible young people. All those sharp, pointy teeth biting soft, smooth-skinned, pulsing necks, releasing warm life-blood, disturbs an excitable youthful subconscious.

At my brother's house, I was not allowed to leave the bedroom door open and there was no bedside light. Fortunately I was tired, so I fell asleep quickly, not expecting to wake again until I heard Barbara's knock on my bedroom door eight hours later at 5 a.m. She always brought a cup of tea that would be carefully deposited on a crocheted lace doily that protected the surface of the highly polished walnut bedside table.

I awoke to hear the handle turning on the bedroom door, so I thought that it was Barbara. I played my usual trick and pretended to be asleep, but even though I had my eyes tightly closed, I wondered why the light hadn't been switched on. I was just about to open my eyes when a crushing weight pinned me to the bed, as if I was being forcibly held down. I struggled against the weight, but found that I couldn't move a muscle. It was as though my entire body was paralyzed, even my eyelids. The pressure on my chest was so heavy that I could hardly draw breath. I thought I was going to die. It was as though a malevolent energy had entered the room, causing the air to thicken until it was impossible to breathe. After what seemed an age, but was probably only about twenty seconds, the weight lessened and the oppressive atmosphere in the room lightened. I leapt out of bed and switched on the light. The room was empty and the house was quiet. I bolted from the room, turning on lights as I fled down the hallway into the kitchen. I was glad that Trevor lived in a bungalow because I'm sure I would have fallen down any stairs that impeded my path. The hands of the electric clock in the kitchen stood at a perfect right angle, 3 a.m. It was a full two hours before I needed to get up, but here I was fully awake, with jelly knees and my feverish mind racing with macabre possibilities. My hands checked my neck for any tell-tale bites. Finding none, I searched for other plausible explanations. Had I been visited by the Devil, like in that new movie that had just come out, *Rosemary's Baby*? A schoolfriend who looked considerably older than her years had seen it with her boyfriend and afterwards had been off school for a week suffering with her 'nerves'. When I phoned her to ask how she was, she couldn't stop talking about the film. Her explanation was so detailed that I thought I'd seen it too by the end of our conversation. Now these richly remembered imaginings ignited my over-heated fantasies like the fires of Hell. The existence of the Devil had never seemed more real.

I never discussed this nocturnal happening with anybody. It was quite a few years before I experienced the phenomenon again and by that time I knew that it was not a demonic visitation, but a brief catatonia that strikes me, usually at times of stress or unease.

Backstage at a Supernatrals gig, 1985

There is a current theory in science that suggests that a substance, dark matter, exists in the universe, but it is invisible. Scientists only know of its existence because they recently discovered that the universe weighs more than it should. This dark matter can pass through us, seemingly without our knowledge. Is it possible that some of us are more sensitive to it than others? Perhaps my supernatural fright was just a few lumps of dark matter weighing me down as they passed on through? Perhaps my disturbing experience on Bond Street tube station was a similar brush with dark matter as I felt its momentary passage weigh heavy on my already freighted soul? Who knows? But I did know that the constant struggle to get my songs heard, or fighting for the scarce black roles in mainstream theatre and TV was wearing me down and often I felt as helpless as when that imaginary force pinned me to the bed so many years ago.

In 1986, in an effort to shrug off my melancholy, I formed a new band, the Supernatrals, which even did a support tour for the Communards, but try as I might I could not get a record company interested in our new material. Eventually I admitted defeat and answered an ad in *The Stage* for a new play that was casting, *Frederick Avery Visits*. It was a profit share, which meant no money, but I didn't care. I had become sick of the auditions that my agent sent me up for in the West End. It had been assumed that musical theatre was my obvious artistic home, given my singing background, but the conservatism of most musicals made me shudder. Brechtian musical theatre I could handle, but not full-on extravaganzas where people burst into insincere song at every opportunity and were constantly hoofing it across the stage with broad cheesy grins on their over-made-up faces. The whole thing was anathema to me, much to the chagrin of my agent.

Frederick Avery Visits was written by Ray Shell, an American actor resident in Britain, whose main claim to fame was as 'Rusty the Engine' in the original cast of *Starlight Express*. The play provided me with a no-pressure outlet for my stymied creative juices and opened to pleasant reviews at the Man in the Moon theatre at the bottom of the King's Road, ironically known as 'World's End'. I consoled myself with the fact that from here on, the only way was up as far as my career was concerned.

During rehearsals for *Frederick Avery*, Ray told me about an open audition for a new play about maverick jazz singer Billie Holiday that the esteemed black writer Caryl Phillips had written, entitled *All or Nothing at All*. In those days, I was unsure how to conduct myself at auditions. Nobody had told me that you were supposed to turn up with a specially prepared song and that you might be asked to learn a dance routine or two. On arrival I queued with other hopefuls, most of whom were clutching sheet music for the song they had prepared. When it was my turn, I apologized for having no sheet music and then promptly launched acappella into the famous Holiday song 'Strange Fruit'. My dramatic rendition was full of passion, but probably way over the top, although I must have impressed somebody, because I was invited to improvise on the melody of 'All of Me' by the musical director, Terry Mortimer. He handed me the sheet music and I followed the top-line melody as accurately as I could, while the piano player banged out the tune with cheery gusto. He prompted me, occasionally suggesting rhythmic patterns that would aid the melodic structure, and I politely complied. I wondered why a black writer had written the piece, but a white musical director was in charge of the music. London was awash with black jazz musicians, surely there was an MD among them.

A few days later I was given a recall. At the next audition I had to improvise some more and read for the part. Then weeks went by before I got a call asking me to prepare the exceedingly difficult Duke Ellington tune, 'Sophisticated Lady'. My agent told me that the recall list had been whittled down to only a few. I approached the audition with a great deal of trepidation. I knew I could act the part, and even look the part very successfully, but I was not sure in those days that

I could sing the part effectively enough. A lot was riding on the ability to phrase and sound like Billie Holiday. Because her technique was unique, I could only suggest her timing and phrasing, I could not do a copy of her inimitable and highly personal style.

The final audition was a solemn affair and I could not gauge how well I had done. The following day, Nick Kent, the artistic director of the Tricycle Theatre, rang to tell me that they had decided to offer me the part, mostly because they thought I could act. It was not a unanimous decision, he explained; apparently the musical director's objection had been overruled. They wanted somebody who could embody Billie Holiday's essence rather than somebody who could copy her jazz singing. I remain eternally grateful to Nick Kent and Caryl Phillips for the opportunity to offer my styling of Ms Holiday on stage. I never did warm to the musical director, but I did my best to overcome his obvious prejudice to the school of music from which I came. In retrospect, I think he could have been so much more helpful, instead of so purist. The person I owe the most to for getting my jazz phrasing on track was the actor who played Lester Young in the play, Alan Cooke. He generously gave me singing and phrasing tuition in his spare time and soon I had the tools to attempt the mammoth task ahead of me. But I'm getting ahead of my story, because the very next day after I accepted the job, the Tricycle Theatre caught fire and burned to the ground. The gods had spoken. It was a very dark matter indeed!

Thus began a two-year wait while money was raised to rebuild the theatre. It was intended that *All or Nothing at All* would reopen the theatre. All I could do in the interim was hope that nobody had a change of heart about offering me the role. It would have seemed so cruel to have come through all the angst and anguish of the auditions to have my brief moment of triumph snatched away so completely. I applied myself to making my acting and singing better in the ensuing period.

Fortunately, I was immediately offered two interesting theatre projects, both Chekhov adaptations, Foco Novo Theatre's production of *The Cape Orchard* – which was basically *The Cherry Orchard* transposed to South Africa, with the larger-than-life personality Norman Beaton in the lead role – and *Trinidad Sisters*, an adaptation by black playwright Mustapha Matura of *The Three Sisters*, directed by Nick Kent, with an all-black cast and produced in collaboration with the Donmar Warehouse.

In *The Cape Orchard* I played Valma, the mixed-race, adopted daughter of her white liberal, land-owning mother. My performance was distinguished by being allowed to roam the stage with a Kalashnikov rifle threatening to kill people. I was brilliant in the role!

The late, great black actor Norman Beaton was the star of the play. He was a total trip to work with. On one particular occasion at Basildon Towngate theatre, the only night that my elderly adoptive mother ever saw me perform on the stage, it was Norman's birthday and he had obviously spent his afternoon having 'a few' in his local before arriving at the theatre just a short time before we went on stage. Norman was often prone to impromptu dialogue improvisation if the mood took him, which was a nightmare for fellow actors, but awe-inspiring to watch as long as you weren't in the scene. The cast was small, so it wasn't too difficult to deal with Norman's ad hoc soliloquies. The play opened with a scene in which Norman depicted a Khoi San bushman in the veldt. The playwright Michael Picardie's deft use of imagery and language allowed Norman to weave his magic spell over the audience, while delivering a long speech about what had been historically lost to the black man in South Africa. Norman took to the stage and gave his soliloquy mostly off script, but turned in a spell-binding performance. Those of us waiting in the wings for our first entrance knew we were in for a bumpy ride that night. Suffice to say, Norman rarely got back on script for the rest of the performance. Those of us in scenes with him attempted to fit our scripted dialogue around his interpretation, which was no mean feat given the intellectual complexity of the text. That night he received a standing ovation for his performance.

Norman had the kind of stature among black actors that meant that, despite his worst excesses, his sheer electric presence and tenacious longevity ensured forgiveness. By the time I was fortunate enough to share a stage with him, his theatrical triumphs were largely behind him. His breakthrough turn as the barber in hit TV sitcom *Desmond's* was fortunately in the future. I was so pleased when his comedy series turned out so well, but I still think it was disgraceful that British theatre so resolutely neglected his talent, that he mostly languished in black adaptations of major theatrical roles. The so-called 'ghettoization' of black theatre in this country was at its height in the '70s and '80s. There was no career ladder for black actors. A black actor could do good work, as did Cathy Tyson in the Oscar winning *Mona Lisa* (albeit as the ubiquitous black prostitute), but that did not mean that other good film roles would follow. No black actors outside the black American Hollywood stable were box-office draws in those days. Norman Beaton was like a British version of the 'voice of CNN' American actor, James Earl Jones, but hardly anybody offered him work that matched his talent.

No one was sadder than I when the play came to the Young Vic in London after a lengthy tour around the country, often playing to full houses on the strength of Norman's name alone, only to find that one night there were more people in the cast of five than in the audience. The performance was cancelled. I had never been in a play where such a thing had happened before. For Norman it was the end. He raged in his dressing room, drinking, cursing and smashing furniture. His wife had to be called to take him home. His tearful, rheumy eyes swam with such a bitterly deep disappointment that I

Appearing as Masha in *Trinidad Sisters*, embracing Patrick Drury

wondered whether he would ever surface from such depths of misery. To his credit, he was back the next day to a much fuller house giving yet another outstanding performance. I learned a valuable lesson that day about weathering career storms and setbacks. As the title of his autobiography suggested, he was always *Unbeaten and Unbowed*. He was a true legend of British theatre.

The best part of the play was at the end when everybody in the company stepped forward, fists raised above our heads in a black power salute, and exhorted the audience to join us in singing the unofficial South African anthem, 'Nkosi Sikelel' iAfrica.' At that time it was the symbol of independence and resistance to apartheid, sung by the majority of the South African population at all anti-apartheid rallies and gatherings. Every night the feeling of solidarity with Black Africa was palpable in the auditorium. It's worth noting that the play asked all the right questions three years before Nelson Mandela eventually walked free from prison. An historical dark matter!

Trinidad Sisters opened on 11 February 1988 and boasted a large, energetic, nearly all-black cast, immaculately dressed in a 1940s wardrobe hired in at considerable expense. The play was transposed from a Russian backwater to Port-au-Prince in Trinidad, just as war had broken out in Europe. The text was spoken with a Trinidadian accent, the musicality of which was hard to negotiate for a non-native speaker like me, but once mastered, added to the beauty of the words. It was a brilliantly conceived West Indian comedy of manners. Patrick Drury (one half of the warring married couple who own the hardware shop in *Father Ted*) was the only white person in the cast and played a British Army major, like the idealistic Lieutenant Colonel Vershinin in the original.

It was a controversial decision to stage this adaptation of a European theatrical 'holy cow'. Most reviewers were especially kind, but one or two were downright hostile – Irving Wardle of *The Times* headlined his review 'Hijacking a Classic', although he did say that 'the playing was extremely capable'.

I thought it was fantastic to be in such a talented ensemble cast playing Chekhov, albeit 'an intrepid colonial hijacking of a European classic', but some black actors were against this ghettoization of black productions. They argued that it just kept black actors in second-rate productions, instead of lobbying white directors at the big institutions to cast black actors in lead roles for the European classics or Shakespeare plays. Laudable comments, but getting angry about perceived injustices in the theatrical world rarely got black people what they wanted and most times reinforced the white prejudicial stereotype that 'all blacks are trouble'. Most black actors agreed that it was better to be in a brilliantly acted version of a well-known play than never doing the so-called 'classic' roles at all. Any actor's worth was increased the more classics they appeared in. Judging by the full houses that we got every night, white theatre-goers were eager to see what black actors could bring to this play and black theatre-goers were overjoyed to see themselves not playing one-dimensional prostitutes, pimps and criminals for once!

There was a joke going around among black actresses when we met up at auditions in those days, which was to quip: 'How many prostitutes have you played this year?' White actresses probably only had to play one in their entire careers. It was tough fighting against the constant stereotyping of black actors by casting directors. I'm glad to say that these days black actors have proved their theatrical worth and are treated more fairly and offered more variety in their roles on stage, TV and film. There is even a healthy modicum of colour-blindness when the big institutions cast the classics. But let's not forget that it has been a fight for recognition every step of the way. I feel extraordinarily proud to have been in the vanguard of that 'all-black experiment'.

For those who think that Black Chekhov is absurd, perhaps it is worth remembering that British actors donning Tsarist cavalry uniforms while speaking in upper-class English and calling each other by long Russian names is no less bizarre!

And once again there were good reviews. 'Pauline Black… cuts a beautiful and stylish figure as Marsha,' wrote Charles Spencer in the *Daily Telegraph*.

Next up was a six-month tour of *Antony and Cleopatra* for a small-scale touring theatre company, ATC. A fellow black actor had once told me that if a director offered you a part, any damn part in a Shakespeare play, then snap it up immediately. Since I didn't think that any director at the RSC was going to offer me the coveted role of Cleopatra any time soon, I took the advice. The director, the sadly departed Malcolm Edwards, wanted me to play Cleopatra as a '40s screen idol; a welcome degree of imagination at last, I thought. The only problem was that we had to enact the whole play with a cast of four! Not only that, we had to set up the scenery and stage every night and tour it to the outermost corners of Great Britain and Northern Ireland, namely Enniskillen and Coleraine.

I have never had so much fun on a tour in my life, even skinny-dipping with the whole cast, director and crew in a basement hotel swimming pool owned by the parents of a splendidly Wildean young Irishman, who was full of the blarney and persuaded us to divest ourselves of our clothes and swim as Nature intended one drunken evening post-performance. I'm sure this young man had an ulterior motive, because I later found out that he sang in a band aptly named The Emperor's New Clothes. Fortunately the days of mobile

Patrick Wilde and me in *Antony and Cleopatra* at the Lyric Hammersmith, 1989

phone cameras and instant photo uploads onto Facebook were far ahead of us.

It was hard work shlepping around the highways and byways of Britain, but our reward, apart from a few heady days performing at the RSC Swan Theatre in Stratford-on-Avon, was a three-week stint at the Lyric Studio Theatre in Hammersmith. I had very good reviews; unfortunately my Antony, played by the excellent actor Patrick Wilde, less so. In fact he was said to be as 'limp as a lettuce leaf' by one uncharitable reviewer. In his defence, he was not best served by the director, who insisted that he wore leather body torso armour over a '40s suit. Such attire only made him look thinner than he was. Antony is supposed to be a grizzled old war-horse, and the incongruous addition of leathery fake muscles made my Antony look as though he was in desperate need of a Charles Atlas body development course. Nonetheless, for a company of only four attempting to do such a huge tragedy, we garnered good reviews for our London stint: 'Pauline Black is every inch the icy temptress,' wrote the *Guardian*. 'Her resolve has a truth and beauty that is majestic, sublime and marvellously affecting,' praised the *Independent*.

While we were at the Lyric Studio, two of my adoptive brothers, Roger and Tony, decided to come and see their little sister in a production. I think they were motivated by the fact that our mother had seen me in *The Cape Orchard* and liked it, and now wanted to see what all the fuss was about. I wasn't sure that either of them had ever seen a Shakespeare play before, but I didn't want to seem unwelcoming, so I booked them some tickets. Unfortunately the audience was thin on the ground and very unresponsive the night they came.

For those unfamiliar with studio theatres, there is usually no recognisable stage or proscenium arch or indeed curtains that open to mark the start of the performance. To make matters worse, our production had no stage set, just an empty floor space bound by rows of chairs on three sides. While I was putting on my make-up for the evening performance in the communal dressing room, my heart sank when one of my fellow performers announced: 'Blimey, we've got Reggie and Ronnie Kray sat in the front row tonight.'

Instantly I knew she had seen my brothers. I went backstage to peer through the black curtains and saw them looking decidedly uncomfortable, fully kitted out in navy three-piece suits, sporting wide, '70s ties, large, gold-plated cufflinks in their immaculate white shirts and freshly polished black lace-up shoes, patiently waiting for the start of the performance. A few more people drifted in and sat in the back row. Simultaneously my brothers craned their necks round to stare at the new arrivals, probably wondering whether they should move further back. The next two and a half hours yawned before me like a bottomless pit. Most of the action would be happening about two feet away from them, much of which was now running through my mind's eye, trying to check for the most embarrassing moments, such as when I had to French kiss Patrick in a particularly passionate embrace. I'm not sure why, but at every performance as soon as we started kissing, my stomach audibly rumbled until we stopped. It was very difficult for us to keep a straight face on stage with such an abdominal cacophony filling the silence, which had on a few nights elicited titters from some audience members. To make matters worse, the director had positioned us at the front of the playing area in the centre, exactly where my brothers were sitting. I made a mental note to ask Patrick to cheat himself further upstage for our romantic clinch.

The small audience was quiet throughout. I just hoped and prayed that they were listening attentively rather than sleeping. My brothers stoically stared forward at all times. Patrick completely forgot to change his position as asked and I have never acted quite so determinedly as when I flew into his arms and found myself looking directly at my brothers as they watched their sister being right-royally Frenched in front of their eyes. As if on cue, an almighty stomach gurgle destroyed the deathly quiet studio theatre. I saw my brothers do a comedy double-take as they looked at each other, perhaps wondering whether the noise emanated from one of them. It was all too much for me, I had to pull away from Patrick and bury my head in his shoulder, in a vain attempt to stifle the giggles that beset me. We hoped that our shoulders looked as though they were heaving with sobs at having to part from each other, rather than uncontrollable laughter.

After my appointment with the asp of death, all four actors returned from the dead to take their bows and the audience, as small as it was, enthusiastically applauded. Both of my brothers were grinning from ear to ear. Phew, I'd got through it. Now for the after-show party!

I had told Roger and Tony to wait for me in the theatre bar after the show while I changed out of my costume. I tore off my stage clothes and dressed as quickly as possible. I was eager to hear what they had thought of their first Shakespearean performance.

Vanessa Redgrave was doing a production in the main house, *A Madhouse in Goa* written by Martin Sherman, which came down fifteen minutes before our play. Every night she joined her fellow actors for a quick drink in the bar before being whisked up the road by taxi to her Chiswick home. At this time I was still very loosely associated with the Marxist Party (it had changed its name by now from the Workers Revolutionary Party) and therefore also with Vanessa and her brother Corin. She found it expedient to have a short chat with me after the show if our paths crossed in the bar. I hadn't seen her for the past few nights, but I desperately hoped that she would have left by the time I got to the bar because I didn't fancy a stilted conversation with her while my brothers were there. My heart sank like a thirsty camel's hump when she hoved into view, all smiles and piercing, ice-blue eyes, and engaged me in conversation. I saw both my brothers' jaws drop as they instantly recognised who was earnestly talking to their baby sister. It's worth noting that all conversation with Vanessa is earnest. In an effort to include them, I made the necessary introductions. I figured that an authentic whiff of Essex working-class folk would do her good. I boldly announced: 'Vanessa, these are my brothers. They came to see tonight's performance.'

It was now her turn to do a comedy double-take, as she looked from my white brothers to me and back again. 'Hello,' she stammered as everybody heartily shook hands, desperately trying to think of something to say. 'So you are Pauline's brothers?' she asked rhetorically.

'Yes,' they chorused, almost standing at attention. I had always noticed that people stood up a little straighter when talking to Vanessa, she just had that effect on them.

'Um, what did you think of your sister's Cleopatra?'

If she had been expecting a learned discourse on the merits of reductive Shakespearean works, then what she got must have come as an all-out assault on her theatrical sensibilities. Roger took up the lull in the conversation.

'First time I've ever been to this kind of theatre,' he announced. 'I've been to Raymond's Revue Bar before, but this was a bit different.'

I could see that her eyes were searching his face to see if he was taking the piss, but Roger stared back at her so star-struck that it was impossible to perceive any malice or amusement in his answer.

'Didn't expect our little sister to be doing all that kissing on stage though, good job our mum didn't see that,' he said, laughing heartily.

At which point I blurted out, presumably by way of explanation: 'Oh, you don't have to worry about that, I think Patrick is gay.'

Unfortunately this was completely the wrong thing to say. As if on cue, both of them leapt towards the bar counter, where they theatrically turned to face me and Vanessa and loudly announced in unison: 'Backs against the walls, boys, backs against the walls.'

Time flowed like treacle. My brothers giving a passable rendition of Tweedle Dee and Tweedle Dumber didn't seem to notice that they had just uttered the kind of tasteless faux pas that even Russell Brand might think twice about. Ms Redgrave proved her Oscar-winning worth by pretending that we had entered a time warp, which rendered my brothers as belonging to a parallel universe, one that had never heard of the term 'PC'. Her elegant mouth twitched upwards at each corner, while her watery blue eyes remained as steadfastly cold as always.

To make matters worse, Patrick appeared at my side, obviously waiting for me to introduce him to the others. My brothers immediately shut up. It was now their turn to enter a parallel universe. I don't think either of them had ever met a gay person before, or for that matter a film star. At least they would have plenty to talk about at family get-togethers in the future. Much to Patrick's chagrin, Vanessa made her excuses and hurried off in search of her taxi, leaving my brothers to handle the thorny problem of shaking hands with Patrick. I hope it was character forming for them. None of my brothers have ever again shown the slightest interest in my acting career.

In August 1989 – at long last – *All or Nothing at All* began rehearsals. The newly rebuilt Tricycle Theatre now stood proudly and newly refurbished on Kilburn High Road. Nicolas Kent, its energetic and fiercely talented artistic director, had fought hard to raise the necessary money to save the theatre and hoped that a strong and stirring new play based on the tragic life of the celebrated Billie Holiday would be a bold opening gesture.

I returned to my hard-won role, suddenly thrust into a situation where I was leading a cast of seventeen people. From the first day of rehearsal I knew I had my work cut out. If I failed to convince as my idol then the play would be a non-starter. I was simultaneously excited and apprehensive.

The play was somewhat unadventurous in that it used the story-telling technique of a series of flashbacks in which Billie Holiday's agent, excellently played by Henry Goodman, and others, reminisced in scenes from her life played out in chronological order. On the plus side, it never descended into the mawkish sentimentality of the Hollywood film version of her life, *Lady Sings the Blues*, starring Diana Ross.

Rehearsals went well for the first couple of weeks, until an unexpected bombshell hit – the author, Caryl or Caz Phillips as he liked to be known, wanted his name removed from the script and posters and refused to have any further contact with his play or the performing cast. Before the assembled actors had fully digested what his actions meant, it was further announced that no words could be changed in the script and lawyers would be sent in on opening night and press night to make sure that this directive was sacrosanct. The effect of these pronouncements on cast morale was devastating. There was an intractable rift between Caz and the director Nick Kent. Nobody knew why.

I tried to intervene, rather foolishly in retrospect. I knew Caz through a mutual friend and had visited his house on one occasion. I took it upon myself to go to his house and try to convince him that what he was doing was detrimental to everybody concerned, particularly because there was a lot riding on the success of the play reopening the theatre. I arrived at his house about 7 p.m., but he was out. So I sat on his doorstep and waited for his return. I'd already waited for two and a half years to make my personal dream of playing Billie Holiday come true, so what difference would a few more hours make? I fervently believed that I could make him see sense and agree to come back on board.

He returned at 10 p.m. He was surprised and embarrassed to see me. To his credit, he invited me in, but would listen to none of my well-rehearsed arguments. After a while, I found his self-righteousness irritating. He was jeopardizing the livelihoods of seventeen cast members and the countless other staff who were working on wardrobe and design. Any appeal to his better nature was resolutely rebuffed. Eventually I lost interest in being a go-between. There is only so much begging that one person can do before you begin to question your self-worth. He didn't seem to care about anybody else caught up in this drama, only himself. To my mind, he never gave a coherent explanation for his actions. I lost a lot of respect for the man on that day. I've never seen him since.

The following day the entire cast was called into the theatre auditorium so that a decision could be made about the future of the project. It was put to us that we could carry on with the project, but any script changes were now out of the question. But I consoled myself with the fact that Billie Holiday had had to surmount bigger difficulties in her lifetime than this relatively minor inconvenience, and in some ways it seemed a fitting tribute to her that a play about her should meet with such an insoluble problem. After all, we are talking about a woman who was raped at nine, a prostitute at twelve, a prison inmate in her thirties and eventually arrested on her death-bed for heroin possession. Even though she had arguably been the greatest female jazz singer ever, she was still hounded to her grave by bad-minded people. Unfortunately, an author who should have known better had chosen to dump on her legacy again.

Three people in the uniformly excellent cast stood out for me in this production: Alan Cooke, Henry Goodman and Colin Salmon, the latter having been discovered busking outside the theatre. Alan took it upon himself to act as my vocal coach and Henry as my acting coach throughout rehearsals. I am very grateful to them both for their unselfish and invaluable help. Colin has my sincere thanks for being such a superb trumpeter and all-round nice guy.

Henry Goodman and me in *All or Nothing at All*, 1989

What fun we had knocking what was left of the imperfect script into shape! Working on a scene with Henry Goodman was a revelation. Until then, I hadn't worked with anybody,

301

actor or director, who applied such exactness to every word in the script. Before Henry would utter a word of the script, he would subject every phrase or sentence to rigorous analysis in a never-ending search for intellectual meaning, nuance and truth. Similarly, he demanded that whoever else was in the scene applied the same dramatic tenets to their lines. Admittedly, this approach was not universally liked, but once you had surrendered to it the possibilities for playing a scene seemed endless. I relished the scenes in which Henry and I were alone on stage. He gave so much as an actor and demanded the same in return. No ego was involved – quite the opposite, he knew that he would shine if the other person did too and that the only way this could be achieved was to get right down to the essence of the scene and serve the play, the written word. How wise such thinking is and I wondered why I hadn't met anybody before who tackled a script in the same manner. Don't get me wrong, I had been in plays where we had all sat round and discussed our objectives and super-objectives à la Konstantin Stanislavsky. All of that had been very useful, but nothing replaces the root-and-branch dissection that Henry brought to a script. My performance owed as much to his attention to detail as it did to Nick Kent's direction.

Opening night was extraordinary. Everything came together and I had one of those curious out-of-body experiences that I get from time to time – not very often, or they would not be special. But I'm sure fellow actors will know what I am talking about – those moments when you can actually observe yourself uttering the lines or singing the songs as though somebody else has momentarily taken over your body. There is nothing more wonderful in the world for a performer than such moments. It is literally as if one

As Billie Holiday: photo shoot for *Vogue*, 1989

is possessed. The performance seems effortless, with no hint of artifice, just a sense of rightness, in that it can be done no other way. One such moment happened on opening night when I was standing in a lonely spotlight singing 'Strange Fruit'. I felt as though Billie Holiday had walked into my being and was mouthing the words of the song for the audience.

The reviews were brilliant, even though the whole of the cast was carrying the unspeakable weight of having to be word-perfect on press night as two lawyers sat in the gods listening out for script inaccuracies or textual changes. With proper work on the script the production could have been brilliant, but as a cast we were left with an imperfect script which sometimes made the production feel like a one-legged person walking unaided.

Lyn Gardner wrote in *City Limits*: 'Pauline Black's magical performance goes way beyond mere impersonation and she's given exceptional support from the entire cast, but particularly Henry Goodman as her agent and Alan Cooke as soulmate, Lester Young. Nicolas Kent directs with customary flair.'

Under the auspices of Nick Kent's brilliant direction, I was nominated for the 1991 *Time Out* Award for best actress. No one could have been more surprised than me when onto the stage strode the satyr-like John Malkovich, who read out the list of nominees and then announced: 'And the winner of best actress for 1990 for her performance as Billie Holiday in *All or Nothing at All* is...Pauline Black.'

I think the whole cast should have been awarded a prize for their sense of support and camaraderie throughout. I've never worked with such wonderful people before or since, and I daresay I never will again. That is what made the production special and a fitting tribute to Lady Day. Thank you.

■ ■ ■

Suddenly I was on a roll; TV roles in the sitcom *Shelley*, cast as a cleaner, albeit an intelligent one, and *The Bill* (as a prostitute's daughter) followed. Then Euston Films cast me as Lexie, the sexy secretary/receptionist in *Shrinks*, a new series for Channel 4 about a group of psychiatrists who ran a private psychiatric clinic in London. It ran for only one season. Its yuppie production values were much the same as a previous late '80s Euston Films failure, *Capital City*, about the day-to-day running of an investment bank. It was now 1991, the heyday of yuppies and 'loadsamoney' lifestyles, but when the shenanigans of a bunch of overpaid private shrinks was paraded before the great British public they voted with the off switch on their TVs. Nobody was interested in rich people's mental health and even the honeyed Scottish tones of Bill Paterson couldn't save this turkey. By the way, a young Kate Winslet appeared in one of the episodes.

I was naturally disappointed with the series demise, but also relieved that I could have a brief respite from a decade of mostly living out of a suitcase in a succession of friends' flats. Terry was beginning to wonder whether he had a wife to share a home with at all. It was okay for me, I had constant interesting work to do, but Terry worked nine to five every day and came home to an empty house in the evening. After such a long time, something had to give in the relationship. One tumultuous row too many made up my mind, and I decided to have a rest and spend some much-needed time at home. Terry and I needed to reconnect with each other.

A chance encounter with Neol Davies, who I hadn't seen for seven years, also led to a musical reconnection. We tentatively began making music together in Neol's newly acquired rehearsal space in the basement of Marks & Spencer in Coventry city centre. Our collaboration swiftly resulted in an acoustic duo appearance on the *Jools Holland Show*. Teaming up together again seemed like a no-brainer. Once it was known that we were back on the music scene, an agent asked us to join Buster's All Stars, which was basically an assemblage of our old 2-Tone compatriots, Bad Manners. With no prior rehearsal, Neol and I did two shows with them, one in Aachen, Germany and the other in Nottingham, at the Rock City venue. It was after these two gigs that Bad Manners bassist Nick Welsh and keyboardist Martin Stewart hatched a plan to dissociate themselves and Bad Manners drummer Perry Melius from Buster Bloodvessel's band. Understandably, having half your band nicked to re-form The Selecter did not go down well with Buster, but fortunately I was not privy to the crafty machinations that went on behind the scenes. The Selecter was reformed and after a one-day rehearsal at the Tic Toc Club in Coventry, we went out on the road and didn't stop, except for brief line-up changes, for another fifteen years.

I carried on acting for TV, film and theatre throughout this period, but I was back in my comfort zone, on stage belting out ska and reggae tunes. The dark matter had passed.

THIRTEEN

WHAT DO YOU HAVE TO DO?

SELECTER

It was late June 1996 and as I stared at myself in the mirror admiring a black Prada jacket that I was trying on in the unflattering light of a fitting room on Sloane Street, I suddenly noticed that my face had gained nose-to-mouth lines, seemingly overnight. My discovery was hardly surprising. I was now forty-two years old. The tiresome fact was that I was growing older. I'd spent the last five years touring worldwide, since reforming The Selecter with Neol Davies. I had also racked up quite a few acting jobs on TV, most recently as a head teacher in a Liverpool comprehensive school alongside actor Christopher Ecclestone, in the Jimmy McGovern scripted *Hearts and Minds*. I'd even played a substantial part in a horror movie, *The Funny Man*, starring Christopher Lee, the year before. For the first time in my life I had enough money to open a deposit account. All this work had not made me rich, far from it, but I continued to create opportunities for work and I secretly prided myself on the fact that I had never had to go back to my day job as a radiographer.

I had a party to go to that night and I felt like splashing some of my hard-earned cash on a snazzy jacket. I wasn't looking forward to the party. It was a media shindig in a trendy warehouse somewhere in Hoxton. An agent had suggested that putting in an appearance might be beneficial for getting the band work. I wasn't convinced, but had agreed to go along.

I usually felt out of place at such events, particularly among the current crop of 'bright young things'. These days House and Britpop music ruled the airwaves. Even the drugs had changed from what I was familiar with. Ecstasy was the current favourite, but I hated the 'loved up' feeling that it engendered. The one and only time that I had taken it, I embarrassed myself after a gig at the Melkweg in Amsterdam. Fortunately I was with a good friend who dragged me away from the young man who had become the object of my attentions. God knows what I'd been thinking. I had no intention of ever being counted among the ranks of that loony, perpetually grinning, bedroom-eyed breed again. What is it about being in a band that seems to stunt one's personal growth? Perhaps the illusion of continuing youth hangs around a tad too long, like Miss Havisham's wedding gown. I'd already seen plenty of my contemporaries ignominiously change their style and start wearing trousers ten sizes too big for them, or piercing their flesh with metal attachments or tattooing their skin to look as though they were still 'really happening'– still current. Forever relegated to the shelves of Apu's store in *The Simpsons*.

For the first time in my life, I had recently begun to feel at odds with my audience. Sure, the old stalwart skins and Mods were there, but they were now paunchier and greyer and tended to parade photos of their teenage kids in front of you, a constant reminder of how much time had passed. Luckily, the band now attracted a new crowd, New Agers, who gleefully packed out our gigs dressed in their trademark colourful, baggy, clown-like clothing. Their seeming healthy disregard for either soap or deodorant made the olfactory experiences in the sweaty confines of small clubs particularly memorable. Don't get me wrong, it was great to be accepted by a new generation's sub-culture, and I still felt passionate about keeping the 2-Tone flame burning by recording and promoting new albums, but I found it impossible to identify with the new fashions as I grew older. As if to underline my antipathy to such stylistic frivolity, it was about this time that I started wearing only black clothes.

A black palette suited me. Just as Johnny Cash sings in 'The Man In Black', there should always be a man upfront dressed in black to keep the rest of us ever mindful that there are plenty of people in this world 'who are held back'. I don't suppose he minded much if a woman got in on his fashion statement!

That song struck a chord with me. I didn't much like the

'good ole boy' status of country music. I loathed the right-wing politics and Bible thumping that went with a lot of it, but oddly enough, I did like Johnny Cash and what he stood for. He seemed to mine a deeper seam in the hillbilly countryside that kept his neck cool and pale, unlike his crowd-pleasing, boot-scooting contemporaries, who never delved below the surface into society's darker underbelly and therefore scorched their necks red raw in the hot Tennessee sun.

Wearing black clothes made a lot of sense on many levels, not just the philosophical. They didn't show the dirt, were instantly slimming and, moreover, mornings were never subjected to that miserable quandary about what colour matched another when trying to dress in a hurry. In the '90s, Prada produced the best black clothes in town.

I bought the jacket and stepped out of the shop's cool interior into the blazing hot sunshine of Knightsbridge. It was such a pleasant day, I decided to walk to Oxford Street via leafy Hyde Park rather than catch the Tube. I fancied a late lunch in Selfridges food hall. I enjoyed the walk, but the sun disappeared behind a huge black cloud by the time I got to Marble Arch. I was wearing only a sleeveless dress, and a chilly breeze was making me shiver as I reached Selfridges. The store's air-conditioning was on full blast, which made me colder than ever. Needing to warm up, I raced up the escalators to the rather swish, second-floor ladies' toilets in order to change into my new jacket. As I slipped it on and once again admired its finely cut proportions in the mirror, a middle-aged, smartly dressed blonde suddenly appeared in my peripheral vision. She addressed my reflection rather than myself and demanded in hysterical patrician tones: 'Why don't you do something useful and make sure the toilets are furnished with toilet paper on a regular basis.'

I was struck by her use of the word 'furnished'. It seemed

such an incongruous word to best describe her access to something as functional as toilet paper. A smile began to form on my lips, which was cut short by her barked order: 'Well, don't just stand there, get me some.'

My immediate impulse was to fly at her and knock her stupid head into the wall and not stop till she was dead. But I didn't. Instead I looked at myself in my new piece of expensive finery and wondered how I could have been mistaken for the cleaner. Tears formed in my eyes and overflowed onto my hot cheeks. Not tears of rage but ones of bitterness and frustration. I wheeled around to face her and stared into her eyes: 'What the fuck do I have to do, eh?' I shouted.

At first she looked at me uncomprehendingly. Then she looked nervously about her, suddenly aware of her potentially dangerous situation. She was alone with a black woman who was acting unpredictably. Her expertly made-up eyes refocused on me, skimming down my body, looking at me closely. A flicker of doubt stole across her face. A light sheen of sweat broke out on her smooth, botoxed brow. She suddenly realized her mistake. A burst of adrenalin spurred me on. I wanted to teach this bitch a lesson that she would never forget. 'Do you think I'm here to clean the toilets?'

The woman began to stutter a makeshift apology: 'I'm sorry, I just thought…'

'You just thought what? Eh? What did you think? Ah, there's a black face, must be the cleaner? Well fuck you, fuck you, fuck you.'

With every 'fuck you', I became a little louder, but also a little less powerful, until I ran out of my righteous energy and just sobbed unashamedly. The woman's jaw dropped in astonishment. Her heavily rouged mouth exposed tiny, unnaturally white, pointed incisors. She resembled a vampire waiting to pounce. I grabbed my handbag and with as much dignity as I could muster, stumbled towards the exit.

'Here, don't forget your carrier bag,' she called after me in a placatory manner, brandishing the white Prada bag that had contained my new jacket.

'You fucking keep it,' I shouted back and fled down the escalators, through the shop and out into the afternoon bustle of Oxford Street, only to find a thunderstorm raging. I ran in the direction of St Christopher's Place, seeking a coffee shop that I hadn't been in for years, but remembered fondly from the early '80s. Mercifully it was still there and even better, empty. The rain on my face mingled with my tears. My jacket was soaked. I was a mess.

Once ensconced in the back of the shop, with an ashtray, a Marlboro Light and a cappuccino, I retraced the events of the toilet battle royal. Why is it that after such a contretemps, it is so easy to think of innumerable one-liners and pithy retorts? I seethed with anger. My body felt hot and stifled. I unbuttoned my new jacket and draped it over the back of my chair to dry. It had seriously lost its shine since I had been mistaken for a janitor while wearing it! So much for Prada, I thought. Yet again, I realized that some white people in Britain still saw blacks as an amorphous mass of sub-humanity simply there to serve. If we were not doing that, then the only other times we were noticed was on the nightly news, usually rioting, raping, murdering, or best of all, conveniently starving to death or dying of Aids somewhere in Africa. Ralph Waldo Ellison had his finger on racist society's pulse when he wrote the classic novel *The Invisible Man*. But that was in 1952. This was 1996.

A strange malaise overcame me as I chain-smoked my way through the next hour and a half. It was as if my identity had been shattered into tiny pieces. I had no idea how I was going to piece my psyche's tenuous mosaic together again. How could a chance encounter with a stranger bring me so low? Perhaps I should have stayed calm and pointed out her mistake, then accompanied her to find the person who was responsible for the cleanliness of the toilets? Of course that's what I should have done, but my tenuous sense of self was not equipped with the necessary social skills to bring off such a feat after such a damning blow. I had never been taught those skills. Who could have taught me them? Certainly my adoptive parents would have been hard-pressed to provide me with such an education. Their only answer to my regular identity crises as a child had been to raise me like a little white girl, in the vain hope that nobody would ever notice the raging bull elephant in the room – my skin colour. Some chance!

A shaft of late-afternoon sunlight cut through the gloomy aftermath of the storm and temporarily lit up my table. Simultaneously, a small voice in my head whispered: 'You know what you have to do? Find your birth parents.' Then my epiphany was gone.

I noticed that the owner of the café, an avuncular Italian gentleman, who had cast concerned looks in my direction ever since my arrival, had finished bringing in the chairs and tables that had been on the pavement outside the café. He looked as though he was eager to close for the afternoon. I looked at my watch. It was 5.30 p.m. Where had the afternoon gone? I wiped my tear-stained cheeks with a red-checked paper napkin, put on my jacket, which had fortunately dried, and took my bill to the counter.

'It will be all right,' he said quietly, as he returned my change. His deep brown Mediterranean eyes twinkled.

I smiled back at him. 'Yes, I think it will be from now on.'

'Nice jacket,' he said. 'Italian-made stuff always is.'

313

FOURTEEN

MISSION IMPOSSIBLE

I abandoned all thoughts about going to the party after such an emotional day. I just wanted to get home as quickly as possible. To avoid the tube's early evening crush, I walked to Euston station. I kept looking at passing black, white, brown, yellow and all-shades-in-between faces, thinking that any one of them might be a relative. The anonymity of swimming along Tottenham Court Road with this tide of humanity made me feel even more determined to seek out the shores of my real origins. I was still way out of my depth, but at least I wasn't drowning any more.

I placed a hasty call to Terry asking him to pick me up at Coventry station in an hour or so. When he expressed concern about my earlier than expected return, I just said, somewhat evasively, 'There's been a change of plan.' Fortunately the train disappeared into a tunnel, cutting off any further communication. He didn't call back. Next I placed a call to my songwriting partner, Selecter bassist and all-round musical linchpin Nick Welsh, telling him that he would have to go to the party on his own. He didn't seem particularly bothered that I was pulling out. I offered no explanation.

Neol Davies and I had found that some wounds are too difficult to heal and had gone our separate ways in 1993. I'd carried on with The Selecter and since Neol's departure we

Neol Davies and me in Selecter, 1993

had released one album, the ironically titled *Happy Album*. It had met with deafening silence from the music industry.

I had co-written the songs for the album with Nick, who was a talented enough bloke, but suffice to say, we did not share the same worldview. He often said in jest, but nonetheless somewhat accusingly: 'You only write about dead black people.'

I found that statement slightly offensive coming from a chubby, thirty-something white bloke, who at that time primarily enjoyed acting like an overgrown school bully, but I let it go because in some ways it was valid criticism. Assuming the maxim that you should always write songs with your audience in mind and given the unnerving fact that 75 per cent of our current audience were chubby white blokes, then perhaps I should have let him write the lyrics. But I still felt passionately about the ethos of 2-Tone and I wanted that reflected in my lyrics. It wasn't my fault that many of the blacks that had helped to shape the history that I wanted to write about had ended up dead.

I had lost count of how many tours we had done since our reunion in 1991. Each year we covered vast swathes of Europe and North America in uncomfortable vans, because the cheap flight, no-frills aerial bonanzas that we enjoy these days hadn't yet begun. Musicians came and went. None of the guitarists were as good as Neol Davies. Indeed, some were seriously maladjusted, unimaginative, sad people. Gaps Hendrickson joined up for a couple of years. It was good to share vocal duties again. But after a furiously heated argument with our Indian tour manager, Vin Gadher, in a German service station restaurant, he was politely asked to leave.

Artistically I felt unfulfilled, but at heart I was a pragmatist about the band. It worked regularly and still seemed to be in demand in most territories, which meant everybody earned

Left to right: Nick Welsh, me, Perry Melius and Neol Davies at The Mean Fiddler, 1992

money, even if the returns had begun to dwindle of late. So why change a winning formula?

There was even a bunch of ska bands doing big business in the USA, who had developed their own brand of super-charged, horn section-heavy ska that was collectively named 'Third Wave'. These energetic young bucks reclassified 2-Tone music as 'Second Wave', and referred to us as 'oldsters'. What goes around comes around; this was exactly how we had treated artists like Prince Buster, the Skatalites and Toots & the Maytals when we were young.

The songs I wrote these days highlighted the downtrodden, the forgotten, the persecuted – those whom people didn't want to look at. The ska audience remained largely unimpressed with my efforts, preferring gigs to be a beer-soaked, nostalgic knees-up showcasing the old hits. The traditional skinheads had largely disappeared back into the woodwork.

If I needed a change of routine or gigs were thin on the ground in the winter season, I accepted an acting job. While not on the road, the other members of the band pursued their own ventures, in which I had little interest. They feigned interest in my theatrical projects, but hardly ever came to any opening nights.

The only time one of them did come to see me in performance was a total disaster. I was acting in a one-woman play, *Let Them Call It Jazz*, an adaptation of a Jean Rhys short story, at the Drill Hall in London. Nick expressed an interest in attending. I arranged a ticket for a Saturday night performance because I wanted him to see it in front of a full audience.

During a harrowing scene in which my character lengthily contemplated suicide, he noisily left his seat in the back row, stumbled down some steps to the front of the stage, walked across it and out the door. Not content with ruining the scene, he came back five minutes later, sniffing loudly, and clambered back up to his seat. As he sat down, his jean shorts, which were always under quite a lot of tension due to his expansive girth, ripped at the crotch. Unfortunately, he had 'gone commando' that night and part of his testicles fell out. The whole audience attempted to stifle their giggles without success. His antics even woke up Vanessa Redgrave, who had been snoozing in the back row. Needless to say, I soldiered on.

Meanwhile my long-suffering husband had put up with my peripatetic lifestyle for longer than he could possibly have expected. We did our best to maintain a home life and, despite sometimes lengthy separations, largely succeeded. But after Terry took early retirement from his job due to ill health in 1991 he preferred me to stay closer to home. We were not a gregarious couple. Our friends could be counted on the fingers of one hand. The neighbours said hello, sometimes commenting on an article about me in the local or national press, or they might have chanced on one of the radio programmes that I intermittently fetched up on, but they rarely invited us into their homes for parties or barbecues.

Perhaps they were uncomfortable with us because we didn't have children. Parents liked to talk about their offspring when the usual topics of conversation about jobs, petrol prices and mortgage repayments had been exhausted. It was difficult to make our pet dog sound that interesting.

The notion of family didn't mean very much to either of us. We always knew that we didn't want children, even from the early days of our relationship. We were both illegitimate, and each of us happily regarded being a bastard as a badge of honour. But lately I noticed that my badge had lost its shine. I was getting older and if I was ever going to find out my

Publicity still from *Let Them Call It Jazz*, 1991

origins, then I had better do so soon. Or perhaps it was just a fact of life that everybody asked the rather dumb question: 'Who am I?' at some point during their sojourn on this blue planet. Almost as much of a cliché as that other three-word favourite, 'I love you'. Perhaps both those phrases might benefit from a question mark after them, I mused as the train pulled into Coventry station.

Terry was dutifully waiting to pick me up in the car. It didn't feel right to launch into the somewhat bizarre story of my day, so I just told him that the party had been cancelled at the last minute. He admired the new jacket and I absent-mindedly listened to his exploits.

We had arrived home from a ten-day holiday in Egypt only a few days earlier, so after dinner Terry spent the evening catching up with correspondence and bill paying. He complained that he felt more tired after a supposedly relaxing holiday than before he went. He always said this after every holiday. Vacations were not his forte. I knew that, but I sadistically persisted in arranging them.

We rarely argued these days, except on holiday when it was the glue that held us together. It made holidays exhausting. We could row about anything: where to eat, what to do, where to go, how to get there, what to drink, you name it, we could argue about it, whereas at home, none of those things even merited much more than a momentary discussion.

However, this latest holiday had disappointed me on a much more profound level. It had been my first trip to the African continent. A mixed-race friend had told me many years earlier that there was an old myth that said when a black person who had been estranged from their homeland took their first steps on African soil, they would hear a bell sound deep in their soul. A particularly fanciful notion, I had thought at the time. I often suspected that he had seen too many episodes of *Roots* for his own good, but the idea must have stuck in my mind, because as I had taken my first step onto the hot tarmac at Cairo airport I had readied myself for a Big Ben moment. Nothing happened! I experienced instant disappointment, which persisted for the rest of the trip, which no amount of pyramids, sphinxes or Valleys of Kings and Queens could eradicate. Africa had not welcomed my sorry black arse home, even though Nigerian blood, courtesy of my father, ran through my veins.

Had today's epiphany been influenced by my less-than-fulfilling African experience? Maybe the obnoxious behaviour of the woman in Selfridges had only been the spark that lit the fuse that had been laid in Egypt. If I wanted to find my father and explore my African heritage, then I would have to find my mother first.

I was tired after such a harrowing day and decided to go to bed early. I hoped that some much-needed sleep would 'knit up my ravelled sleeve of care'. That night I had a dream. I was alone in a small rowing boat, seemingly adrift in the fog. All around I could hear the giant tuba honks of large ships, some sounding perilously close. But I didn't feel afraid, because in the distance I could hear the sound of a huge bell. I steered towards it, knowing that even though I was in dangerous uncharted waters, the bell would keep me safe.

I awoke to a bright sunny day. It was 7:30 a.m. In those first bleary moments of wakefulness, Terry's snoring momentarily merged with the ships' giant tuba honks in my dream. A swift poke in the ribs with my right elbow dispatched the offending snorer a little further across the bed, allowing the dog to wriggle into the gap between us, his favourite place in the early morning.

I lay in bed for a while thinking about the dream. Perhaps it was prophetic? All sorts of whimsical interpretations crowded my waking thoughts. Perhaps Africa was calling me home after all? Who knew? One thing I did know, today I was going to start searching for my mother.

While Terry and I chatted about our individual plans for the day over breakfast, I was acutely aware of the fact that I hadn't told him anything about my latest decision. I usually shared most things, but for now this was out of bounds.

Terry had searched for his real father once, without success. Would I suffer the same ignominy? Perhaps we were both safer not knowing our origins? That way, our own beginnings were a clean slate, unsullied by the indiscretions and fleeting dalliances of profligate parents. More importantly, it made us the same, united by the damage that had been done to us in our earlier lives. Maybe that delicate balance would be upset if I suddenly turned up with a full set of real parents who might come crashing into our carefully constructed lives with all kinds of preconceptions and needs and wants? Would we, as a couple, be strong enough to stave off such a concerted onslaught?

We had got used to the fact that the remnants of our respective families largely left us alone. We liked it like that. Or I had done, until recently. Perhaps it was time to embrace the notion of a 'real family', instead of the 'cuckoo's nest' in which I'd been reared?

As I understood it, I began life as a 'British' egg, impregnated by a 'Nigerian' sperm in 1953. Put like this, one wonders whether the egg and the sperm were flying the national colours at the time. I imagined the tiny sperm with a green bulbous head and white wiggly tail, racing up the birth canal ahead of the pack, vigorously wriggling itself into a red, white and blue egg. Once inside, it spent the next nine months working against the clock, to successfully scramble the yolk into me. I imagined myself as a freshly arrived newborn waving a black and white chequered flag backwards and forwards, signifying the end of this human Grand Prix, with a new mixed race baby. The beginning of the end for white racial purity in post-war Britain!

In today's 'multicultural' society, the sight of a brown baby swinging on a woman's hip is almost seen as trendy. In 1953 such obvious evidence of miscegenation was viewed with fear and suspicion but, just as night follows day, it's impossible to stop people fucking, particularly when the motherland's gene pool was expanding with such interesting and colourful new arrivals from the colonies.

Great Britain enjoyed two of the greatest achievements in world history in 1953: the discovery of the structure of DNA by Crick and Watson, who fearlessly charted organic life in the micro-world of biochemistry, and the discovery by Sir Edmund Hillary and Sherpa Tensing of what it felt like to majestically stand on top of the macro world. These kinds of triumphs are the mark of a civilised society, but at that time, most rented accommodation in London bore the very uncivilised sign: 'No Irish, no dogs, no blacks'.

Please note that even dogs were further up the pecking order than blacks!

Even in the US blacks had only just won the right to sit at lunch counters in Washington DC by a ruling of the Supreme Court. South of the Mason-Dixon line, such a right was unheard of and even talking about such rights, if you were black, could get you strung high in a tree.

It was a world where racism was explicit. There was no hidden agenda, no code words to enable white folk to discriminate without being caught out. No, you could come right out and say it, as did most graffiti on redbrick walls: 'Wogs Out'.

My birth mother had been only sixteen when she got

pregnant, so given the circumstances it was a wonder that I was born at all. I could have ended up being flushed down the toilet after a botched back-street abortion. My guess was that when her pregnancy could no longer be concealed, she was removed from Dagenham's cockney prying eyes to an unmarried mother's home (ingenuously called 'Mother and Baby Homes' back then). I had read somewhere that young mothers in such places were discouraged from breastfeeding, in case they formed an attachment to their babies.

I had only one vital clue to my origin: the empty, khaki-coloured, registered envelope that I had found when I was eight years old, bearing my real mother's name, Eileen Magnus, and an address in Dagenham, Essex.

After my adoptive mother Ivy died in 1988 in Romford's general hospital, I rushed back to her house and riffled through the same drawer as I had when a child. Sure enough the envelope was in exactly the same place, wrapped inside the court papers dealing with my adoption. The box of little bullets that had so puzzled my younger self were still there too, except I now knew that they were vaginal pessaries!

Such an action, so soon after her demise, may sound rather callous, as if I did not care about Ivy's passing, but the truth is I was moved more than I can say when I saw her lying freshly dead in her hospital bed. Her hand was still warm when I touched it, but she had gone. One small blue eye was still half open in the palsied side of her face, as if she wanted one last glimpse of her daughter. 'I know what you will do now,' she seemed to say accusingly.

And she was right, and although I hurried to the drawer, I wouldn't act on what I found there immediately; not, in fact, for another eight years. I couldn't let go of Ivy's memory that quickly in favour of finding a replacement mother, not after all the years we had spent together. But I'd known I needed the last vestiges of my former self that were still in her possession. I needed them badly, because I knew my four adoptive brothers would soon be riffling through her personal effects, hoping that there might be something worth having. I had to get there before they did, just in case the envelope got thrown out with the rubbish. More importantly, I couldn't be sure whether I had remembered the name and address correctly, though I should have known that it had been emblazoned on my memory since the first time I saw it.

Among her possessions I also found two huge scrapbooks containing a wealth of press cuttings about me that she had painstakingly kept over the years. Reviews good or bad were dated and meticulously catalogued in order. When I mentioned this extraordinary find to my brother Tony, he said that she carted these scrapbooks about in a large plastic carrier bag to any weddings, funerals and christenings that she was invited to. She delightedly displayed their contents to those unfortunate enough to be waylaid at such events. I'd had no idea that she had been so proud of me in the last decade of her life. She hadn't responded particularly favourably when she'd seen the early photos of The Selecter that I showed her. Too many black men, I supposed. Rather tellingly, she had only kept individual photos of myself from that period. The memory of Janet Sparks had stayed with her until the end.

Eight years later the buff-coloured envelope that I had retrieved the day she died now lay on my kitchen table, still reluctant to offer up any more secrets. It occurred to me that my best plan of action was to compile a list of all the people named Magnus who lived in the Dagenham area and beyond. But how was I going to do this without travelling to Essex? Go to the City Library.

Coventry Library and I go back a long way. Back in 1979 the building that now housed the local library had been one of the liveliest city-centre venues. Unfortunately it was named Tiffany's, possibly suggesting that it was frequented with permed young ladies wearing fur coats, white stilettos and matching handbags, the latter items artfully placed on the floor for the sole purpose of being danced around. Tiffany's was the only decent-sized dance hall in Coventry apart from the main halls at the Lanchester Poly and Warwick University. Back then the entrance had been via a huge glass tower and it had boasted a revolving stage.

It is a strange experience to stand in a place that is now carpeted, hushed and filled with swotting students, or the elderly sheltering from the cold, knowing I once bounded around the stage dressed like a rude boy, indulging in mock fights, creating loud music in a tightly packed hall filled to the sweaty rafters with screaming punters.

I climbed up the four flights of stairs to reception, walked past the issues and returns counter and made my way towards the reference shelves. I was very pleased to discover a well-stocked shelf of regional telephone directories covering the whole of Great Britain. Excitedly, I pulled down the directory for South-East London and thumbed through the pages until I found the entries for the name Magnus. My hands shook, making it difficult to read the words on the page. My eyes nervously skimmed over names and numbers until I found what I was looking for. There were so many entries for the name Magnus, but none magically read E. Magnus. Worse still, it was a reference book, so I couldn't take it out of the library. I contemplated popping it in my bag and then bringing it back at a later date, but decided that was too risky and knowing my luck, I would get caught. So I just sat there with an A4 pad and laboriously copied out all fifty-three of them, one by one. I considered it fortunate that her surname was not Smith.

It was lunchtime when I got home. I grabbed a coffee and a cheese sandwich and sat down at the kitchen table where Terry was noisily slurping vegetable soup, eyed by our attentive dog, who always got to lick the bowl when he finished. I put the A4 pad on the table and began writing out a short text for what I might say to any of these anonymous Magnus people when I called them. I wanted to put them at their ease immediately, because an unsolicited nuisance caller could be mistaken for a telesalesperson.

'You're very quiet today,' Terry murmured. 'What's that you've got there?'

'Oh, nothing,' I replied.

'Looks like a lot of nothing.'

'Well...' I trailed off, suddenly unable to continue without bursting into tears. I couldn't understand why I was feeling so emotional.

'Are you okay?'

'No, not really.' The silence hung heavily between us. I felt overwhelmed by the enormity of the task that lay ahead. 'I've decided to find my real mother,' I blurted out.

Terry put his spoon down on the table. The dog looked concerned. 'How are you going to do that?'

I could tell from the guarded look on his face that my news was a shock. 'I'm going to ring everybody named Magnus on this list and see if anybody knows her.'

It all seemed so obvious when I spoke the words out loud. Of course, somebody would know her or at the very least have heard of her. My emotional turmoil abated.

'Hope you know what you're letting yourself in for. You're

on your own for this one.' He got up from his chair, leaving the bowl of vegetable soup half-empty, and went out into the back garden. The dog looked even more concerned.

Terry's response came as no real surprise. There was no malice intended. After all, he must have experienced the same emotional rollercoaster when he had unsuccessfully looked for his father. I knew that he didn't want to see me disappointed in the same way.

I felt relief. I had shared the secret. Ever since I had decided to embark on the journey to find my mother, I felt like a character in the famous '60s espionage thriller, *Mission: Impossible*. I kept hearing the voice on the tape from the show's opening sequence permanently on repeat: 'Your mission, should you decide to accept it...'

I knew that, just like the cast in the TV series, I would have to use guile, manipulation and deception to get the result I desired. What better way to get started than perfecting my cold-calling technique on fifty-three strangers? I only hoped that I wouldn't self-destruct in five seconds like the taped voice.

FIFTEEN

THE MAGNUS EFFECT

I chose the box-room bedroom of the house to carry on my covert operation. Terry and I had converted it into an office space, complete with an office chair, large oak desk, computer, phone and fax. It was ideal for my current needs.

I decided to trust my instincts regarding what I might say if anybody answered. I told myself that it couldn't be that much different from improvisational techniques that I'd used in acting classes. Best thing to do was dive straight in. I should have dialled the first number on my list, A. Magnus, but I was so eager that I scanned down the list until I found the only entry that read E. Magnus. Logically, it seemed a no-brainer to start with this name. Somebody picked up after about ten rings. A female voice answered: 'If that's you, Stacey, get fucking lost. You know not to ring at this time.'

Completely thrown by the greeting, I blurted out: 'Oh, I'm not Stacey, I'm Pauline. Sorry. Is that Mrs Magnus?'

'Yeah, what about it?' she suspiciously replied.

I blundered on: 'Well, you don't know me, but I'm trying to look for somebody named Eileen Magnus. She lived in Dagenham about forty years ago, but might have moved by now, but since you share the same surname, I wondered if you might know somebody with that name?'

Apart from the sound of heavy breathing, there was silence at the other end of the line, but just as I was about to continue, I heard a loud male voice, possibly emanating from another room in the woman's house, shouting: 'You gonna watch this crap or what?'

This question seemed to zap the woman into life and she barked at me in a cockney accent: 'You selling or somefink? 'Cos if you are then you can piss right off.'

'No, nothing like that. I'm looking for a relative,' I hastily replied, not wishing to antagonise her any more than I obviously had already.

'Well, why didn't you say so in the first place. Can you ring me back in five minutes, 'cos I'm watching *Home and Away* and it's a good one today.'

I couldn't imagine *Home and Away* ever being good on any day, but I said I would and put the phone down.

So much for those acting lessons! My confidence was shattered. I hadn't been prepared for such a hostile exchange. Why on earth I thought that everybody would be helpful, I cannot imagine. I could see that I was in for a very long haul indeed.

Five minutes later, I redialled the number as asked and the man, whose voice I had heard earlier, answered. 'Are you the person who rang just now?'

'Yes,' I answered.

'Well, she don't know no one called Aileen, all right?'

'It was Eileen actually.' But he'd put the phone down already. I didn't dare ring again.

'One down, fifty-two to go,' I murmured to nobody in particular. I crossed E. Magnus off the list.

It took me the rest of the afternoon and early evening to call everybody on the list. Quite a lot were no answer. I left messages if they had an answering machine, but I didn't expect anybody would call back.

Cold-calling is an illuminating way of eavesdropping on other peoples' lives. Some of the conversations were heart-wrenching, in that I suspected that the elderly lady or gentleman on the other end of the phone really just wanted to reminisce about the old days with somebody who might be interested in them. They really didn't care much who I was. I didn't have the heart to cut them off as soon as they said that they had never heard of anyone called Eileen Magnus. It never ceased to amaze me how much information some people will give up to an entire stranger just to have a bit of conversation and not feel so lonely within their four-wall prisons.

Several people were so eager to be of use that they offered to ring around their other relatives and see if they knew anybody of that name. I would leave them my number and they would promise to ring back if they found out any further information, but I never heard from any of them again.

I concluded from such a generally positive response that people love to be helpful if they can and, more importantly, they adore a mystery, particularly if they can be part of the solution.

One man I spoke to in the East End of London, H. Magnus, asked me if I knew that the name Magnus was Jewish. He thought that maybe my mother might belong to a family of bookmakers in the East End. He said that this extended Stepney family branch was very large, so there was a good chance one of them might know her. Apart from that nugget of information, he could throw no more light on the whereabouts of Eileen Magnus.

It had never occurred to me that Magnus was a Jewish name. I had always thought of Magnus Magnusson when considering the origins of the name. I thought perhaps my mother was Scottish, Irish or perhaps even Norwegian in origin, but not Jewish.

My adoptive mother, Ivy, had always been very suspicious of Jews. Mind you, she was impartial. She had been suspicious of any foreigner.

When I was a very young child, my adoptive dad had been a coalman. Part of his delivery route was in Gants Hill and Redbridge, which had a sizeable Jewish population in those days. My mother would always complain to anybody who would listen that Jewish families never paid their bills. Often they would offer my father things in lieu of payment, like the faded crimson velvet curtains complete with gold braid-edged pelmets that adorned the bay window in our living room. They really had seen better days, and were discoloured where the folds overlapped, but my dad liked them. Ivy was never convinced, although she hung them as requested. Dad thought they looked classy. They did look as though they had been very expensive once upon a time.

On another occasion, he arrived home carrying a huge doll's house whose roof had collapsed. I loved it on sight. It even had some of the furniture rattling around inside the four rooms. He never did fix the roof as promised. Another time he brought home a beautiful, carved wooden rocking horse. When I look back I think most of my toys originated in the homes of Jewish boys and girls. Ivy made it plain to my dad that she thought he should be tougher and demand proper payment instead of other people's cast-offs. It probably never occurred to her that maybe they didn't have enough money to pay for their coal, particularly if they were Jewish émigrés from post-war Europe. I was too young to offer an opinion on the matter. I just loved to get the 'presents' that my dad brought home.

Her dislike of Jews was even more inexplicable when

coupled with the fact that our neighbours on the opposite side to the Green family were Jewish. Dr Biro ran a surgery next door to us and they lived in the house adjoining. Rumour had it that he and his wife were Jewish émigrés from the continent.

Anybody else who lived next door to a doctor's surgery would have considered themselves very lucky, particularly when illness struck, but not Ivy. She never registered with Dr Biro. Oh no, she caught a bus to her favourite Scottish doctor's surgery over three miles away, even if she was half dead with the flu.

Mrs Biro spent much of her day peering through the net curtains of her sitting-room window, noting the comings and goings of her neighbours. Every year, usually on Christmas Eve, she would beckon to me from her open front door if she saw me passing the house. Dutifully I hurried up her sloping garden path.

She was a tiny, wizened woman, old beyond her years, but always immaculately made-up and stylishly dressed. I was in awe of her. She sported the same fancily winged, horn-rimmed glasses as Marjorie Proops, the famous gossip columnist, which gave her leathery face an owlish appearance.

I stood on her doorstep, uncomfortably smiling as she stroked my cheeks with her arthritic hands, softly murmuring, '*Mein Liebchen, mein Liebchen.*'

She always looked as though she might burst into tears at any moment. Then she would give me a small, hand-made, drawstring gingham bag, full of tiny iced gingerbread cookies to take home. '*Für Mutti,*' she said and shut the door.

My mother invariably turned her nose up at these annual goodies. 'I'm not eating that foreign muck.'

But I loved them. They tasted so much more exotic than

Ivy's favourite custard cream biscuits. Secretly I wished I could be Jewish.

A year after I had left home, Ivy told me that Mr and Mrs Biro had been found dead together in their bed. They had committed suicide. Mrs Biro had an incurable disease and her husband, unable to live without her, decided to help her die and then kill himself. They must have been very old by this time and I found myself feeling inexplicably sad about this, despite the fact that I didn't really know either of them. Somebody told me much later that both of them had had their families wiped out in the concentration camp at Auschwitz. They had managed to escape, but Mrs Biro had never recovered from the trauma of the Second World War.

Would my mother be like the tiny tragic figure of Mrs Biro? Was she waiting for me somewhere with a tiny bag of cookies? The ringing of an insistent phone broke my romantic reverie. I hastily picked up the receiver.

'Hello. Did you leave a message asking about an Eileen Magnus?' a woman asked.

Yes I had, I'd left many messages, all with my phone number in case they wanted to get back to me. Nobody had, yet.

'Well, I might know somebody who knows her.'

Thank goodness I was sitting down because my knees had turned to jelly. Could it really have taken only one afternoon to find her? I couldn't believe my luck. I forced myself to stay calm and make light conversation.

'Whereabouts do you live?' I asked as casually as I could.

'South Ockendon,' she said. 'I know someone who's got an Eileen Magnus in his family. Her dad used to live in Dagenham years ago. Think she's a cousin. I'll have to wait until he gets in from work to be sure.'

'Really,' I said, trying hard not to regurgitate my cheese

sandwich. My stomach was flip-flopping as if it was on a fairground ride.

'Can you ring back later?' she continued.

'Of course,' I said politely. 'What's the number?'

She gave it to me and I scanned my list looking for an accompanying address. I discovered that she was phoning from a caravan park. I asked her if the address was correct.

'Oh yes, we live on a caravan site, love, there's only one phone in the caretaker's office. The caretaker's my husband. I pop in now and again just to check for messages. Ring about nine. He should be back by then. He's got a scrap metal business down Tilbury way and he gets busy in the evenings. If it's the woman I'm thinking of, I think she lives on a caravan site over Thurrock way. All right, love, talk to you later.'

Then she was gone. I hadn't even had a chance to ask her name. I looked at my watch. It was 8 p.m. Where had the day gone?

Terry knocked on the door and asked me if I wanted some food. I'd completely forgotten about eating. He offered to make baked beans on toast, which I gratefully accepted. All I could think about was how I was going to survive for the next hour without self-destructing.

I mentioned what had happened with the South Ockendon connection over the makeshift dinner. He looked up from his plate and peered over the top of his glasses.

'You do know what you might be letting yourself in for, don't you?' he said gravely. 'You don't know who she might be associated with. Living in a caravan park hardly sounds as though she's made much of a life for herself. Be careful.'

I had to confess that I hadn't looked at this new discovery in quite the same way. I had happily glossed over the bits of information that would ordinarily make me sit up and take notice. So what if she lived in a caravan park? She was still my mother. But I didn't dare utter those words, because I could see where he was coming from.

I slipped back upstairs at the earliest opportunity to collect my thoughts before ringing back at nine o'clock. At the appointed hour I dialled the number. It rang for five minutes. Nobody picked up. I continued ringing every fifteen minutes, but all to no avail.

My mind reeled with possibilities. South Ockendon, Tilbury, Grays, Thurrock. I remembered those place names from the destination signs on the red London buses that had passed through Romford town centre. In our family these places had been seen as East London's badlands. It was generally accepted among my adoptive brothers that a different breed of 'cowboy' lived there. Maybe the fact that somebody was looking for Eileen Magnus had sparked suspicion in her family. They might have put two and two together and now wished to remain undiscovered. What could I do? Nothing, just keep phoning.

I had accepted that the probability of this family being my long-lost relatives was fairly high. I imagined a family falling on hard times, and gradually sinking, through no fault of their own, other than poverty, from a council estate in Dagenham to a cold, damp caravan park in the Essex hinterland. I envisaged a Dickensian scene with them all huddled around a campfire late at night, discussing whether they knew an Eileen Magnus or not.

I began to wonder whether I was making a mistake. Perhaps ignorance was bliss. What manner of people were they? Perhaps they were gypsies or travellers. Then I chastised myself. Whoever they were, they were my most helpful lead so far and indeed had said that they would ask around for me.

I decided that I would have to take what came. There was no pick-and-mixing to be done when tracing relatives.

I knew when I started that it was unlikely that I was a rich person's child. Such people did not live in Dagenham. But at the back of my mind was a nagging voice saying: 'But there is poor and poor.'

Suddenly it dawned upon me that my future relationship with my mother, if I was to find her, might come with various responsibilities. What if I found my mother in a run-down, leaky caravan with no money? What if she was sick or incurably ill? Would I be callous enough to find her, not like what I saw, and then just walk away? I didn't know the answers to these questions. What had started out as a simple premise – find your mother – had become a complicated web of thoughts and feelings. I'd only been searching for half a day. What would I feel like if it went on for months?

At 10.30 p.m. somebody picked up. 'Hello, I don't know if you remember me, but I rang earlier looking for somebody named…'

I didn't get a chance to finish. The woman I spoke to before answered. 'Oh, hello, love. I had a word with him and his cousin Ellen's dad lived in Ilford, not Dagenham. Sorry.'

'Ellen?' I repeated numbly.

'Yeah, it was Ellen you said, wasn't it?'

I didn't have the heart to tell her it was Eileen. I thanked her for her help and put the phone down.

Did anybody in the entire world ever really listen? Or did we just hear whatever fitted our agenda at the time? I was exhausted and none the wiser. I showered and slipped into bed. Terry was blissfully asleep, with the dog snuggled in beside him. I lay there dozing for a while, but by 2 a.m. I admitted defeat as far as sleep was concerned and got up.

I find that the best cure for insomnia is to watch an Open University lecture in the middle of the night. It never fails; better than any sleeping pill. That night's offering was a module on advanced engineering, delivered by a young mullet-haired professor. As the camera focus pulled back to show him in full view, I was amazed to see that he was wearing flares. He looked as though he was an extra in *The Sweeney* TV series.

I absent-mindedly stared at graphs, pie charts and crudely drawn diagrams showing the forces exerted upon a spinning ball in a given medium and the resultant whirlpool that it creates. My ears pricked up when he explained that this was due to the 'Magnus Effect'. For a moment I thought that I was so preoccupied with the name Magnus that I must have misheard, but then he repeated the phrase. He said that most footballers tried to bend the ball into the net when they took a corner. The curve of the ball was a direct result of the Magnus Effect.

I'm a great believer in serendipity, but this discovery was almost unbelievable. The chances of stumbling upon this particular programme in the middle of the night, when you had spent all day being a victim of the 'Magnus Effect', had to be a million to one.

It was as if a giant, unseen boot had already applied itself to my rear end with a force that was propelling me towards my ultimate goal. Perhaps I should just bend with the Magnus Effect, instead of trying to impose my own linear trajectory. I needed more information about my birth, my mother and her family. The best place to find that was in St Catherine's House in London, the national repository of records of births, marriages and deaths.

I switched off the TV, returned to bed and slept like a baby.

SIXTEEN

HOW DO YOU SOLVE A PROBLEM LIKE BELINDA?

The following day I returned to London. I needed tangible legal evidence that Belinda and Eileen Magnus existed. The only way to get that was by looking at birth records. If I knew my mother's date of birth, then I could look in the marriage records to see who she married. Maybe this would give me an insight into her world and possibly the greatest prize of all, a current address.

It was an early train full of commuters. Next to me a well-upholstered woman was wedged into her seat. An open Tupperware box rested on the table in front of her, from which she continually extracted biscuits, which she nibbled like a hamster for the entire journey. A well-dressed businessman sat opposite me, poring over documents, occasionally adjusting his tight white collar with the fingers of his right hand. Next to him was a short, blond man, probably in his mid-thirties, who had the tiny arms and hands of a thalidomide sufferer. I was acutely aware that he kept surreptitiously peering at me when he thought I wasn't looking. His bottle-bottomed glasses made his eyes look twice as big. To avoid his gaze I put on my sunglasses and pretended to be asleep.

At Watford Junction, the large woman beside me poked me in the arm and said, 'Excuse me,' in the high, fluting voice that people use to tell a child to do something.

She manoeuvred her bulk from the seat that she had shoehorned herself into, forcing me into the aisle. As I sat back down, the man opposite leaned forward and said loudly in a broad Yorkshire accent: 'Are you that singer that used to be in a ska band in the '80s? The Specials, right?'

'Um, it was The Selecter,' I replied, embarrassed by the fact that all the people in the immediate vicinity had turned to look at me.

'You're Pauline Black, aren't you? You were right good,' he announced in response. 'Do you remember me?'

Damn, he had uttered the four most deadly words known to an ex-pop star. I hardly remembered somebody I met yesterday, yet alone back in 1980. 'Uh, where did I meet you?' I said quickly, hoping for a clue.

'Bradford. You were playing St George's Hall. We chatted for ages. Remember?'

I gave the usual response in such situations, which went something like: 'I'm afraid I met an awful lot of people that year.' I could almost feel the disapproval of the nearby passengers who were all earwigging the conversation by this time, obviously attracted by the unusual spectacle of an extremely discomfited, very minor celebrity.

Like all fans, he had a story to tell about our encounter and proceeded to do so in such a loud voice that I reckoned they could have heard him in First Class. 'You said you were hungry and asked me to go and get you some fish and chips.'

'Wow,' I said, 'that was kind of you.'

'Yeah, but when I came back with them, you moaned 'cos there wasn't enough salt and vinegar on them.'

The words hung in the air like a cartoon conversation bubble. Passengers' eyes swivelled accusingly towards me, probably thinking: 'What a callous bitch.' Unable to give a good account of my behaviour, I laughed. I don't know why, because it was a completely inappropriate response.

'I'm really sorry about that,' I said, trying to contain my giggles. Mercifully the long horizontal sign that says 'Euston station 1 mile' came into view through the carriage window. 'Hope to see you at a gig soon,' I said as a parting shot. I got up and fled down the aisle towards the front of the train.

'I always liked Madness best out of you lot anyways,' he said to my departing back. Some people just have to have the last word!

I could see that it was a fine day outside the station concourse, so, not wanting any more embarrassing encounters, I decided to walk to my destination.

My brisk pace rapidly took me through leafy Russell Square past Talawa Theatre, where I had starred in a play, *From the Mississippi Delta*, a few years before. I had discovered the Holborn area on exploratory walks to fill the time between matinee and evening performances on Wednesdays and Saturdays.

The man's words kept echoing in my head as I walked along: 'You're Pauline Black, aren't you?' he'd said.

'Was I?' I wondered out loud, much to the consternation of passers-by.

Who was I? My first conscious identity had been as Pauline Vickers. Not happy with that, I'd changed my name by deed poll to Pauline Black, when I was twenty-six. Now I was about to reclaim my given birth name of Belinda Magnus. So who did that make me? Confused was the answer.

I had often passed St Catherine's House, but I had never ventured inside. It occupied a corner plot on the intersection of the Strand and Kingsway, an imposing, wedge-shaped building with a Portland stone and granite façade and large glass doors that swished gently as they were pushed open to the thickly carpeted inner sanctum. Once inside, it was like being hermetically sealed in a tomb.

It was only 10.30 a.m., but already the place was a hive of activity. The occupants were mostly silent, or talking in hushed voices. The soft rustle of pages turning and the solid clonking of books being put back on shelves were the only sounds that disturbed the overwhelming quiet.

These hushed enclaves are called 'search rooms'. Here is the proof that humanity exists in Great Britain and beyond since records began; the proof that we are not figments of each other's imaginations. All of life's main events are recorded here in large slab-like tomes, burgundy-coloured for births, green for marriages and black for deaths.

Each one represents a quarter of a year. They contain numbered codes that are useful when searching for lost relatives. Humanity reduced to letters of the alphabet and numbers. There is nothing to illustrate the accompanying information on each page: no happy photos of married couples or chubby-cheeked new arrivals on Earth. No photos of gravestones, mausoleums and follies, or worse, an unmarked pauper's grave. There was nothing to say whether these people were loved, hated, did bad or good things. In this giant repository of human misery and happiness, equality reigned supreme.

But in reality these millions of pages contained lots of dirty little secrets. I was one of them. In my opinion, adoption is legalised identity theft. How many children were trapped in this paper limbo-land, our real identities strangled at birth, reduced to a cross-referenced number, which enabled officialdom to bury our origins in an inaccessible grave, as if we didn't exist. Many of us would never be found, but perhaps I could liberate Belinda Magnus from this closeted hell. She had been patiently waiting for forty-two years.

Identity is the soul of a person. The adoption process is like having your soul written on a piece of paper and given to somebody else. Remember the *Simpsons* episode 'Bart Sells His Soul' in the seventh series? He writes 'Bart Simpson's Soul' on a piece of paper and sells it to Milhouse for $5, who then sells it on to the comic book guy for some comics. Afterwards Bart has a nightmare where he and his friends are each rowing their boats across a misty river. The difference between Bart and everybody else is that each of his friends has another self – or soul – who helps row the boat. But Milhouse has his other self and the soul of Bart rowing for him so he does not have to do any work at all. Bart is doomed to the much harder task of rowing with both oars. That's how it feels to be adopted. The business of life is much more hard work.

I lifted the heavy book for the last quarter of 1953 from the shelf. I turned the neatly handwritten pages until I found the tenth month and the twenty-third day. Three-quarters of the way down the page, neatly recorded in blue script, was evidence of my stolen soul, two words, Belinda Magnus. She existed again. I was almost whole.

The process of reclaiming my name seemed a natural rite of passage. I can't explain the sudden joy I felt. Thus invigorated, I decided to look for my mother's birth registration. I had been told that she was sixteen when she had me. I looked in all four quarterly books for the year 1937. I found her in the last quarter. With this positive identification and a birth date, I set about looking in every marriage registry from 1953 to 1996. I got to 1973 and gave up. Nothing. Perhaps she was dead? I stared at the black-bound death registers and decided that I didn't dare begin.

By now it was mid-afternoon. To satisfy my curiosity, I went back to marriages and looked through the registries until the present day. There was no record of a marriage for

Eileen Magnus. Therefore at the age of fifty-eight, she was either a spinster, dead or in another country.

It was almost five-thirty and the place was nearly empty. A security man was standing by the door intent on letting nobody else in and hoping those who were still present would soon leave. I reluctantly admitted defeat.

On my return journey to Coventry I mulled over my discoveries and decided they didn't really amount to much. Then I had an idea. The solution to my problem was so simple that I wondered why I hadn't thought of it before: 'Go to the last known address for Eileen Magnus.' Of course! Even if she no longer lived there, perhaps the present occupants or a neighbour might be able to shed some light on her whereabouts.

Then a glimmer of doubt crept into my plan. If I went to the address, there might be an embarrassing or even distressing incident if she still lived there. Or worse, there might be relatives who knew about me still living there. Perhaps they might not want me to know where she was? The idea was fraught with untold dangers.

I'd read many pamphlets, articles and internet pages about searches for birth parents that had gone horribly wrong. The reader was constantly warned that the estranged son or daughter in question had not followed the guidelines for a successful reunion. There was always an official address at the end of such articles exhorting any adoptees to get professional help before embarking upon their journey.

I knew these organisations had only the best intentions, but I decided that it was precisely the best intentions of such organisations that had got me into this predicament in the first place, so why should I trust them to get me out of it? Besides, I preferred a 'hands-on' approach. At least I could see what was happening on a daily basis. I didn't fancy sitting around, possibly for years, before a letter dropped through my letter box saying that my mother would like to meet me. If the mountain won't come to Mohammed, then Mohammed must go to the mountain!

I did have one trump card still up my sleeve – my adoptive brother Ken, himself adopted, lived in my mother's home town, Dagenham, with his second wife and young son Daniel. I would ask him to make some enquiries. He was white, middle-aged and had the gift of the gab: excellent credentials for the job. As our adoptive mother often said: 'He can charm the birds out of the trees when he puts his mind to it.' I resolved to phone him as soon as I got home.

My brother Ken was a kindred spirit. Even though he was twelve years older than me, the glue that united us was our adoptee status in the Vickers family. Unlike myself, nobody would have guessed that he had been adopted. He even looked similar to my other adoptive brothers. In his early thirties, he got wind of a rumour from our elderly aunt Lily that maybe our adoptive dad was actually his real dad. This bombshell caused a crater-like division in the family for a while, especially after he traced his real mother, Edna. It was quite natural that he wanted to find out if the rumour was true and since mothers know best, Edna was best placed to provide verification. All she would admit to was that she had had an affair with our adoptive dad, but she didn't think that he was Ken's father. Unresolved questions are worse than an unexpected answer. Our dad died soon after and took the secret, if indeed there was one, to his grave.

I was the first person that Ken told when he embarked on his search. He explicitly swore me to secrecy, because he knew that it would upset Ivy and the rest of the family. During an argument with Ivy about how she couldn't boss me about because she wasn't my real mother, I viciously blurted out that Ken had found his real mum and I intended to do the same. If I had felled her with a cricket bat I couldn't have inflicted a worse hurt. Ivy became hysterical and cried for a week. Our small family world fell apart. I was hit from all sides about how malicious, heartless and uncaring I had been to divulge Ken's secret to her. The fallout put my own search back about twenty years.

Ken and I didn't speak for a few years. He was naturally very angry with me. In time we had got past this obstacle, but things were never quite the same between us. I think I was simply acting out of jealousy. I envied him finding his real mother. My lack made me cruel.

When I phoned Ken later that evening, he would have been well within his rights to say: 'Go do it yourself. I did.' But he didn't. He offered to help in any way that he could. We chatted for a while about possible strategies, but eventually decided that it was best just to wait and see what happened when he knocked on the door. He agreed to go the following evening.

The night and the following day dragged on interminably. I told Terry what I had done. 'What did you involve Ken for? I would have gone round there for you.'

I felt guilty that I hadn't even thought to ask him. I didn't dare say that I thought Ken was better suited to the job, because he was friendly and chatty, whereas Terry could be very undiplomatic sometimes.

'I should have thought,' I said, as a placatory gesture. 'I didn't think you wanted to get involved.'

'Well, I don't really, but I promise to support you in whatever comes of this.'

'Let's just wait and see what happens,' I said lightly.

We settled down in front of the TV to watch a video of *The Shawshank Redemption* for the fourth time. Usually this movie was a guaranteed tearjerker, but I was so emotionally pent-up that I wasn't even crying by the end credits. What was happening to me?

I wasn't good at waiting, so by the time the phone rang the following evening at 7.30, I was almost chewing the wallpaper.

'Hello, little sister,' Ken said, sounding very pleased with himself. Immediately he cut to the chase. 'I think I've got a bit of a result for you.'

My heart lurched like a playful puppy.

'Eileen doesn't live there, if that's what you're thinking.'

'Oh.' My heart sank like a drowned puppy.

'But the present owner of the house had a look at his deeds and it was sold to him by a couple with a Polish name. Have you got a pencil?'

I grabbed a pen and paper.

'Are you ready? I'll spell the name, because I'm not sure how you say it correctly. B O B O L E C K I.'

'Did the house owner know who they were?' I asked tentatively, not sure what to make of this new piece of information.

'He thinks the husband was Polish and the wife was Eileen's older sister. Apparently he married one of three sisters. He can't remember her name, but he's pretty sure that it wasn't Eileen. But he thinks their parents were named Magnus.'

'Does he know where they went?' I asked urgently.

'Oh yes, I knew there was something else I had to tell you. He thinks they went to Surrey.'

Surrey? Hadn't expected that, certainly not after living in Dagenham.

'All right, love. I'll leave you to it then. My dinner's on the table. Good luck,' he said cheerily. He loved his food.

I thanked him profusely and hung up.

There was a lot to be said in praise of family, no matter how you came by them. That old adage, 'They stick by you through thick and thin,' is absolutely true in the case of the Vickers family. Would I find the same willingness in this new one? I didn't know the answer to that, but I hoped to very soon.

I sat by the phone, staring at the nine capital letters on the page. Was this the key to the mystery or just a red herring? Whatever it was, I needed to know how to pronounce the name, before I could do any more with it. So I phoned my friend David Box in London. His mother, Hanna, was a Polish Jew. She was sure to know how to say the name.

Fortunately he picked up after a couple of rings. I briefly explained my problem to him. He ran the name by his mum, who pronounced it exactly as it was written.

'Do you know where they live?' David asked.

'Not really. Somewhere in Surrey is as far as I've got.'

'Oh, that's in the London area. Let me have a look in the phone directory and I'll get back to you.' He hung up.

I sat with both hands on the receiver, willing the phone to ring. Surely, it wasn't going to be as easy as looking in a phone book to find my mum? After a few minutes the phone rang again. It was David.

'Hold on to your hat, Pauline,' he said jokingly. 'You're in luck. There's only one Bobolecki listed in the Surrey phone book. So there's a good chance that it might be them. Do you want the number and their address?'

Of course I want the bloody number and address, I wanted to scream!

'Good luck. Let me know how you get on.'

And there it was, probably the most important piece of information that I'd ever written down in my life – the telephone number of my prospective aunt in Surrey. I was almost home.

■ ■ ■

The upwardly mobile leap from Dagenham, Essex to Worcester Park, Surrey, was encouraging. It was more heart-warming than finding your mother on a run-down caravan site in South Ockendon.

It was too late to phone. Besides, I had to think of a plausible story before I went barging into a potential aunt and uncle's lives. How could I get them to deliver the answer to my 64,000-dollar question without giving away my real identity? I knew that I would have to resort to a temporary subterfuge to find out what I needed.

By the time I had finished phoning all the Magnuses in the East London phone book I had perfected a plausible white lie. Generally, lies are seldom foolproof, but the one I had constructed had held up under heavy scrutiny. I just hoped that it wouldn't receive too much analysis in the morning. For all I knew, any mention of the name Eileen Magnus might raise alarm bells.

I tried to imagine what my aunt would be like. It was likely that she was older than my mother, but I couldn't be sure. Did my aunt know about me? It was possible that she didn't, although unlikely. A big sister tended to notice if their little sister gave birth to a black baby in 1953. Therefore if somebody enquired about the whereabouts of Eileen, would she be alerted to the possibility that this baby had come looking for its mother? I hoped that so much time had passed that she had forgotten that I ever existed.

What if she was racist? People of her generation were often uncomfortable about black people. When I was the radiographer on night duty at Walsgrave Hospital in the mid-'70s, very occasionally I would have to X-ray an elderly patient who refused to be touched by a black person. I would patiently explain to them that I was the only person on duty in the middle of the night and that they would have to let me do it or wait until the morning. Some of them eventually saw sense, but some preferred to suffer their agonies until a white person turned up to do the job in the morning. I found these experiences totally humiliating.

Was my aunt like that? If she was Jewish, then I hoped that she would be like David's mother Hanna, who was one of the most enlightened women I knew.

The following morning I was unusually nervous. Breakfast was a meagre affair, just coffee and buttered toast. I kept pacing up and down the kitchen, practising what I was going to say on the phone, unable to sit still. Terry was unusually quiet when he came downstairs. I had shared the previous night's news with him. It had taken him by surprise. I could tell that he had thought that my enterprise would take weeks, not days. He murmured some vague words of encouragement, but we hadn't discussed the implications it had for us. He let the dog out into the garden before switching on the kettle to make his customary cup of tea. A pall of silence hung over the kitchen. We occupied the same space, but seemed to be living in two separate worlds. It was almost as if my mother had become a taboo subject between us. I couldn't pinpoint exactly when this had happened, but I knew that the train of events that was bringing me closer to my mother seemed to be pushing me further apart from my husband. I wasn't exactly sure why. Perhaps he was afraid that if I found this new family then I would have less need for him?

Something similar had happened when I joined The Selecter. The band was like a surrogate family, albeit a dysfunctional one. For two years it was all-possessing and all-encompassing. Outsiders, even spouses, were largely unwelcome in our tight little world. I did my best not to exclude Terry from decisions I made concerning my future, but sometimes I could see the hurt in his face when I ignored his advice and joined in the band consensus over an important issue. Our relationship suffered so much that we argued most of the time. It was only after the demise of the band that things settled down enough for us to make a fresh start. We were both younger then and more adaptable. I wasn't sure that we could take that kind of strain again.

'I'm taking the dog for a long walk,' he suddenly announced.

As soon as the front door shut, I went upstairs to the office and prepared to make the phone call that I hoped would change my life. I placed a notepad and pencil beside the phone so that I could note down all the twists and turns of the conversation. I was so nervous that I mis-dialled twice. It rang five times before it was picked up. The inside of my mouth was so dry that I could barely part my lips. I fought an overwhelming urge to hang up.

'Hello,' a crisp female voice said.

'Hello,' I answered. 'I wonder if you could help me?' was my opening gambit.

'That depends on what you're selling,' came the instant retort. She didn't sound friendly.

I suddenly realised that it was a big assumption on my part that this was actually my aunt. It could just as well have been her daughter, daughter-in-law or, indeed, my actual mother. I decided to tread carefully. 'I'm not selling.'

'That's what they all say,' she rejoined.

It wasn't going at all to plan. I decided to quit the small talk and get to the point as quickly as possible. 'My mother recently died and left a package in her will for an Eileen Magnus, but unfortunately no forwarding address. I'm trying to track down this person. Do you know her?'

If they bit down hard on this piece of information, which most people did when they heard the words 'package' and 'will' in the same sentence, they usually asked for this fictitious mother's name. Which she did.

351

'Ivy,' I said truthfully. 'I think my mother worked with Eileen when she was very young. I'm not sure where.'

'Did your mother work in London?'

'Yes,' I replied with as much confidence as I could muster. I just hoped that it wasn't a trick question. Then I moved in for the kill. 'I think it's mostly photos and old postcards in the parcel, but I'm not sure, there might be some jewellery.'

At the mention of something substantial, she dropped her guard and said, 'Oh, Eileen would love that. She loves anything to do with dear old Blighty. She doesn't live here any more, you know. She's been in Australia for years. Would you like her address?'

No wonder I couldn't find any evidence of her existence. She wasn't here. She was halfway around the world. Before I knew what was happening I was copying down the address of my mother in Australia and not only that, her telephone number too. After that there was very little to say. I thought it was better to cut short the call, just in case she asked any probing questions, like how had I made the connection between her and Eileen, given that they had different surnames.

I bade her goodbye and promised to let her know how I got on. After replacing the receiver, I did wonder whether she would phone my mum in Australia and discuss the strange conversation that we just had. Perhaps they would put two and two together and come up with me. I didn't think that I had said anything to arouse her suspicion, but it was impossible to know what conclusions she would make after mulling over such a strange conversation.

Australia. I hadn't expected that. Talk about a curve ball! I wondered how she had got there? I guessed that she had probably gone out there on the 'assisted passages' scheme, usually referred to as 'the ten-pound pom'. She had certainly put some distance between us.

My adoptive parents had once considered emigrating when it was all the rage in the '60s. They knew a family, the Hemmingses, who decided to join the long queue of ten-pound Poms. Mr Hemmings had been my dad's drinking buddy, a work-shy loudmouth, who drank too much and made too many children. Mrs Hemmings had befriended Ivy on the pub steps as they waited for their drunken husbands to be thrown out late one Saturday night. She was a rumpled bed of a woman, with a sagging belly from too many pregnancies and pink-rimmed National Health spectacles held together with pink plasters. Her untidy, unkempt house was a stone's throw from the pub and opposite Romford bus garage. Ivy often visited her with me in tow. The house seemed to be overflowing with small boys in grey-worsted short trousers, and girls in dirty pink pinafores, all sporting the same pale pink National Health specs as their Mum. I think I once counted seven children in total.

Mr Hemmings had tried to convince my dad to get out of the rat race too and go with them. I think my dad was very interested in the idea, but there was one little problem – me. Back in those days, black people were not welcome in Australia. You could go there as long as you were white. I think Dad got as far as filling in some preliminary forms because I remember a lengthy discussion about emigration that he had with my two elder brothers around the kitchen table. Curious to know what was so hush-hush, I eavesdropped from the adjoining living room. One of my brothers said: 'They won't take Pauline, you know.' Nothing came of it. We stayed in Romford.

The intervening years had firmed up my poor opinion of the Australian government and the shabby way it had treated the indigenous population of Aborigines in the past. Everybody in Britain loved the irascible Rolf Harris, but I used to cringe as a child when I heard him sing 'Tie Me Kangaroo Down, Sport', particularly the line about an Aboriginal man who is dismissively referred to with a derogatory name.

How come a bespectacled white comedian introduced us to the didgeridoo? It was supposed to be a sacred instrument for the Aborigines, not a cheap comic turn on TV variety shows. Australian history was concerned only with the white man and how he had conquered the inhospitable terrain and made it habitable. The fact that it was already habitable to the Aborigines had been conveniently forgotten, just like the stolen Aboriginal children who were forcibly removed from their parents from 1869 to 1969 and made to skivvy for poor white families in the outback.

'Of all the countries in the world she could have gone to, she had to go to Australia,' I said out loud. I was elated and disappointed all at the same time.

Soon afterwards Terry returned with the dog. 'Why the long face?' he asked.

I showed him the piece of paper with my mother's name, address and telephone number on it. 'Because she's in Australia,' I said.

He immediately hugged me. 'So what,' he said. 'That's brilliant, Pauline. I knew you'd do it.'

In that moment I realized why I loved this man and no other. He dashed to the bookshelf in the living room and grabbed a *World Atlas*. Like excited teenagers, we traced the New South Wales coastline with our fingers, eventually stopping at Tarrawanna, a tiny dot on the map, beside the much bigger dot of Wollongong, which we estimated was about sixty miles from Sydney. She lived almost by the Pacific Ocean.

We agreed that I shouldn't phone my mother. So I went into town and bought the most expensive stationery that I could find and spent the afternoon composing a letter. Cherry-picking one's own forty-two-year-old life for interesting facts to tell your mother is a nigh-on impossible task. I wrote fifteen drafts before I was happy with it. I enclosed some photos; a couple of baby shots, one of me with an Afro hairdo when I was twenty and a newspaper clipping from The Selecter's heyday. I took it to the post office to catch the last post of the day. I was dismayed to find out that it would take seven days to reach its destination. The final cruelty!

I woke a week later to an insistently ringing phone. I looked at the alarm clock. It was 5 a.m., who the hell was ringing at this hour? Blearily I groped around on the bedside table for the phone. 'Hello,' I mumbled, rubbing sleep out of my eyes.

'Hello, is that you, Belinda?'

'Yes,' my soul blurted, before I could stop the word. I was suddenly super-alert.

'It's Mummy, darling.'

I couldn't help thinking that my mother sounded alarmingly like Dame Edna Everage!

My mum, 1996

SEVENTEEN

CRASH LANDING

To lose one parent . . . may be regarded as a misfortune; to lose both looks like carelessness.

Lady Bracknell, Act 1, *The Importance of Being Earnest*, Oscar Wilde

With the acquisition of my real mum, I had entered the hallowed ranks of the merely misfortunate, according to Oscar Wilde. The countless clichés, previously guaranteed to cause my emotional meltdown, such as listening to the old mournful spiritual 'Motherless Child' sung by Mahalia Jackson, watching Kizzy being torn from her mother's arms in *Roots* or the comedic appearance of the 'handbag' near the end of *The Importance of Being Earnest*, were now rendered as harmless, dead and defunct as a Norwegian Blue parrot. It was mid-July, the height of summer and the living was easy.

But having spent much of my life fantasizing about what my real mum looked like, the reality of seeing her photo enclosed in her first letter was shocking in its simplicity. I searched the photo for a vestige of similarity between us, but sadly there was nothing of immediate significance. I saw a bespectacled, grey-haired, blue-eyed woman with smooth skin, an engaging smile, a neat knitted cardie and sensible dress and shoes. What had I expected, an ageing sexpot, Sophia Loren? Maybe. Sensible had never come to mind whenever I thought about my mum.

I was reminded of a Mike Leigh film, *Secrets and Lies*, that I had seen on its release in 1996. It too described the reuniting of an adopted black daughter with her white birth mother. Many people I met around this time alluded to this film whenever I told them my story. Indeed, perhaps I was influenced by the movie to go in search of my parents, but not directly so, because when I first saw the film I thought it was rather fanciful, even if it did have excellent performances from all the actors involved. It was difficult to buy the idea that a white woman in Britain in the late '60s, however young and downtrodden, could actually forget giving birth to a black child. It made for a nice comedic feelgood moment for white audiences, but didn't ring true for me. But the bigger idea of making the mother's well-heeled brother a photographer, intent on displaying the real world as a pleasant illusion, while the adopted daughter is an optometrist, intent on helping people to see more clearly, was inspired. It effectively showed how normal everyday folk reacted when their worlds were turned upside down.

But what was happening to me was no movie. There was no handy blueprint for how everybody was supposed to behave. I had come crashing into their antipodean lives and a maelstrom of emotion had been unleashed, most of it not mine. This crash landing had the effect of fragmenting the entire construct of two separate families. Mum's older sister, Aunt Jeanette, who lived only a few miles away from her, told me in our first telephone conversation that my mum had fought to keep me after I was born, but eventually had to give me up for adoption, causing her to have a nervous breakdown. These few new facts were like being given jewelled pieces of a mosaic that I had to hastily assemble into a coherent picture.

The three sisters Aunt Jeanette, Mum, Aunt Margaret, *c.* 1942

My mum was served with the same task as I tumbled and jumbled my thoughts and feelings into a flurry of letters to match her abundant communiqués. There was so much to say, but how to say it?

Sometimes I wanted to pick up the phone and scream at her: 'Why did you abandon me and then move to the other end of the Earth?' and other times I wanted to soothe any anguish she might still feel and write about how lucky I was that she had found me two loving adoptive parents. I felt pulled every which way, one half of me trying to quell the hurt, needy child inside and the other half trying to act like a considerate and understanding adult. Every sentence had to be weighed carefully in case it might be read the wrong way or cause offence. Unfortunately, diplomacy had never been my strongest trait.

I don't know if my mum felt the same as I did. Her early letters mostly stressed how pleased she was that she had 'done the right thing' and made sure that I was given to a loving family. I certainly couldn't pretend otherwise, but there were many layers to my childhood that I instinctively knew were better not discussed with her. Perhaps I would be able to do that when I met her. In my mum's very first letter she vowed to write every week and she has never gone back on her word. I vowed to do the same and largely I've met that goal. In this day and age, snail mail seems so antiquated, but emailing my mum would feel like a betrayal. She types her letters, somehow lending an emotional distance to the words. Her subject matter always remains stolidly in the present, very rarely discussing the past. In an effort to please her, I do the same. It's as if we need to be very clear and precise about what we reveal to each other. Perhaps we worry that the sprawl of personal handwriting might subliminally allow unpleasant past memories and feelings of recrimination to creep between the words.

I was brutally made to realize that mums rarely come singly, they fetch up with all kinds of other people. After all, forty-two years had gone by, ample time to replenish a family nest with countless relations, or 'relos' as they were affectionately referred to in Australia. I had a brother and sister, one niece, seven cousins and twelve second cousins, plus numerous in-laws. These enthusiastic relos wrote or phoned, eager to be included in this new family drama. At the oddest hours of the night, the ringing of the telephone would elicit yet another new family member with a tenuous grasp of time zones, who was eager to fill me in on themselves and welcome me into the family. The initial conversations would then be followed up by a letter full of photos of healthy, grinning faces resplendent in the New South Wales sunshine. They overwhelmed me with often conflicting stories and gossip. Their good intentions were legion. Their newsy letters, full of eager curiosity and the minutiae of family life, crossed the equator on an almost daily basis. People who I had never known existed the previous week suddenly bared their souls just on the strength of a half-blood relationship. It was an extraordinary and exciting time.

My mum had had some explaining to do when I turned up. As I carefully pieced together a montage of conversational snippets, I realized that her generation knew about me, but the generation that she and her two sisters had produced did not. This obviously came as a shock to my newly acquired thirty-five-year-old brother Cornelius, shortened to Little Con for family purposes, and my thirty-three-year-old sister Sally-Ann. Con sent me a seven-page letter outlining his life to date on paper torn out of a spiral notebook. The ragged edges of the lined paper, bearing his neat handwriting, mirrored the tearing apart of the fiction he had been told about his mum's youth from his newly revised reality. His first words were: 'Words cannot express my happiness at the news that I have an older sister.'

I fell in love with my newly acquired brother immediately. He worked for Northparkes copper and gold mines near his hometown of Parkes, a seven-hour drive inland from Sydney. After the first couple of pages telling me about his partner and seven-year-old daughter Cree, he launched into the story of his musical career. I was amazed to discover that he had been a bass player in three punk bands in the early '80s, Suicide Squad, The Kelpies and Soggy Porridge. He had released records with each band too. What joy, a fellow musician, somebody who I shared half my genes with understood the creative and working life of a musician. His astonishing postscript said that Parkes, where he lived, was the official 'sister' city of Coventry. Such extraordinary coincidences boded well for our future relationship. I longed to meet him.

Con Murphy playing bass in 1981, channelling Sid Vicious

Sally-Ann was more sedate, recently married and worked in a bank. She sent short faxes or telephoned. Her speech patterns were full of long drawn-out vowel sounds, as if talking was an immense effort. Con was the opposite and hardly paused for breath, as though his life was in a constant rush, as indeed it was. Within eight short years he was dead from a heart attack. In photos both siblings were naturally blond, blue-eyed, big-boned and strong like their Irish father Cornelius, Big Con.

For the first four weeks I was immersed in family history. The three Magnus sisters had certainly been eager to enlarge their gene pools beyond post-war Dagenham. Aunt Margaret had married a Pole, Aunt Jeanette had married

Sally-Ann on her wedding day

a Scotsman, and Mum had married an Irishman from Clonakilty, Michael Collins's hometown. Obviously my mum had been the most adventurous of the three, having sampled Nigeria along the way. My recently bereaved Aunt Jeanette, the matriarch of the Australian side of the family, imparted some interesting historical revelations. My maternal grandfather had been a bare-knuckle fighter in his youth and a couple of his cousins had sung in the D'Oyly Carte opera. Not a bad set of genes to have inherited in order to deal with the cut and thrust of the music business. Sadly, within a week of my crash landing, her Scottish husband, Charley, had died of a sudden heart attack. He had written one letter to me which ended by exhorting me to read Luke 15, chapters 4–6. I fished out an old school Bible from the bottom of a drawer and dutifully looked up the reference:

What man of you, having an hundred sheep, if he lose one of them, doth not leave the ninety and nine in the wilderness and go after that which is lost, until he find it? And when he hath found it, he layeth it on his shoulders rejoicing.

And when he cometh home, he calleth together his friends and neighbours, saying unto them, rejoice with me; for I have found my sheep which was lost.

I accepted this biblical quote in the spirit in which it was meant. It seemed churlish to point out that nobody had come looking for me, but I couldn't deny that once they had found me they certainly appeared to be rejoicing. Now that the secret was out, it seemed like everybody could relax and get on with their lives, complete and unburdened. The skeleton was laid bare and the cupboard was empty. Or so I thought. There was one bombshell left to drop and it came from the most unlikely quarter.

Terry and I decided to visit our new family for most of the month of November. The holiday would be book-ended by a European tour with The Selecter in October and the start of rehearsals for *A Midsummer Night's Dream* at the Lyric Hammersmith, playing Titania, in December. I was eager to see my new family in the flesh. This news was met with excitement in Australia. Letters took on a fresh intensity as everybody discussed what we would do on our month-long holiday and what clothes to bring for the changeable spring weather. Amid the avalanche of letters, I received one written on bright yellow paper bordered with colourful drawings of sea birds and turtles from my thirteen-year-old second cousin Krystel, who excitedly told me how much she and her five siblings were looking forward to our imminent arrival.

Then she proudly announced 'I'm one of the Jehovah's Witnesses like my nanny, aunty, uncles, cousins and more of my relatives.' The sentence after this declaration was: 'Sorry if my letter is boring…' Out of the mouths of babes!

Whoah! This couldn't be happening. I felt as though I had been given a perfectly wrapped present only to have it snatched back before I had time to open it. Jehovah's Witnesses? I dimly remembered my adoptive mother talking to strangers on the doorstep when I was a kid, sometimes for more than an hour, before buying a copy of their publication *The Watchtower*. I used to read it to her, but a comment she made about the contents always stuck in my mind: '144,000 people get to go to heaven. Must be full up by now. Why do they want more people to join?'

My mother's logic did seem to have a point. She also took exception to their attitude on blood transfusions, vociferously saying: 'I wouldn't be here now if it wasn't for a blood transfusion.' Whereupon she would relate for the umpteenth time, in blissful anatomical ignorance, her 'I had it all taken away' story about her botched hysterectomy in the late '50s, which had required her to be given eight pints of blood. However, in the catastrophic wake of thousands of haemophiliacs who had contracted Aids from infected blood transfusions in the '90s, perhaps they were not as crazy as secular society supposed?

I read some information about Jehovah's Witnesses on the Internet, but discovered little to allay my fears. Their lives seemed circumscribed by tenets that I could not believe in, however hard I tried. How could we have been on Earth for only 6,000 years? I was a Darwinian through and through. Evolutionary theory worked. I mistrusted anybody who couldn't bring themselves to admit in the wake of Charles

Darwin's ideas that humankind was descended from apes and had probably been wandering the Earth for the past 200,000 years. But on the other hand, I discovered that people of this faith were sent to the concentration camps in Nazi Germany, just like the Marxists, trade unionists, gays, disabled and Jews. They would not fight in any manmade wars or enter into any manmade politics. Laudable aims. They seemed so contradictory. But then hadn't much of my life thrived on contradiction? Why had I thought that finding my mum would be problem-free?

Perhaps my mum wasn't one? She'd married an Irishman from County Cork in a Roman Catholic church in Clonakilty. I had the photo to prove it. The likelihood was that she was a Roman Catholic and the aunty that my little cousin had referred to was an aunt on her Chilean mother's side. I tried to convince myself of this, but somehow I knew that Krystel had included my mum in her list of faithful adherents. I felt angry and betrayed that my mum or Aunt Jeanette hadn't mentioned anything in their letters about their beliefs. Uncle Charles's biblical quote suddenly made sense in the light of this new knowledge. Anytime any Jehovah's Witness had knocked on my door and I had entered into discussion with them, I was always impressed by how they had a biblical quote for every eventuality.

'Why can't people just be honest with me? Why do they have to lie?' I screamed, throwing the letter down onto the kitchen table, where Terry calmly sat eating his breakfast. 'That's it, I'm not going to Australia,' I announced.

'They haven't lied,' Terry answered. 'They just don't see this information as the most important thing about themselves. Just like you didn't want them to think that the only important thing about you was being black.'

The voice of reason had spoken and he was right. I'd spent my whole life being judged by society's stereotypes and here I was doing exactly the same thing to good and welcoming people who I'd only known for a few joyous weeks. 'So stop acting like a spoilt, ungrateful child and let's go to the travel agent in town and book the tickets today.'

Two hours later we possessed two return Qantas Airways tickets to Sydney. Terry bought a T-shirt in Coventry market too. It comically depicted the five stages of evolution of Homer Simpson, beginning with a picture of a banana-eating monkey scratching its hairy bum entitled *monkey eatalotis* and ending with a picture of Homer scratching his white underpants-clad backside with one hand while eating a banana with his other, entitled *Homersapiens*. He promised to wear it en route to Sydney. It's at times like these that I realize why I married him.

The following week I went on tour with The Selecter to America. We began on the west coast. On the evening before our first show, I stood on the Pacific shoreline in Santa Barbara watching the sunset set fire to the distant horizon, knowing that diagonally across that vast ocean my mum was watching it rise. From her letters I had learned that she enjoyed getting up at sunrise to walk the dog and going to bed at sunset, an inconvenience that I was soon to learn at first hand. I felt closer to her. I was almost halfway there.

I had written to her before I flew out to California, asking why she had omitted to tell me that many of the family were Jehovah's Witnesses. When I returned from The Selecter's ten-day tour, her return letter was waiting for me. She wrote:

About my faith and that of Sally, her husband, Aunt Jeanette and your second cousins. Yes we are witnesses.

There is always such a lot of adverse publicity about
religion, that I wanted to let you get to know us and see us
all and meet with us before I mentioned anything about
religion. Usually that and politics can be so explosive for
some people. Anyway like you said, there will be lots to
talk about. If you have asked people that you know about
Jehovah's Witnesses you will get all sorts of opinions and
some will be scary. That's what I mean when I say just take
it easy and wait to hear about it from us. Don't be anxious,
just come and enjoy your holiday and stay with us.

I breathed a sigh of relief that she hadn't mentioned that my
brother Con was a Witness. But I was still like a dog with
a bone. I couldn't pretend that I didn't feel uncomfortable
about my mum's faith. Almost in a tit-for-tat display of
defiance, I decided to ask my mum an uncomfortable
question, one that we had both been avoiding. Aunt Jeanette
had warned me that my mum didn't like remembering the
events surrounding my birth. She said that the original
Magnus family settlers in Britain had been Jewish traders
from Greece, who had probably arrived in the middle of
the nineteenth century. This meant that part of my genetic
make-up was indeed Sephardic Jew. But who provided the
other half of my DNA double helix? Who coloured me black?
I couldn't have complete closure on my newfound identity
until I understood the enigma that was my father. Curiosity
got the better of my sensitivity during a phone conversation
with my mum and I popped the question: 'Do you know who
my father is?'

'Yes, dear, he is Nigerian. His name is Gordon Adenle. He
was an engineering student studying in London when I knew
him.'

Bingo!

I wasted no time at all discovering everybody with the surname Adenle in the London telephone directory. Africans usually have huge extended families. I reckoned that there was a good chance that if I could find somebody with that name, then they might be able to point me in the right direction. This premise proved correct. There were two entries. The first entry turned out to be my father's second wife, Irene. I rang her immediately.

'Hello, is that Mrs Adenle?'

'Yes, who is this?'

'I'm trying to contact somebody named Gordon Adenle. Do you know anybody of that name?'

'Oh, Gordon,' she said familiarly. My heart skipped a beat. 'Oh, he died last year of liver cancer.'

Silence. I was devastated.

'Who are you?'

'I think I'm his daughter.'

'Why didn't you say, I thought you were one of his girlfriends. Sorry you had to hear the news like that, my dear.'

I can't remember much else that was said. She insisted that I visit her as soon as possible. She gave me her address in Waterloo. The next day I took a train to London. She lived in a flat at the top of one of the Peabody Buildings in Duchy Street. She spontaneously burst into tears as I came into sight on the last flight of stairs.

'Oh, yes, yes, you are Gordon's daughter,' she hiccupped between sobs. 'Come in, come in.'

A plump, elderly lady, walking with the rolling gait of somebody who had endured hip replacements, led me into her tiny, sparsely furnished living room. Above the wood-surround electric fire was a huge ornately framed black and

Irene Adenle, Oba Samuel Adenle (my grandfather), Prince Gordon Olodosu Adenle (my father) in the 1960s

white photograph. I bore more than a passing resemblance to the opulently robed seated man in the picture.

'That's your father,' she said, still crying. 'Wasn't he handsome?'

My father was Prince Gordon Olodosu Adenle, firstborn son of Deborah Iyo Adenle, first wife of Oba Samuel Adenle I of Oshogbo. An Oba is a tribal king. He is the ruler of his particular fiefdom within the Yoruba tribe. My grandfather had over twenty wives and probably sired more than a hundred children. Since my father was a prince, Irene reliably informed me that made me a princess. That certainly put a whole new spin on being called a 'Jewish Princess'!

The information came thick and fast. Most of it seemed

My father

too fantastical to take seriously. Irene was a flurry of activity, despite her infirmity. At last she had somebody that she could talk to about the love of her life. She delved into drawers and cupboards, extracting bits and pieces of memorabilia and African artefacts to illustrate her story.

A leather belt, a piece of obviously expensive woven cloth, a traditional horsehair fly swat with an elaborately carved handle, my father's obituary pamphlet, newspaper cuttings of my grandfather's state funeral, which was attended by Nigerian Premier General Obasanju, no less, and scenic postcards in my father's handwriting from Ibadan and Lagos were piled high on the coffee table. As I admired each item in turn, she said: 'They're yours, dear. He would have wanted you to have them.'

'But how can you be so sure I'm his daughter?' I asked.

'It's in the eyes, dear. All in the eyes.'

And she was right. When I looked into the eyes of the man in the giant photo on the wall, it was like looking into my own in a mirror. As a mixed-race person, it was easier for me to identify with the black side of my family than the white family in Australia. Society defines me as black by virtue of my skin colour. It would be absurd for me to say: 'I'm half white.'

I also looked like him. I recognised the assertive way that he held his head, his poker-straight back, the sardonic set of his mouth. I felt a physical connection with him, which I hadn't felt when I saw photos of my mum.

Once I had agreed with Michael Jackson when he sang 'I don't want to spend my life being a colour' in his hit 'Black or White', but as I strode down the street to Waterloo tube station I wondered, why not? I'd named myself by that very colour. Why not wear it with pride? For the first time in my life I was perfectly comfortable in my black skin, particularly now that it was a snug fit. If it was good enough for my father, then it was good enough for me.

■ ■ ■

Terry and I flew to Australia on 16 November 1996. Somewhere between Singapore and Sydney I had a crisis of confidence and fled to the cramped toilets on the Qantas flight to change my clothes. I opted for a new, conservative, navy-blue mid-calf dress that I'd packed in my hand luggage instead of the edgy black trousers and shirt ensemble that I was wearing. Then I took a brush to my short, straightened hairstyle and with the aid of water fashioned a small neat Afro. Most of the passengers were asleep, but if any had observed me on my way to the toilet, they would not have recognised me as the person who reappeared fifteen minutes later. I looked unnervingly like my younger self in one of the photos that I had sent my mum with my introductory letter. She had commented favourably on this particular photo, so I think my subconscious asserted itself and hastily manufactured a transformation once I was over Australian airspace, so that I could give the most favourable first impression to my mum.

Pathetic really, but I think I was desperate for her to like me. I couldn't bear the thought of her rejection again. Terry did a double-take as I sat down beside him in my aisle seat, but, probably recognising the uptight look on my face, decided not to say anything. The plane landed in Australia on time at 6.35 a.m. The interminable wait in Sydney's draconian Customs Hall increased my anxiety threshold tenfold, so that by the time we found ourselves outside in the passenger terminal, we were half-asleep and rather fractious.

If I am honest, I did what everybody does when something is about to happen of paramount importance – I built a perfect fantasy. The drama queen in me scripted the tumultuous event that was about to happen; it went something like this:

Sydney airport interior, early morning.

Pauline immediately recognises Mother among the throng of people, a broad smile breaks out on her face as she rushes into her outstretched arms.

Mother sobs uncontrollably.

Soft focus camera, slow motion close-up. Paul Simon strums 'Mother & Child Reunion' as background music.

You get the gist? I needed to assign an easy narrative to the reunion. And then in crashed reality, in the shape of a tall, sturdily built woman, large of bosom and big of smile, with piercing blue eyes and a messy grey-haired up-do, striding towards me at breakneck speed. It was the eyes I noticed first – piercing, watchful and sea-blue. In that moment I floundered in their depths like a freshly hooked fish before it is landed. Would I be found wanting? Did she look disappointed? Did I look too much like my father? Would that upset her? Deeply unsettling questions whirred in my mind, until suddenly she broke into a broad smile and warmly declared: 'Daaaaaaaahling.'

Next thing I was enveloped in forty-two years worth of unreserved love. The surrounding hustle and bustle receded and I felt as though I had entered an unexpected limbo land, where everything that had previously happened to me and my mum was put on hold, while we selfishly tried to backtrack and sew together the ends of the severed umbilical cord that once united us. But the passage of time had worn the frayed ends too much for such easy closure. The moment passed. Wonder dissolved into incredulity. I just couldn't get to grips with her living, breathing self. Terry looked similarly overwhelmed at being embraced by a mother-in-law who was only two years older than him. If she noticed his T-shirt, she said nothing.

Behind my mum stood a plump young woman with blonde, bobbed hair. Her ruddy cheeks framed a nervous, uncertain smile as my Mum introduced me to my sister Sally-Ann. Polite embraces were made, but I sensed a wary distance. Normality reasserted itself, as our luggage was piled onto a cart that Sally had found and Mum paid for a car park ticket. The moment that I had waited a lifetime for had passed and now everything that happened seemed so prosaic, so curiously underwhelming, as if nothing else could match the intensity of that first mother and daughter meeting. I felt as though I was observing everything, not in it or of it, but out of it, looking on. I couldn't shake this feeling on the short drive to my sister's house, a neat one-storey home she shared with her husband Greg in the Sydney suburbs.

On arrival, my mum's husband Cornelius, ten years her senior, was waiting at the house and immediately enveloped me with pure spontaneous love, murmuring my name 'Belinda' in his soft Irish brogue, his accent undiminished even after thirty-eight years in Australia. His warm, emotional reaction to Terry and me was totally unexpected. Under the circumstances, I thought that he might appear a bit stand-offish, but not a bit of it. He was so happy, he cried like a baby. Then everything settled down for a while as presents were exchanged and cups of tea made and drunk. A short potted history gushed forth from my mum, about how different society's attitudes had been when I was born. How her family hadn't been equipped to have her and her new baby at home. It was like listening to a fairy story, a different fairy story than I'd been told by Ivy, my adoptive mother, but still a fairy story, albeit much closer to the truth. I felt that it was being said more for Sally's benefit than for mine.

Then it was off to Wollongong, ninety kilometres south of

My mum and her husband, Big Con

Sydney, to my mum's house. A small house, with perfectly tended gardens front and back, greeted us. Everything was spotlessly utilitarian throughout. Back then Terry and I both smoked and my mum wasted no time in telling us that Jehovah's Witnesses did not smoke. If we wanted to smoke then it would have to be done in the back garden. Fortunately, much of the Australian lifestyle is spent in the back garden, soaking up the sun and barbecuing large slabs of raw meat accompanied by a few bottles or 'stubbies' of Toohey's beer. Our need for nicotine was so high that Terry and I spent much of our visit in the garden, only entering the house for ablutions or sleep.

For the next month my mum and I attempted to bridge the yawning gap of forty-two years and establish a relationship. 'Just be yourselves,' she had said to both of us on arrival.

Easier said than done. I wasn't sure who 'myself' was

375

any more. Normally our chosen line of work defines us for others, but I found it difficult to talk about touring with The Selecter. My oldest cousin Gavin, Aunt Jeanette's son, who bore a distinct resemblance to the pony-tailed actor Steven Seagal, had usefully found a 'live' version of me singing one of The Selecter's hits, 'Three Minute Hero', where I insert the word 'fucking' into the lyrics. On the same CD was a version of 'My Collie (Not A Dog)', extolling the virtues of smoking copious quantities of sensimilla. Hardly heinous crimes, but he wasted no time in telling me that a degree of consternation had been engendered in Mum and Aunt Jeanette when they had heard these songs.

I don't think that there was much love lost between him and my mum. Once he had been a staunch Jehovah's Witness. His Chilean wife had reared five of his children, but he had also fathered another out of wedlock. This and his general louche conduct around town were too much for the local Kingdom Hall members who, after repeated warnings, had delivered the ultimate punishment and dis-fellowshipped him. When I turned up out of the blue, my cousin decided that his previous behaviour was as nothing compared with the uncovered hypocrisy of the family's older generation. He told me many things that I did not want to hear, but I understood why he felt the need to tell me.

He said that Little Con had eschewed the faith in his teens and left home to live in the seedier districts of Sydney. He joined a punk band, much to the dismay of Mum. Unfortunately, the lead singer of this band, the son of good friends of Mum, had turned into a heroin junkie somewhere along the way. Therefore bands and drugs and bad behaviour were inextricably linked in her mind. The fact that The Selecter had been relatively successful and had a small but significant worldwide fan base was of no consequence to her, because as far as she was concerned the subject matter of the songs left much to be desired.

As if to illustrate how Mum wanted to present me to her friends, a large framed poster which I had sent her, of me dressed as Billie Holiday, singing into an old-style, square, 1950s microphone, advertising the *All or Nothing at All* production, hung in pride of place on her living-room wall. This was my acceptable face, not the be-hatted and suited, gender-bending stage persona of Pauline Black of The Selecter, photos of which I had also sent. The strange thing was that neither of these personal constructs was essentially me. Whoever that was seemed to have been temporarily lost over the Indian Ocean.

I was eager to show her the photos of my new Nigerian family, which had now expanded to include seventeen half-siblings and numerous aunts and uncles. She visibly blanched when she saw photos of my father, but she gamely entered into conversation about her recollections of him and even showed the photos to visiting relatives and friends. She tellingly recounted her first meeting with him: 'He followed me all the way home to Dagenham Heathway station. I knew I couldn't take him home.'

I didn't pry any more after that.

Little Con arrived five days later, flamboyantly clad in a full length Drizabone coat, white T-shirt, tight black trousers and black winklepicker boots, with my young niece Cree, in a noisy blue pick-up truck that Aussies refer to as a 'Ute'. He sported an Akubra hat on his dirty-blond, mulletted hairdo and carried a large plain wood didgeridoo under his arm. What an entrance. We hit it off immediately. He was a huge bear of a man with a jaw like Desperate Dan and hands like shovels, a typical Aussie from the outback. He smoked, drank and stayed up late. Terry and I had dutifully found ourselves in bed at about 7.30 p.m. most nights prior to his arrival, because that's when Big Con and my mum retired. The size and layout of the house precluded making too much noise if people wanted to sleep, so if we tried staying up later we were reduced to whispering to each other in a darkened living room. When evening arrived on the first day of Con's visit, he had none of this and kept the television blaring into the small hours. The following day he dragged us out to a local pub to meet up with Gavin, who introduced us to his impish younger brother Robert. The two cousins and Con were like a comedy act, constantly telling jokes and irreverent family stories. Having been in a pressure-cooker environment since our arrival, it was a welcome chance for Terry and me to let off steam.

The following morning, I finally persuaded a hungover Con to play the didgeridoo. Fascinated by the strange, unearthly sound of this fine Aboriginal instrument, I purchased another. We spent hours blowing into our respective carved wooden tubes, much to the curious wonderment of the staid neighbours. It was almost like a primal bonding ritual.

I met nobody on the entire visit who expressed anything less than joy and admiration at our story. After a while I even got used to everybody calling me Belinda. It was strange at first to be renamed, particularly after so many years had gone by, but we were starting again, so it felt right to start with a clean slate. Fourteen years later, my mum has finally been persuaded to call me Pauline instead, but I know it doesn't feel natural to her.

I have visited the family four times in Australia in the intervening years. The more I have got to know my mum, the

Rob Hamilton (cousin), Aunt Jeanette, Mum, me, Gavin, Terry, Karen and James (Rob's wife and eldest son), 1996

more I can see myself in her. We don't look similar, but we share a few idiosyncrasies. We laugh exactly alike, routinely slip from one accent to another, sometimes within the same sentence (I have no idea why, it just makes talking more interesting) and enjoy casually standing in the third ballet position. Silly things, but like somebody once said, 'It's all in the detail.' In 2009 Mum finally saw me perform on stage in Sydney when I toured there with the Neville Staple Band. I felt very proud that night and I think she did too. Largely we have succeeded in avoiding discussions about religious faith or politics. Tolerance about such issues has been intermittently tested in both hemispheres but has withstood undue pressure so far. As my mum once said, 'Life is a journey and we are in it for the long haul, Belinda.'

Terry and I no longer smoke, so I suppose more of her way of life has rubbed off on us than ours has rubbed off on her. It's been an interesting journey so far. I am eternally grateful to both of the people who have mothered me in their different but ultimately loving ways. I am a product of their collective nurture and both of them did the best they knew how.

Often I find myself studying a small photo of my father that Irene kindly gave me at our first meeting. He looks so handsome, like a young Eddie Murphy in the movie *Coming to America*. He is dressed in a pure white lace dashiki suit with a matching kufi on his head. Even though he is shaking somebody's hand by way of introduction, his imperious gaze is directed at the camera lens. I always have the unmistakable feeling that he is looking at me. The kinship between us seems almost tangible. For a brief second I can feel myself under his skin, as if we have become one. It is an unnerving moment, when it happens, but one that I have come to welcome over the intervening years. It's almost as if he comes to visit, just to remind me that I am his. But the feeling is fleeting and soon gone. Perhaps it doesn't really happen at all?

Without his physical presence, the only way I can ever know about his personality is from what others who knew him choose to tell me. I must trust that he was a good man, despite the fact that he was already married when he made an attractive, flame-haired sixteen-year-old pregnant with me and then abandoned her to her fate. I find it hard to love this man, because he showed no love to me or Mum, but listening to Irene's stories about him, I can tell that she passionately loved him.

When I think about my journey so far, I am reminded of a discussion between two toys in the children's book *The Velveteen Rabbit* by Margery Williams.

'What is REAL?' asked the Rabbit one day, when they were lying side by side near the nursery fender, before Nana came to tidy the room. 'Does it mean having things that buzz inside you and a stick-out handle?'

'Real isn't how you are made,' said the Skin Horse. 'It's a thing that happens to you. When a child loves you for a long, long time, not just to play with, but REALLY loves you, then you become Real.'

'Does it hurt?' asked the Rabbit.

'Sometimes,' said the Skin Horse, for he was always truthful. 'When you are Real, you don't mind being hurt.'

'Does it happen all at once, like being wound up,' he asked, 'or bit by bit?'

'It doesn't happen all at once,' said the Skin Horse. 'You become. It takes a long time. That's why it doesn't often happen to people who break easily, or have sharp edges, or have to be carefully kept. Generally, by the time you are Real, most of your hair has dropped out and you get loose in the joints and very shabby. But these things don't matter at all, because once you are Real you can't be ugly, except to people who don't understand.'

It has taken a long time, but the more I have learned about my families' histories and where I fit into the puzzle that I had been trying to solve from the age of four, the more real I have become. There isn't a neat ending to my story. Allowing strangers with whom I share my blood into my world hasn't healed all those early wounds, but it has made sense of what happened to me.

You see, my story isn't just about finding my real identity, although that was very important. Knowing my true origins made me feel better about myself, answered some fundamental questions at last and offered yet more people to feel a sense of kinship with on this earth. Primarily, this story is about a search for love, the search that all of us have to make, and in my case the search for the unconditional love that is the birthright of all children. That love is usually given upon entering this world, but if it isn't, or is taken away for some reason, then some of us are impelled to find it, if at all possible, and in so doing maybe make hard choices and change ourselves along the way. I was born mixed race and because of my circumstances, mixed up, but rather than have my somewhat inconvenient origins airbrushed out of existence, I chose to embrace that part of my heritage in as much of my life as possible. I have never regretted that decision. The racial identity that marks me out in society is worn beneath my skin every day. My father's colour envelops me and that is unconditional love of a kind. Indeed, one almost might say black by design.

EIGHTEEN

A RAISIN IN THE SUN: WOMEN DON'T RESIGN!

Musicians don't retire; they stop when there's no more music in them.

Louis Armstrong

Onstage at 229 –The Venue, London 17 March 2012. Photo © Nathalie de Bruyne

It is a year since this book was first published in 2011, and like many new writers, I have been engaged in the business of promoting it since its arrival in bookstores. The promotional experience has been illuminating, often humbling, frequently emotional, seldom combative, but most surprisingly, not at all what I had expected.

For me, reading has always been a very private experience, occasionally I might discuss a book with friends or acquaintances, but mostly I ruminate on its contents alone, hoping to divine what is at the heart of an author's story. It has never occurred to me to go to an author's reading or patiently queue at a bookstore for an autograph. Somehow, the private world between the author and me has already been established and I do not feel that discussing the contents with them will make my experience any more fulfilling. Therefore, I approached my first reading and discussion with some trepidation.

Housmans, a radical bookshop on Caledonian Road, near Kings Cross station in London, was chosen as a first venue both to launch this book and for me to talk about it. It was mid-July and I'd just finished a challenging interview with Lisa Tarbuck for her early evening show on BBC Radio 2. I could tell by the questions she asked that she had actually read it. We had a delightfully animated chat, despite the fact that my mobile phone kept burping and buzzing in my handbag during our on-air discussion. I pretended that I didn't know what the noise was.

I was on a tight schedule and a taxi whisked me from the BBC to Housmans with minutes to spare. I fetched up outside the bookshop, hoping there would be a few people there, knowing that I could always rely on some stalwart Selecter fans, but I was surprised to find people queuing out the door. There were a few familiar faces, but mostly they were people I didn't know. It's sobering to be confronted with total strangers, all of whom are intent on discussing the words that you put on a page to describe your existence. The worst part of it was that I was late and, having drunk many cups of coffee during the afternoon, I desperately needed a toilet which, I was told, was at the back of the shop.

A microphone had been set up on the raised step toward the rear. I was rather dismayed to find that the toilet was close by, and probably within amplified earshot of the assembled audience. To make things worse, a hush descended as I walked the green mile towards the facilities.

Much relieved, but fearing that any dignity I had acquired through my writings was now somewhat diminished, I took a deep breath before stepping up to the microphone and entering the heady world of book readings. And to my delight, I found I loved it, particularly the discussion afterwards.

In my experience people are very reluctant to ask questions at meetings, so I expected the proceedings to be wrapped up soon after I had finished my reading. Then I hoped to grab a white wine from the makeshift party table in the corner and chat to some of my friends and family who were there in support. However, people were so eager to talk about anything and everything to do with the racial makeup of society that I barely paused for breath for the next hour. One woman almost came to blows with somebody else over a particularly thorny racial issue; I had to step in to the fray and announce quite loudly, 'Hey, all I did was write a book.'

And that is precisely the point that I am trying to make, the power of books should never be underestimated.

When I decided to put this memoir into the public domain, it was very much because I felt that the story of mixed-race people in this country tended to be hidden, perhaps because our origins are sometimes difficult to explain to a society that, despite its mutterings about having dealt with institutional racism, still manages to remain colour sensitive, a sensitivity that is in danger of breaking out again during our present economic hardships. The media largely assume that people with non-white skins have come to this country from another. They are seen as foreign, as other. But those of us born here, consider ourselves as British as our white counterparts. Like so many European countries, we now live in a multi-ethnic environment. Multiculturalism is the supposed new ideal for a successful society in the twenty-first century, but sadly, not everybody is on message.

In January 2011, I took part in a BBC4 series *Reggae Britannia*, an episode of which was filmed at a two-hour live music show at the Barbican in London. Reggae luminaries such as Rico Rodriguez, Dave Barker, Dennis Al Capone, Big Youth, Janet Kay and Carroll Thompson performed and the master of ceremonies was dub producer Dennis Bovell.

On the day it was filmed, the fascist English Defence League had provocatively marched in Luton. That afternoon, as if on cue, Prime Minister David Cameron made a distressing statement. He declared that multiculturalism had failed in Britain. I found his choice of words a curious indictment of the intelligence of the British public, a cross section of who were present in abundance at the Barbican on that particular evening. As I walked on stage to perform, I vividly remember looking out at the audience and feeling wonderfully uplifted at the array of skin colours on show, all of these people brought together by the power of Jamaican music. Jamaica may be only a small Caribbean island in the Atlantic Ocean, but its music has a giant outreach the world over. We were there to celebrate how that music had successfully crossed both the sea and the racial divide in modern Britain. Far from being dead, multiculturalism on that evening was demonstrably alive and kicking and a testament to the spiritual resilience of human beings on this fragile planet of ours.

Just before I opened my mouth to sing, a thought bubbled up in my head that I blurted out in the Tourette-like manner that often assails me in times of nervousness, 'Multiculturalism rules!' I asserted and then launched into a Selecter hit, 'Three Minute Hero', a song that bewails the tedium of some working people's lives.

I thought nothing more about what I had said, content just to enjoy the moment and honoured to be among such a powerful showing of my heroes and peers. But when the concert was reviewed in the newspapers the following week, both the *Independent*, the *Guardian* and the *Evening Standard* picked up on it. Even the often divisive shilly-shallying and malign media manoeuvring of hard-bitten journalists could not ignore the audience's racial spectrum and enthusiasm for reggae music. The concert suggested that maybe, just maybe, there had been a paradigm shift in Britain and perhaps finally racism was on the wane. Wasn't it better to celebrate those things that united us as a people rather than constantly bigging-up the nonsense that divides us? British people seem far more sophisticated these days about understanding the intricacies of racism than in the period in which I grew up.

The Barbican concert was the catalyst I needed to put The Selecter firmly back on the road, and not just be content to do a few reunion concerts, like those we had played in October and November 2010. Why not abandon altogether the accepted shibboleth for bands of our age, which held fast to the belief that regurgitating the old hits was all we were good for? Instead of reformation, why not strive for a renaissance?

I had already approached Arthur 'Gaps' Hendrickson to join The Selecter again in spring 2010. Luckily, he needed little persuasion. I sensed he wanted to do more than just get back together again.

For me, what had set The Selecter apart from our 2-Tone contemporaries was the dynamic of a band fronted by a male/female duo. Usually with duos, one person takes precedence over the other, but with Arthur 'Gaps' Hendrickson and myself, it was very much about both of us trading strengths, meshing harmonies, swapping looks, instinctively knowing what the other was thinking and, most importantly, communicating our uncompromising message to a receptive audience.

As autumn approached, rehearsals began with a fantastic group of musicians, some of whom I have known since

Arthur 'Gaps' Hendrickson. Photo © Natalie de Bruyne

1991 and grown with over the years. I'm a great believer in bringing a band together in an organic way, people either fit or they don't. Even if they fit musically, sometimes their personalities do not and, since bands have to spend many hours together not making music, it is very important that people get along with each other. From the off this was the case. It was like a breath of fresh air that people were kind and considerate to each other and listened to each other's opinions. The rehearsal period was a joy and eventually our numbers swelled to eight and sported, for the first time in Selecter history, a horn section led by all-round musician/ producer Neil Pyzer.

Our first performance had been at the 'Sinners Day Festival' at the Ethias Arena in Hasselt, Belgium on Halloween 2010 and headlined by Nina Hagen, The Fall and Echo and The Bunnymen. Our early evening slot met with a fantastic response and the band looked and sounded its very best.

Onstage just before us was the great Jah Wobble and I introduced myself to him in the dining area backstage after we performed. He had also written an autobiography, the incorrigible *Memoirs of a Geezer*, and we discovered that we shared a publisher, Serpent's Tail. John Wardle, as he is known to his mother, was eager to say hello and we said, what most musos say when they first meet each other, 'It would be really good to do some songwriting together.'

The only difference was that John actually meant it, but more of that later.

Two weeks later The Selecter debuted in London to a packed auditorium at a very emotional gig at Bloomsbury Ballroom. Was that it, I wondered? We had celebrated The Selecter's thirtieth anniversary, but where did we go from there?

It wasn't until the aftermath of the *Reggae Britannia* concert that I discovered my raison d'être for putting The Selecter back on the road. It was simple: nobody, least of all our 2-Tone contemporaries, were talking about multiculturalism. This new checkerboard of humanity peopled the communities we lived in, and hopefully The Selecter could make it our future constituency.

Like many good ideas, once my eureka mood passed, I realised that breathing life into the band again was going to be much more difficult in my mid-fifties than it had been in my late thirties.

I have this theory that many women in the media spotlight reach an age – usually somewhere between forty-five and fifty-five as the menopause beckons – when the powers-that-be, rather undiplomatically, reckon that their faces are now more suited to radio. If you are a singer like me then you find that promoters demand current photos, just to make sure that you are still relatively 'easy on the eye'. Faced with such unwelcome scrutiny, many women give up the stage or TV and film and occupy themselves with other creative pursuits, like writing, photography or painting.

There are some mavericks, who battle on in the visual entertainment industry once youth has flown, but so many look nipped, tucked and botoxed that it is distressing rather than empowering to watch them parade their taut, surgically enhanced, shop-dummy visages on television; films, at this age, are considered totally out of bounds, because faces in close up on a large screen are not helpful if trying to hide wrinkles or hairline scars. The smallest blemish is magnified to foot-high proportions. Likewise HD television has not been kind to anyone past the age of thirty-five. Very few women in music, TV or film are allowed or perhaps are prepared to show everybody how a woman looks at a *certain age*, but so many men, Mick Jagger, Ronnie Wood, Rod Stewart and Clint Eastwood, to name but a few, are allowed to wrinkle or sag with impunity. Rather unfairly, they are still considered attractive way past traditional retirement age.

In 2001 I performed the role of Yvette in Berthold Brecht's *Mother Courage* alongside Hollywood actress Tyne Daly in the title role. She fetched up in Dublin for rehearsal, sporting two long, thick grey-haired plaits, a comfortable plus-sized body and an imperious, untouched face. She looked perfectly happy with herself and announced over a rehearsal lunch: 'When I walk into a party in Hollywood, I am every woman's worst nightmare. They look at me and know this is how they would look, if nature had been allowed to take its course.'

What she meant was that she was considered unpopular because she refused to don the accepted over-plumped facial look that is all pervasive in La-la land. Ms. Daley is to be applauded for her services to womanhood.

So far, the use of hair dye has been my only deviation from the hallowed path for middle-aged women set by Ms Daley. As oestrogen levels diminish, so women's energy lessens in direct proportion. I thought that the menopause ought to be a rite of passage for a woman, not a rush for oestrogen replacement therapy. Sooner or later it would have to be faced, whatever palliative drugs were taken to stave off the inevitable. Although the menopause is an unwelcome physical shift, it is more about coming to terms with the psychological shift. I had taken a hiatus from performing with The Selecter in November 2006 so that I could undergo this mind reset in private.

By then, I felt completely dried out, like the 'raisin in the sun' in Langston Hughes' poem 'A Dream Deferred'. Content just to coast for a while, but not sure what to do, I adjusted badly to self-enforced idleness. Eventually I regained some balance by starting to write this book in 2009. This activity coincided with a mooted reunion of the original band for our thirtieth anniversary, but the usual antagonisms had reasserted themselves. I didn't have the energy to fight, so that dream was deferred yet again.

I may have felt like a dried-out raisin, but as the next year passed, I gradually began to feel a little sweeter inside; sweet with the promise of songs unsung and thoughts unwritten.

While we were away from the music scene, it had moved on and there was now a new terminology to describe us - heritage band. It appeared that we had suddenly metamorphosed into a very minor stately home; some might even have said a very small country house in need of some repair, but nonetheless, it meant that for brief stints in the spring, summer and autumn, our flowering lawns were opened up to the public, who could come inside the house and poke about in the drawers entitled 'old hits'. Therein lay the dilemma: did I want to build a band that only played the debut album and the hits, or was it possible to rebuild a band brave enough to create new material, when most of our contemporaries were content to follow the former option?

It was eagerly pointed out to us by many promoters that the Specials were content to offer up their past to tens of thousands of old, cuddly reconstructed skinheads. Not only that, but they had single-handedly improved the coffers of Fred Perry ten-fold, while churning out the hits, which amounted to a whole heap more than those of The Selecter. We had almost lurched into the forgotten band of 2-Tone status. We were not one-hit wonders, but were certainly closer to that precarious fate than the Specials or Madness.

If I wanted to put The Selecter back on the gig map, then I needed a plan.

I'd just finished reading a book, *Race of a Lifetime* by John Heilemann and Mark Halperin, about how Barack Obama planned his campaign for the presidency of the USA. I figured that one-mixed race woman in Britain could probably learn a lot from one mixed-race man, who contrary to all expectations had seized the time and become the most powerful man in the world. I avidly pored over the book, which gave a blow-by-blow account of how he won the Iowa caucus and built a path to the White House against almost overwhelming odds. The mantra for this amazing feat in the book was, 'Build a strategy, stick to it and everything will follow.'

I'd been in the music business for over thirty years, but I had never seen so much meaning distilled into so few words. It's probably common practice for others, but I'd never planned any long-term strategy for my career. Usually good ideas came along and they were cobbled together in an ad hoc way and often the result was pleasing and occasionally it was a disaster. I seemed to live in the space between those two outcomes. I decided that it was time to change that approach.

The older a band gets, the deeper the nostalgia that surrounds them. People stop believing that you might have anything new to say and are content just to explore the shallow pools of their memories. I don't mind talking about the old days if some degree of analysis is applied to it, but this is not the case for most fans and indeed why should it be? Most of us listen to music because it reminds us of our youth, the good times, our first love affair, our marriage, our first child, any and all of these things attach themselves to a particular soundscape that the popular music industry has to offer. I hope that plenty of young people in 1979 got a bit more than they bargained for when they decided to tribally follow the 2-Tone movement. It was unlikely that 'Too Much Pressure' was going to be the backdrop to any weddings or births, even though realistically it was probably more pertinent than Etta James' 'At Last'. 'Missing Words', our third hit as a band, was as close as The Selecter ever managed to get towards a love song in the early days. Most people only knew us for our first hit, 'On My Radio'.

What the band needed was new hard-hitting material that was unafraid to question the emergence of the English Defence League and other European far-right groups, or Britain's foreign policies, or the global recession, or the meaning of modern-day multiculturalism.

For a while, I had been toying with the idea of revamping Woody Guthrie's well-known song, 'All You Fascists Bound To Lose'. Woody was a US folk singer from the '30s who sang and played a mean acoustic guitar with 'this machine kills fascists' scrawled on it. I'm an avid fan of any artist who says what they mean and Woody definitely hit the nail squarely on the head with that slogan.

We played around with the song's chorus for a while and came up with a storming horn riff and the rocksteady style backing track. As soon as Gaps and I started laying down the vocals it became apparent that this song was on the right track.

You can always tell when an idea works, because the recording process is enjoyable; nobody is searching for ideas, they just flow. Gaps delivered the *coup de grace*, when he came up with the phrase 'big in the body, small in the mind'. It fitted the song and some of the new updated lyrics that I had written. We had kept some of the original lyrics, but in the second decade of a new millennium they were a bit archaic, particularly when you took into account that the world's banks were tottering in the midst of a full-blown global recession. Derivatives and hedge funds hadn't been invented in Guthrie's era. The phrase 'greed has got to go' described perfectly what needed to be done to the banking industry. The financial infrastructure had failed and suddenly, according to the government, we were all in their sorry mess together. Strange how when they are making millions they don't seem to be in quite such an inclusive mood.

Another song that I had been singing for the past year, the aptly titled 'Back To Black' that Amy Winehouse had written and sung so eloquently was mooted as a possible double 'A' side single with 'Big in the Body', as it was now known. A darkly foreboding reggae version was fashioned from the song's raw material. Gaps provided a toasting section in the middle of the song that elevated it into a more profound milieu, it was no longer just an unrequited love song.

We decided that 'Big in the Body – Small in the Mind' would be released in May 2011 on our producer, multi-instrumentalist and erstwhile Selecter tenor saxophonist, Neil Pyzer's imprint, Vocaphone Records, followed by 'Back to Black' a few months later. Two covers for sure, but given an excellent spin by The Selecter.

A London promoter, who had organised our 'comeback' show at the Bloomsbury Ballroom the previous autumn, offered us another London show at the 02 Islington Academy on July 23rd. I was not sure about this venue. I'd played it in the past and found it strangely soulless. We always play best in a venue that has some character and I do not mean beer-sodden carpets and Elvis memorabilia behind the bar. But a London gig was a useful prelude to our coveted festival date, Camp Bestival, a week later. We hoped to release two singles by the end of July, which would lead to audience interest in a new album. Whatever, we were on the road. We had a plan. The added bonus was that I had the book coming out in early August and hopefully that would boost our profile.

Our London promoter then suggested that I meet with a PR company that he used to publicise his shows. I knew that PR would be useful, but also very expensive. We were not commanding huge fees for our gigs, so it was a leap of faith to contemplate using them. I knew that a strategy was not enough, it had to be implemented and, short of handing out leaflets and walking up and down Oxford St with a billboard announcing 'The Selecter are back', I had no better idea to achieve our goal.

The meeting was predictable: those who are trying to sell their wares promise the earth and then realise about 10 per cent of it. The head honcho, an affable bloke who reminded me of actor Joe Mantegna, made his sales pitch and offered to pull together a strategy to promote the book and our London date. They thought it would be easier to get publicity for the book than any new Selecter music. I had no choice but to remain silent about their attitude to our musical wares. Acute deafness assailed those at the table, when I talked about promoting our two potential singles, although there was a glimmer of interest in our recording of 'Back To Black'.

'These days, only albums sell. The singles market is dead,' I was told. Not the most inspiring opinion of our strategy. But what was there to lose? Only a large sum of money. I said I would think about their terms and left to meet Jah Wobble in a recording studio just off Oxford Street.

True to his word, John had phoned me a few months after the 'Sinner's Day Festival'. The short conversation mostly consisted of him shouting, 'Come 'ere, Tyson' to his Staffie dog, while they enjoyed an invigorating morning stroll on some blasted heath in the north-west. We agreed that he would send me a backing track to which I would add a melody and lyrics. Within a day, an mp3 consisting of a roaring piece of bass-driven music dropped into my inbox. I instantly liked the all-consuming energy of the track and for some reason decided to title it 'Rockers'. Within a few hours I had a vocal melody and lyrics that I hoped the wonderful Mr Wobble might find suitable for his track.

During our allotted recording time, we chatted easily about our respective future plans. I mentioned the meeting I had just been to and discussed some of my misgivings about the proposed strategy for The Selecter. After I finished talking, he fixed me with his electric-blue eyes and said, in his gloriously rapscallion manner, 'What you got to lose, Pauline? You got to keep on exercising the craft.'

I couldn't argue with him. Past performance did not necessarily have any bearing on future performance. The most exciting thing about writing songs is that at any moment you may just write the song that turns into a classic. It was a very persuasive argument. John had not stopped making music after Public Image folded. It didn't matter to him whether the public were interested or indifferent towards his music; he still made it. I respected that.

After the recording John and I attended a party to say goodbye to an editor who was leaving our book publisher. At this party were a lot of very bookish people who sipped wine and ate deliciously dainty vegetarian finger food. Among the guests was Viv Albertine of the Slits, whom I hadn't met in person since a now-legendary photo shoot by Michael Putland of the so-called rock goddesses of 1980, which included Siouxsie Sioux, Debbie Harry, Chrissie Hynde and

Poly Styrene. We began chatting about the writing process because she was thinking about writing her memoir. Our discussion culminated in what we thought about Patti Smith's recently published book *Just Kids*. Viv hadn't particularly enjoyed the book. I, on the other hand, thought that her book elegantly encapsulated her heady, youthful days with Robert Mapplethorpe. Her dramatic stage persona had opened up a new pathway for female musical expression in the '70s– one which had undoubtedly made mine and Viv's musical explorations more easily accepted by the buying public. I had a scheduled train to catch, so I left early. As I made my goodbyes, she gave me a copy of her recently recorded EP. I listened to it on the return journey to Coventry. It was a lovely piece of work, as brightly unique as she was.

I relate these three events because they were absolutely pivotal to everything I did the following week. On arriving home, I walked through the door of my house, tuned up my guitar and began writing songs. I didn't stop until I had enough material to fill nearly three- quarters of a 10- track album. The process felt almost effortless. Whatever writer's block had temporarily dammed my creativity was gone; words came tumbling out onto the page and tunes came zinging out of my mouth. I stopped only to walk the dog, sleep and occasionally cook some food for my husband. My immediate imperative was to make music, not just any music, but new music. By Monday morning, I wrote a Selecter press release for our new publicity agent, entitled *Made In Britain*. I had the concept, the songs and the manifesto. But more than anything, I believed in what I was saying.

I sent the rudimentary songs to Neil Pyzer, who put together some backing tracks and moved the songs on to their next stage. We were still a couple of songs short, but

I knew that Gaps had written something that he was very eager to record, the intriguingly titled 'My Good Bad-Minded Friends'. I also suggested that he record a version of Dandy Livingstone's 'Think About That' because I thought that it would suit his vocal styling. We had our album.

By the end of the week I accepted the PR company's terms and enthusiastically told them that they would now be promoting a new album entitled *Made in Britain* due for release 4 September and two single releases for 31 May t and 31 July, all available on iTunes download. They probably thought I was joking or mad, possibly both, because there had been no album on the cards at our intial meeting. I didn't care whether they took me seriously or not, I was paying them and I felt on a roll; any scepticism on their part was the least of my problems. I knew we had a strategy, all we had to do was realise it.

It's extraordinary how people get behind an idea when it is presented to them as a fait accompli. People love a story; particularly if they don't have to write it and can simply regurgitate it. And that is exactly what happened. But stories are not enough; a strong visual image is an asset too. So who better to bring on board our new project but the mighty former 2-Tone graphic designer from Chrysalis' art department, John Sims. John now lived in Folkestone and had his own graphic design business. He gladly accepted our challenge after I talked to him about our basic concept for our first single 'Big in the Body, Small in the Mind'. He introduced me to the artwork of Gardar Eide Einarrson, a young New York artist of Norwegian origin, who works mainly in black and white and uses drip techniques to explore sub-cultures, oppression, authority and resistance. His work was thought-provoking and contained an uncomfortable streak of violence that was perfectly attuned to what we needed. John worked on a concept based on some of Einarrson's techniques. Within a few weeks he sent me several proofs, but one idea stood out above the rest, an arresting design that pictorially embodied the fight against fascism – in The Selecter's distinctive colour palette: black, white and red.

Buoyed by his obvious enthusiasm to continue his artistic legacy with us, I commissioned him to work on another design for the next single 'Back to Black'. Using the drip technique he made the cover look as though a space invaders game was in process, the black drips from the title's words built a checkersboard below it. It was inspired and again exactly what we wanted.

I was excited. I was in the midst of proofreading my book before it went to print, an arduous but necessary task, but rereading my story again after several months was useful because I saw how its overall message dovetailed very neatly with the music we had produced. I believed that The Selecter hadn't created such a synergy since the days of the Too Much Pressure album. Our gigs were going well, thanks to the enthusiasm of our booking agent, Zac Peters at Midnight Mango. Gradually people remembered who we were and what we once stood for. At the very least, their interest was piqued.

A postman in Jersey, Kevin Crowther made contact and offered to form a fan group on Facebook. Within a week we had nearly 5000 members, all clamouring to know release dates, and asking whether the new music would be available on CD or the again popular vinyl format. Most were dismayed to hear that initially it would only be available as a download on iTunes.

We made a low-budget video for 'Big in the Body', and posted it on YouTube. It got our message across loud and clear. I felt like a child trying to acquaint myself with all the new technological ways to network the band to our fans.

On 31 May our single was released and our ardent fan base downloaded their copies, not in numbers that set the charts on fire, but enough to keep interest in our endeavours burning. We added the song to our set and audiences mostly quit their dancing while listening to it, before leaping up and down again when we played one of our hits immediately after. It was obvious that the successful introduction of new material was going to be a slow process.

With chorus lyrics 'all you fascists bound to lose', the single had no chance of being played on mainstream radio. Why is it that everybody thinks that racism is a really bad idea, but nobody will ever do anything to promote music that flies directly in the face of it? It is said that you can't have your cake and eat it, but the media do and I wholeheartedly hope that one day they choke on it.

A Brazilian priest, Dom Helder Camara famously said: 'When I gave food to the poor, I was a saint, but when I asked why they were hungry, I was told I was a communist.'

While all of us assuage our guilt by lobbing a quid into a plastic bucket for this or that cause, we take our eye off the ball marked 'inequality'. If we put half as much energy into making our leaders accountable for the policies that underlie such fundamental inequity in the world, then we might get somewhere towards solving it. Charity is part of the problem, and at best is only a short-term solution.

As the months rolled on and we entered the summer festival season, we thought it would be a good idea to further our cottage-industry endeavours and plan for a release of a double 'A' side vinyl single, 'Big in the Body b/w Back to Black' to coincide with the release of the first edition of this book.

John Sim's artwork was so beautiful that it seemed a shame to waste it as tiny jpgs on web pages.

Vinyl had become the medium for musical connoisseurs and Neil Pyzer thought that it would be a good move to release the single in a wholly different way. I liked vinyl, but I was worried that perhaps it was too retro for us. Then I remembered Steve 'Cardboard' Eaton, a colourful local DJ, always immaculately and flamboyantly suited and booted in vintage '60s suits, footwear and headgear who had departed this life back in March. Steve had been the young man whose photo on the front cover of *Too Much Pressure* had famously captured a dejected youth leaning against a wall with his trilby on the ground. His vast collection of old vinyl spanned the ska, rocksteady, reggae & 2-Tone genres. Locally he was held in such high esteem that his funeral cortege was lead into Nuneaton's Heart Of England Crematorium by a large phalanx of scooterists from local scooter clubs. Like all funerals, one is surprised when one listens to the eulogy by how little one knew about somebody who was integral to one's past and whose image was known as far afield as America, Australia and Japan. It was the passing of an era. Steve encapsulated all that was good about 2-Tone, loving the music, before we got to bickering and were unable to stay together. It felt as though the music stood for something then.

I wanted to recapture that moment again and what better way to do it than releasing a vinyl single with artwork by John Sims, who had been at that initial photo shoot with Steve in 1979.

On 23 July 2011, a Saturday, we took delivery of a consignment of 7-inch vinyl double 'A' side singles, 'Big in the Body b/w Back to Black' at London's 02 Islington Academy. The previous day 'Back to Black' had had a rave review in

Metro and a number of radio shows had been lined up to promote it. None of us expected a hit single, but it was proving to be the kind of single that interested radio stations in The Selecter again. Our strategy was working; then the bombshell of Amy's death hit.

Our timing could not have been worse. There was nothing to do except pull the release of the single. It was like a repeat of 1981 when The Selecter had released our second album *Celebrate the Bullet* at the same time as the assassination attempt on President Reagan. We hadn't pulled the album back then, but radio stations would not play it, because of the title.

As if to compound the irony of the other side of the single, 'Big in the Body, Small in the Mind', the day before, on 22 July, a Norwegian fascist sympathiser, Anders Breivik, had gunned down 77 people, most of them young, on Utoya Island in Oslo. Nothing but death seemed to surround our vinyl single.

These two events profoundly upset us, and what should have been the pinnacle of our summer campaign, Camp Bestival, seemed almost frivolous as we turned up a week later on 31 July to a frothy pink and yellow colour scheme resembling a kids playground. Fortunately the audience enjoyed our version of 'Back to Black', which was generous of them, because the whole of the weekend had been given over to various artists paying tribute to Amy Winehouse.

Despite having our singles' choices legitimated in such horrific ways, there was nothing else to do but forge ahead with our album release, *Made in Britain*. We intended showcasing five new songs from the album at Folkestone Skabour Festival on 1 September 2011, three days before its release. *Uncut* and *Record Collector* magazines had given us excellent album reviews. Journalists and interviewers were keen to pick up on our positive thoughts about multiculturalism. And then the summer riots happened.

They began in Tottenham, North London on 6 August after a peaceful local protest following the death of a young black man, Mark Duggan, who had been shot by the police on 4 August. In the following days similar scenes spread to many other parts of London and to other major cities – Birmingham, Manchester, Bristol, Salford, Nottingham, Wolverhampton and Liverpool. Between 6–10 August, five people died, at least 16 others were injured and an estimated £200 million worth of damage was perpetrated. All police leave was cancelled, MPs returned from their holidays to debate the issue in Parliament and the media poured hatred upon the perpetrators, mainly black and white youth, in an unprecedented tirade of venom designed to appeal to the vengeance seekers of middle England. Over 3000 people were rounded up and summarily expedited through the criminal justice system, or named and shamed in the newspapers. Any apologists for their behaviour were shouted down by the baying howl of the people who thought that these people should have been sent to some far-off salt mines.

Having been in a band at the time of the 1980-81 riots, and seen the effect that they had on communities, I knew there was more involved than the simplistic overview of the media and government. It was ironic that only a few months before I had been part of a panel, organised by the British Music Experience at the Millennium dome and chaired by Michael Riley of Steel Pulse, debating that very same unrest and the role that music had played in it. Celebrated photographer Pogus Caesar showed his harrowing photos captured at the frontline in Handsworth, Birmingham, to an audience of young and old who had forgotten what had happened back then. Although it had been thirty years ago, the parallels were plain to see. A lost generation of youth, many with no job prospects, brainwashed to revere the bling that gives you status in your yard, living in areas with failing schools and communities of fragmented families, had spontaneously gone on the rampage. If the daily news shows fat-cat bankers living the life of Riley while the government exhorts us to tighten our belts, is it any wonder that the over 90 unexplained deaths of young black men in custody in the past ten years, was a bone of contention among such communities and that eventually their dissatisfaction is expressed violently? No, is the answer to that.

Riots have happened throughout history, always seemingly over just one event, but it's like a suppurating abscess, eventually it finds its way to the surface and erupts, not caring where the pus hits.

What shocked me more than anything was the level of animosity expressed by people I knew, people actively involved in promoting the legacy of 2-Tone, many of whom displayed a profound level of ignorance that I could only gasp at. Yes, rioting is messy, yes rioting mostly has devastating consequences, yes, it can often appear and is usually reported as mindless violence, but all it really means is that some people somewhere have had enough and are intent on knocking those with a more comfortable existence off their stools for a week or two. As many contemporaries tutted, clucked and chattered, I wondered what had happened to them in the past thirty odd years, to make them move so far to the right. Had 2-Tone been de-politicised and rendered toothless, just some music to feel worthy about and jump around to at drunken parties?

In the aftermath of the riots, it was difficult to think about putting out an album entitled *Made in Britain*, celebrating

The Selecter at 229 – The Venue, Londo, 17 March 2012 on their *Made in Britain* tour. Photo © Nathalie de Bruyne

multiculturalism. By this time thousands had been arrested, summarily charged and brought before the courts, and many given heavy prison sentences. But as the band discussed the problem, it became clear to us that it was more necessary than ever to produce such an album. It represented our journey from *Too Much Pressure* in 1979 to now, but from the events that had just happened, we wondered if much had actually changed. As if on cue, *Mojo* magazine wrote: '*Made in Britain* sits comfortably side by side with Selecter's first album *Too Much Pressure*'. At least somebody had got it.

Our strategy is still in place and The Selecter continues to gather speed on its musical journey. *Made in Britain* may not be kicking out the jams, but I like to think that we are putting a dent in the wishes of the far right.

This woman is not for resigning!